SlimCalmSexy
DIET

Slim Calm Sexy
DIET

365
PROVEN FOOD STRATEGIES FOR MIND/BODY BLISS

Keri Glassman, MS, RD, CDN
CONTRIBUTING EDITOR
Women'sHealth

WITH SARAH MAHONEY

RODALE.

**Book design by Mike Smith,
with George Karabotsos, design director of
Men's Health and *Women's Health* Books**

**Cover photography by Rainer Hosch
Interior photography by Beth Bischoff,
with the exception of pages 178–195
by Ayla Christman, and pages 218–259
by Thomas MacDonald**

Library of Congress Cataloging-in-Publication Data

Glassman, Keri.
    The slim calm sexy diet : 365 proven food strategies for mind/body bliss / Keri Glassman with Sarah Mahoney.
        p.   cm.
    Includes index.
    ISBN 978-1-60961-749-3 direct hardcover
        1. Reducing diets—Psychological aspects.   2. Behavior modification.   3. Food habits.   4. Exercise.   5. Reducing diets—Recipes.
I. Mahoney, Sarah.   II. Title.
    RM222.2.G53768   2011
    613.2′5—dc23   2011040014

2 4 6 8 10 9 7 5 3 1 hardcover

RODALE

We inspire and enable people to improve their lives and the world around them.
For more of our products visit **rodalestore.com** or call 800-848-4735

To all of the slim, calm, and sexy
women I am so very blessed
to have in my life . . .

contents

acknowledgments

Thank you to Maria Rodale and everyone at Rodale
who tirelessly puts their energy and efforts into making millions
of lives better and healthier each day.

To everyone at Rodale Books, *Women's Health,* and *Men's Health,* thank you all for providing me
with a place to share my passion and wisdom. I am honored to be part of such an extraordinary team.
To Michele Promaulayko, you are an inspiration, a friend, and a rock star editor in chief!

To Dave Zinczenko for the opportunity to be part of such an incredible place and project,
and Steve Perrine for your belief in this book (and me!) from our very first meeting.
To my editor Ursula Cary, I am truly going to miss our working sessions. You are beyond
amazing at what you do. And, to Debbie McHugh for keeping us on track! A huge thank you
to George Karabotsos, whose brilliant design direction makes all things beautiful. Also, thanks
to Mike Smith, Erin Williams, Chris Krogermeier, Ayla Christman, Rainer Hosch, Beth Bischoff,
Thomas MacDonald, Susan Hindman, and Maureen Klier for all of their hard work.

To Karen Rinaldi and Shannon Welch for getting me involved and for supporting me
on *Slim Calm Sexy Diet* and my other books.

Allison Keane, thank you for your friendship, your incredible diligence,
and for being the amazing you.

Sarah Mahoney, you are my writing partner rock. On to the next! You are a dream to work
with and I have the utmost respect for everything you do. Therese Baran, thanks for
being the foodie that you are and creating recipes that I can't get enough of. Thanks also to
Rachel Cosgrove, Mandy Ingber, and Jenifer Nyp for their incredible fitness expertise,
and to Nancy Kalish for pulling it all together.

To the team in my office, thank you for your passion, commitment, and energy for our incredible field
as well as all of your friendships. Karen Rogers, my director of operations, thank you for running
the show and letting me do my thing. I appreciate everything that you do and no one could do it
better. Lara Metz, Stacia Helfand, Amanda Buthmann, and Tiffany Mendell, you are gifts to the field of
nutrition! Also, thanks to all of the interns who put so much energy into assisting me on this
project, especially Joey Damommio.

To everyone at WME, including Strand Conover, Jeff Googel, and Bethany Dick,
and Chloe Leeson for all of their hard work. Mel Berger, no books would happen without you.
Thank you! Ken Slotnick, there are no words!

To my parents, once again, thank you for your neverending, utmost support and always being there.

Thank you, Brett Glassman! And, of course, thank you to the loves of my life,
Rex and Maizy, for making everything all good every day. I LOVE YOU!

Slim. Calm. Sexy.
Is it really possible to feel this way all the time?

As a nutritionist, I have a ringside seat to what makes some women feel slim, calm, and sexy, and others feel fat, frumpy, and frazzled. It doesn't matter if you're 5, 10, or 50 pounds overweight—when you're unhappy with your body, you're miserable. And I know exactly how this feels.

As a kid growing up in the Boston area, I loved gymnastics and worked extra hard to get the slender, muscular body I envied in the other girls. On the drive home, I'd be so famished that my mom would take me to McDonald's, where I'd feast on Chicken McNuggets with honey-mustard dipping sauce. My nutrition habits continued to yo-yo. I certainly wasn't obese, but just before I went off to college, I looked in the mirror with dismay. "I'm fat," I thought. I was zeroing in on body parts I didn't like—my tummy, my thighs.

My initiation into the world's biggest club—women on

a diet—was by way of the Scarsdale diet. Between the grapefruits and the dry toast, I lost 15 pounds in the last few weeks of my summer vacation, and I went off to college skinnier than ever and feeling invincible about food. Then I downed big bowls of sugary cereal, late-night pizzas, and giant chocolate chip cookies. I usually had a bag of Swedish Fish in my pocket. I was still playing sports, but I fueled myself with not-so-smart snacks. As a result, I spent most of my college years weighing between 15 and 20 pounds more than I wanted to. I didn't like the way my clothes fit or the way the extra weight made me feel.

I moved to New York City, and I spiraled further into the yo-yo diet trap. I felt like I was either starving or overeating, but I wasn't sure why. I was fascinated by health magazines and found myself reading up on nutrition news whenever I could. I decided I wanted to study it more seriously, and enrolled in the master's degree program at New York University. As I learned how to interpret nutrition research, the basic components of food, and even micro-nutrients, my outlook on diet shifted dramatically. The science of nutrition had suddenly become … personal. After years of thinking, "I can't eat the cake, I can't eat the cake," a switch flipped, and I thought, "I can eat blueberries!"

I now saw the world of food as my own personal board game, like Candy Land but tastier. It wasn't that I swore off cake, exactly—in fact, I didn't make a conscious decision to say goodbye to any foods. I just started saying hello to more of them. I found myself experimenting with delicious new foods, from kale to salmon to cashews. I tore through the produce aisle the way some women work sample sales or flea markets. What hidden treasures would I find? Kumquats? Bok choy? Star fruit? Lemongrass?

Before long, I was slim. Effortlessly. The scale was in the right place (give or take a few pounds, which, I promise, is totally normal). I fit easily into my favorite jeans, month after month, even year after year. I was no longer at the mercy of whether or not fried wontons were served at cocktail hour or how fast the waiter brought a new bread basket. I had finally stepped away from the black-and-white world of seeing food as "bad" or "good." I knew I could have extra bread, if I wanted. In fact, the more I learned about food, the more empowered I became.

I enjoyed my workouts at the gym and my runs, focusing on my strength and times instead of every little fat bulge, imperfection, or how many calories I burned.

And you know what happened? I relaxed. I felt calm and in control, even in the face of total chaos. I was in charge of my own fork, dinner plate, and any other aspect of my life. I nourished myself with the right foods, and in turn, I looked—and felt—amazing. Self-confident. Sexy. I was finally the real me. I felt amazing, and there are even those days when I feel downright fab! Even after two kids, I feel better than I did 10 years ago. (Of course, we all have bad days, and I'm no exception. But I've learned to take those bumps in stride—and you will, too.) Some of my self-assurance, of course, is just part of growing up and settling into a wonderfully full life. But most of it was learning what to eat, when, and why.

My own slim, calm, sexy journey took several decades—and while I can't give you age and experience, I can give you the tools to find empowerment through food and find your perfect balance within. At Nutritious Life, my practice in New York, I work with thousands of clients and watch them "flip the switch," just as I did. Today, I share my passion with an even broader audience—on TV, in magazines, and in published books—and I can't wait to share it with you.

follow me to the
SLIM, CALM, SEXY YOU!

6 weeks to a
slimmer, calmer, sexier you!

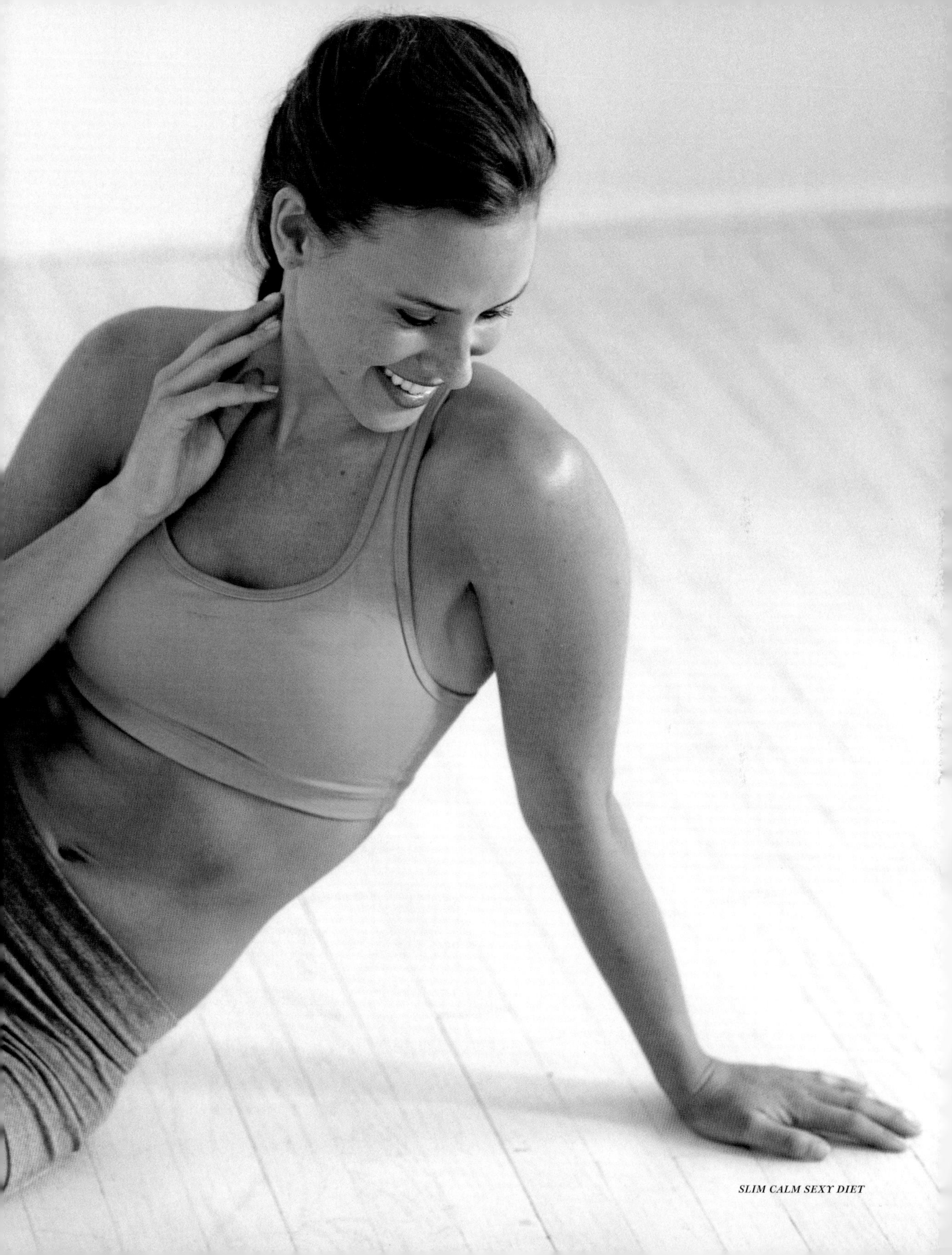

There

are certain relationships that, once they go bad, should be cut off completely—a bad-news boyfriend or a needy acquaintance who sucks the energy out of you like a vampire. Some people have a relationship with cigarettes, too, and when they quit, it is totally over. But you can't break up with food that way. You have to have a relationship with food, and I want to make that relationship as happy as possible.

At Nutritious Life, my practice in New York, I've learned that really transforming someone's relationship with food is not just about slimming down, but it's also about quieting those internal, mental food fights. Getting to the root of that tension and healing it is the secret to making peace with your body and achieving your goal weight.

For me, redefining that relationship was so important—and so interesting—that I wound up with a degree in nutrition and a thriving practice as a registered dietitian. I even get to appear on TV regularly to talk about food, and I contribute to magazines. I'm excited to teach you everything you need to know in the following pages. I'll explain, first and foremost, why a slimmer, calmer, and sexier you is so crucial to your overall health and well-being. And then I'll show you just how easy that weight loss transformation can be. The diet plan itself couldn't be simpler. You'll eat three meals and three snacks each day, centered on:

The Perfect Balance

No worrying about how much carbs, protein, or fat to eat. I've created each day to be roughly one-third each of carbs, protein, and fat: the most nourishing whole grains (even bread); lean and satisfying meat, chicken, and fish, so critical to success-ful weight loss; calcium-rich dairy foods; and the types of fats your body needs most, mainly from antioxidant-rich plant sources such as olives, nuts, and avocados.

100 Percent Real Foods

If there's one thing we know, it's that made-in-the-lab fats, artificial sweeteners, and bucket loads of chemicals and pre-servatives don't help anyone lose weight. The foods in the Slim Calm Sexy Diet are the real thing, with an emphasis on fiber, antioxidants, and omega-3s. In other words, they're coming straight from the farm, not thefactory. As much as possible, I've chosen organic items, because they're better for you and for the planet.

Slimming Science

Fruits, vegetables, and other healthy foods (even fat!) promote weight loss on their own merits. But that could be said of hun-dreds of diets. What makes the Slim Calm Sexy Diet so special is that I've chosen the perfect combination of these healthy, deli-cious foods—and the timing of when you eat them—as well as included special in-gredients with added slimming power. This unique approach is what helps you lose weight faster and keep it off for good.

This Plan Will Make You Slimmer

• • •   And healthier! Everyone thinks that losing weight will cause a huge change in their life, and they are right. Nothing beats the feeling of sliding into a bathing suit, a pair of jeans, or a little black dress and knowing you look amazing—even before you check yourself out in the mirror.

Not that I'm knocking vanity or anything, but slimming down is even more transformative in how it improves your health. Shedding just 5 to 10 percent of your body weight—if you're 5 feet 4 inches and 160 pounds, that means losing 16 pounds and crossing from the "over-weight" to "healthy weight" threshold of your body mass index—reduces your risk of heart disease, high blood pressure, diabetes, gallbladder disease, sleep apnea, and certain cancers, reports the National Institutes of Health. In fact, every time you lose just 2 pounds, you reduce your risk of getting diabetes by 16 percent, according to researchers from Indiana University. Losing weight cleans up the heart risks in your blood, too: It can help you lower your LDL, or "lousy," cholesterol; raise your HDL, or "happy," cholesterol; and reduce the amount of triglycerides. (That's especially important, says the National Institutes of Health's National Heart, Lung, and Blood Institute, if you are what's known as an "apple" and tend to gain weight in your middle or if you have a waist measurement that is greater than 35 inches.)

The specific slimming foods I've chosen for you in this plan deliver all those benefits, as well as many more. Take berries, which you'll be hearing a lot about. Yes, they'll help you achieve those weight loss goals. But brand-new research from the Harvard School of Public Health shows that the flavonoids in them—a type of healthy antioxidant also known as vitamin P—are so protective of blood vessels that they can actually lower blood pressure. Over a 14-year period, women who regularly munched strawberries and blueberries had blood pressure that was 8 percent lower than women who didn't.

And, of course, that's just the inside of your body—you're going to look better, too. As the bloating, dimpled excess fat recedes, you'll see more of your beautiful sleek self in the mirror every day. In fact, I encourage you to track those changes. (See "Find Your Benchmarks" on page 16.) While there's no cure for cellulite (at least not yet, but when we find it, I'm sure there will be a stampede for it), researchers at the University of Cincinnati do know that weight loss does seem to improve it for many women.

This Plan Will Make You Calmer

• • •   As I'll discuss in detail later in this chapter, stress is one of the biggest obstacles to maintaining a healthy weight. Often, women think they can separate the two, and say things like, "I'll lose weight when the stress from _____ dies down" or "Losing weight will reduce my stress—life will be easier when I'm thin." But I know from experience that unless you make stress management a core part of your diet, losing weight will be much tougher than it has to be. I've created this plan to inject as much calmness as possible into the way you eat, and I'm betting that with each passing day, you'll feel more and more in control of not just what you put on your plate, but also how you react to the stress around you.

In fact, stress-busting is a main mission of the Slim Calm Sexy Diet, and I've loaded the menu with all kinds of little powerhouses, like the pistachio. A Penn State University study found that eating 1.5 ounces a day (about 74 of the cute little green guys) for just 4 weeks lowered the amount of stress subjects experienced. (Researchers measured this by giving them extra-hard math problems.) In addition to specifically calming foods, the Slim Calm Sexy Diet will also keep you snacking, a strategy that works to keep you on an even keel in two ways. First, there's the irrefutable physiology: When your blood sugar stays even, so do your spirits. Second, it makes it easy for even the busiest people on their most hectic days to stay calm and make good eating choices. Then, you won't have to put up with that terrible "I'm too busy to eat" frazzled feeling or, worse, the demoralizing guilt that comes from eating too much of the wrong food. You'll turn crazy-busy and crazy-hungry into a calm, confident state of mind.

This Plan Will Make You Sexier

• • •   Weighing too much hobbles your love life, too. I know a lot of women wish their sex life could be more satisfying (and plenty just wish they had a sex life). Again, it's easy to think these bedroom blahs have nothing to do with the way we eat, but we know that is simply not true. So I've written this diet in a way that addresses that—not just by helping you lose enough weight so that you can rediscover that vital spark in yourself, but also by adding plenty of foods that address the biology of your libido.

The problem isn't just that women who are overweight are more likely to avoid getting naked and make excuses to avoid sex (although we all do that). Up to 30 percent of obese people also suffer from low libido, according to research from Duke University, and it turns out the problem is almost as complex physiologically as it is emotionally. High cholesterol levels and insulin resistance, which are early warning signs of type 2 diabetes and all too common among overweight and obese people, affect performance: Researchers say the itty-bitty arteries that surround the clitoris are affected, making it tougher to achieve orgasm. That's not good. Orgasms are supposed to relieve stress, not cause it!

Being overweight also increases the levels of sex hormone binding globulin, or SHBG. It binds to the sex hormone testosterone—so important to both men's and women's sexual response—so there's less available to make us feel frisky. Even though we usually think of testosterone as the stuff that causes men to crave sex, women make some, too, and we need the free version of it—not the bound version—in order to get in the mood. (That's not just a theory: A study in the United Kingdom asked women to track how many times a day they thought about sex. The more free testosterone they had in their blood, the more naughty thoughts they had. And, not so surprisingly, the more they thought about sex, the more they actually did the deed.)

The Slim-Calm Connection

• • •   Let me ask you a question: In one word, why do you struggle with your weight?

That's easy, clients will tell me. Overeating. Or, bread. Or maybe, fat or portions. Lots of times, I'll get a two-word response. Ice cream. Business travel. My kids. Fast food. Or four words: I eat too much.

What if I told you that there really is a single word behind your problem and that it isn't a food word at all? It's stress. All kinds of stress. First, there's the whole litany of stresses that we all deal with, to one degree or another, when too many demands are made on us at once: traffic delays, crabby bosses, in-laws, deadlines. You know, life. Then there's the stress that comes from the constant little digs you make at yourself as a result: "I look terrible." "I feel fat." "I hate my tummy." (Seriously, referring to yourself as Thunder Thighs damages your morale more than you'd think.) Layer onto that the stress of the love-hate relationship so many women have with food, and you've got a serious problem.

A whopping 68 percent of American adults are either overweight or obese. And while the stress epidemic isn't quite as bad, it's close. In the latest findings from the American Psychological Association, 47 percent say stress looms so large in their life that it keeps them up at night.

Biologically, it's also bad news. First, the human body doesn't do very well at categorizing stress. Our bodies are programmed to react the same way to each demand (even a short meeting with a difficult co-worker): as if it's a full-on, life-or-death assault. Our breath gets shallow. Our muscles tense. Our digestive system shuts down, and our glands fire up, cranking out stress hormones like cortisol, adrenaline, and norepinephrin. Some of those hormones, of course, are good for us. (Without a little excitement now and then, we'd more or less be dead!) And our bodies are designed to tidily break those juices down as soon as the crisis of the moment passes. When it works right, it's pretty much a perfect system.

But some of us are in constant stress overdrive—whether from actual events, endless deadlines, illness, pain, or even general unhappiness (yes, it's true, being blue is really stressful)—with no downtime to process those hormones. Our stress hormone levels never have time to reset and go back to normal. On a cellular level, it's like living inside the world's busiest fire station.

You may already be shrugging and saying, "I know I'm stressed. So what?" I need for you to understand that this chronic stress—even though it may feel psychological or emotional—is physical. And it's standing in the way of the slimmer you, the calmer you, and the sexier you.

Whether you choose to admit it or not, that excess stress is creating hormonal upheaval in your bloodstream and in many of the cells in your body—the most basic building blocks of you. By now, medical researchers have documented dozens of ways that these physical stress reactions mess us up. They increase the risk and severity of killer diseases like cardiovascular ailments, cancer, and diabetes, as well as heartbreaking problems like depression and even infertility. And they certainly zap a girl's sexual energy.

Simply put, stress makes it easy for people to gain weight and hard for them to lose it.

When stress disrupts the natural rhythm of cortisol (it comes from glands on our kidneys and is normally cranked out at its highest levels in the morning), it makes us hungry, causing us to overeat and gain weight. And if that's not bad enough, we gain it in the worst possible place: in our bellies, packed tightly around our organs. Researchers have consistently found this connection between high cortisol levels and central weight gain to be especially true for women.

It's hard to overstate the importance of this cortisol connection. Over the years, much attention has been focused on insulin (and insulin resistance, which we'll discuss at length later) because it is the body's primary hormonal control over both weight loss and weight gain. But cortisol is the only other hormone we secrete that has that power.

Mother Nature then plays a really nasty trick. Once a person is over-weight, cortisol continues to monkey around with insulin sensitivity, causing a craving for more calories. You've heard that expression, "the rich get richer"? Well, in the cortisol derby, unfortunately, the stressed gain weight, and overweight people get more overweight. Researchers from the Kaiser Permanente Center for Health Research in Portland, Oregon, for example, recently studied a group of more than 470 over-weight people for a period of 6 months, measuring exercise and food intake. Those who entered the study with the lowest level of stress lost the most weight, and those who felt they were getting a better handle on stress through the study's weekly counseling sessions, which included stress-management techniques, lost more than those who didn't feel they were tackling their stress issues.

So, as stress continues to make our systems more inflamed—both from the cortisol and the demands of the new weight—we further change our behaviors to try to soothe that inflammation. Instead of eating healthier foods and moving more, our bodies trick us into eating "comfort foods." I promise, your arteries do not take comfort in bacon or mac and cheese.

And that's just the biology of stress. There's another kind of stress that leads to overeating, and it is one of the main reasons I wanted to write this book, because I feel so strongly about it. It's more subtle and harder to measure. It's the emotional assault you feel from constantly being at war with food. Hating the way you look in a fitting room mirror. Dreading summer's sleeveless shirts. Refusing to bring a bathing suit on a beach vacation. The tug-of-war that happens in many women's heads when they open a restaurant menu: "Extra-cheesy quesadilla or salad? Herbal tea or the Molten Chocolate Lava Cake?"

All of this "noise" is exhausting. I'm tired for you!

I wrote this book to help women everywhere find their slimmer, calmer, sexier selves. And the secret lies in transforming that one little word—stress—into something that can spark true change. Starting right now, you'll escape that negative cycle of body-bashing and weight gain, and you'll begin your journey to a lifetime of healthy, happy, empowered eating. At Nutritious Life, the first lesson I teach clients is that we take this journey one bite at a time.

How the Slim Calm Sexy Diet Works

• • • So, how can you get from fat, frazzled, and frumpy to slim, calm, and sexy? It's easier than you think, and I'll guide you every step of the way. It works like this: For 3 days, you'll follow a diet that will gently cleanse your body of all its stress baggage. Don't worry, this isn't a severe fast. You'll eat simple, clean foods—natural, with nothing fake or artificial. And you'll eat lots of them. You won't feel hungry or deprived.

Once you've completed the cleanse, you'll embark on a menu of even more delicious foods: succulent pork tenderloin, wholesome breads, tangy fish tacos, delicious cheeses (even mozzarella and feta), and a quinoa-pistachio salad that will make your mouth water.

You'll slim down fast. But you'll lose more than weight. Bad habits, cravings, and a lot of that negative eating stress will just melt away. I expect you'll lose 17 to 18 pounds over those first 6 weeks and continue to lose about 2 pounds a week after that until you've reached your desired weight. You'll be eating generous portions of some of the most nutritious foods on Earth that also have the power to trim your waistline and soothe away stress.

Wonder where I came up with dozens of these miraculous foods? I was fierce. Only ultra-healthy foods made the cut for this meal plan— no fake this or artificial that. They are laden with healthy, natural anti-oxidants and, whenever possible, are organic and fresh. That's important to maximize nutrition and minimize preservatives and other chemicals. It's better for our health and better for the planet. (There's nothing calming about ingesting anything with 16-syllable ingredients.) These foods are the same ones that transform my clients at Nutritious Life. They're so packed with natural nutrition that they start soothing, healing, and reshaping you almost as soon as you start chewing them.

But that wasn't the only criteria. To make the cut, these foods also had to have been shown to possess some special ability to slim you down. I know your main goal is to lose weight, and you will.

In fact, every single meal will include a food that's specifically slim-ming—from succulent produce (like berries, spinach, and citrus fruit), to wake-up-your-mouth herbs and spices, to the so-rich-they're-almost-naughty goodies like coconut and deep, dark chocolate. (If I got you at "deep, dark chocolate" and you're ready to begin, feel free to jump right into the plan by turning to page 54.) Many of these are what I describe as dietary superpowers. They are among the most nutrient-dense foods on Earth.

Besides telling you what to eat, the Slim Calm Sexy Diet will tell you when to eat, one of the main reasons it is so effective. That's because in my world, hunger is the total opposite of calm. When I'm hungry, I get cranky and agitated. I can't focus on anything or even form a thought for a coherent e-mail. The whole family knows to get out of my way! This plan is designed specifically to keep you satisfied. Each day, you'll eat three full meals and two snacks—and a third Happy Hour snack—and yes, you can eat them in any order you'd like (I'll show you how to find your own personal eating rhythm). Often, clients will tell me that they're shocked by how much food I expect them to eat. "How will I lose weight if I'm always eating?" they'll ask. It all comes down to a key concept: satiety. That's the scientific word for the perfect balance in our bellies— not hungry, not overfull, but just right. Snacking promotes that kind of satisfaction, which helps you lose weight.

Is there some kind of magic in meal frequency? You bet. Because the nutrient-dense foods provide such a potent one-two punch of nutrition and satisfaction, snacking on them sends you into the next meal with a much better sense of appetite control. And since I can't protect you from all the bad food choices that are out there by whisking you away to a spa (sorry!), I like knowing that I'm sending you out in the world fortified with those snacks, making it easier for you to make smart decisions throughout the day.

One of my favorite studies was done on healthy women at the University of Wales. Some were fed breakfast, and some breakfast and a snack. Obviously, the snackers reported less hunger throughout the morning. But what impressed researchers is that they also functioned better, scoring higher on a series of word-recall tests. Better still? The snackers were in a better mood all morning long. I'm a huge believer in the Happy Camper philosophy: When your mood hums along, so will your weight loss.

As your body gets used to this new style of eating, you'll see other changes, too. You'll have to get used to the compliments as your skin begins to glow and your eyes get brighter. You will likely drop two sizes and look and feel better in all your clothes. As your energy level readjusts, thanks to all this healthy noshing, you'll likely wake up smiling and ready to bounce out of bed. The snooze button will be a thing of the past. And of course, all this will lead to an undeniably sexy self-confidence that may just transform you into the goddess you were always meant to be!

Slim, Calm, Sexy ... and More

• • • Even if you've tried and failed dozens of times to lose weight or keep it off, I know you can win with the Slim Calm Sexy Diet. (In fact, the latest behavioral research tells us that you haven't been failing in those prior attempts to lose—you've been learning and building your toolbox.) This time will be different, because this plan approaches weight loss not as a fad or a quick fix, but as a complete approach to a nutritious life. Yes, you'll lose some of the extra pounds that are tormenting you, but you'll gain something even better: a total mind-body transformation. Here are some of the added benefits you'll enjoy.

Your Mind

• • • You're probably already in love with the "Calm" part of the plan— who wouldn't like a little relief from a stress-packed life? But in addition to the built-in soothers like folate-rich grains, blood-pressure-lowering avocados, and lots of lean proteins (which have plenty of the calming substance tryptophan), there are foods that sharpen your thinking, as well. Many of these foods are loaded with a special constellation of antioxidants that have been shown to sharpen focus and cognition, including fatty fish, berries, chocolate, and tea. Others, including walnuts, help sharpen your memory. Even spices and seasonings help. Nutmeg can take the edge off anxiety, for example, and cinnamon boosts alertness.

Your Sleep

• • • One of the most exciting areas of nutrition research in the past decade has been about how sleep, or lack of it, correlates to added pounds. Researchers now know that too little sleep—a chronic problem for many people, especially us type A personalities who like to squeeze as much into a day as possible—interferes with our hunger hormones. It decreases the secretion of leptin, a hormone that gives us a feeling of satisfaction and signals us to stop eating. And it jacks up the

nutritious *life-ism*

Focus on eating better, one meal at a time. Otherwise, it's too easy to get discouraged, whether it's because you're worried about what you might eat next weekend, or how long it may take to lose 25 pounds. Forget it! Your only mission: Make the next meal you eat healthy, balanced, and satisfying. In other words, think of every meal as a "Monday morning."

secretion of the hormone ghrelin, so we feel hungry even when we're not, according to research from Stanford University.

So that means sleeping more will help you lose weight. And weight loss may help you sleep more deeply. Those who are overweight or obese have a higher incidence of sleep apnea. This disorder—most commonly found in men until age 50, when it turns into an equal opportunity health risk—is tricky to diagnose, because so many people have it and don't realize it. Sleep apnea causes them to sleep fitfully and wake up frequently during the night, so they're not really resting. (If you're the kind of person who sleeps 9 hours a night but still feels zonked, please ask your doctor about this.) While an estimated 70 percent of obese people have it, there are many risk factors. For example, Chinese women and African American women are more vulnerable.

Because you'll be eating such a well-rounded, healthy diet, you'll also find yourself backing off caffeine and sugar—things we naturally crave when our energy levels crash. (Don't worry, I won't ask you to give up coffee—I couldn't live without my morning cup of joe.) But studies have shown that the less caffeine you drink in the afternoon, the more restful your evening zzz's will be. And I promise, you'll be getting so much natural energy from your diet that you won't even need that 4 p.m. Starbucks run.

Your Workout

As much as experts love to talk about the obesity crisis, I wish more of them would talk about knee traumas. Being only 10 pounds overweight increases the force on the knee by 30 to 60 pounds with each step, reports the Johns Hopkins Arthritis Center. As someone who regularly lifts small children, I can tell you that 30 to 60 pounds of extra weight is a lot. Those extra pounds are hard not just on your knees but also on your breasts and bladder. (I need all the help I can get staying perky!) For every 11 pounds a woman loses, her risk of developing knee arthritis falls by more than 50 percent. Losing 10 pounds is often all that's needed to turn an exercise hater into someone who loves it, or to turn a reluctant walker into an avid runner. I love to watch the way weight loss changes my clients' attitude about working out.

Research has shown that the people who are most successful at maintaining their weight loss are those who also exercise regularly. I think you are going to love the workouts in Chapter 9. We created them to work perfectly with the diet, easing you into the right activities as you progress. Initially, these yoga-based and strength-training moves will feel great to everyone; heavier people will start with lower-impact cardio and then increase the intensity as their fitness levels improve and they lose weight.

Your Skin

• • •   Be prepared to take in the compliments, because one of the benefits of the Slim Calm Sexy Diet is that your skin will look better than it has in a long time. Any dryness will disappear, fine lines will soften, and you will see a lovely glow. (We even debated calling this book *Slim Calm Sexy Beautiful Diet*.) First, your skin will respond immediately to being properly nourished and hydrated from the inside. Remember, you're eating pure, healthy foods with nutrients known to have antiaging properties—from green tea to strawberries to avocados—that are also proven to have a cosmetic as well as a nutritional benefit. Second, the exercise and sleep components of the program will boost circulation and relaxation. Your mother was right: Getting plenty of "beauty sleep" does makes you look prettier.

Your Metabolism

• • •   Once you've begun losing weight on the Slim Calm Sexy Diet, you'll soon see that your metabolism (which is one of the most mis-understood words in the weight loss world, right up there with "carbs" and "ideal body weight") isn't your enemy—even if you've been saying that for years. You'll discover, as the pounds come off, that your metabo-lism is your very best friend. As you lose fat and gain muscle, your me-tabolism constantly recalibrates, figuring out how much energy it takes to sneeze, finish your expense report, or perfect your Dancing Warrior.

  And, yes, as you lose weight, you'll burn fewer calories. A smaller machine burns less fuel, right? I'll show you how to get your body used to constant small adjustments so you can keep zapping those pounds. I'll also help you learn how to adjust by age, too. Unless you're making some major changes in the way you exercise, in general, most women burn about 100 calories per day less each decade. So, at age 35, you need to eat less than you did at 25, and so on. Calorie calculations are by nature a little imprecise and don't always take into consideration how active or sedentary a person is. But in general, nutritionists estimate that for every 10 pounds you lose, you'll need to cut about 100 calories out of your regular daily diet. Small snacks throughout the day—a cornerstone of this diet—and a muscle-building workout routine mean your metabolism will be constantly revved and burning at its maximum capacity.

Your Life Span

• • •   You may not be thinking as long-term as most health researchers, and it's okay with me if your sights are set on a class reunion or a dress you want to fit back into. But I'd be slacking if I didn't tell you that the

Slim Calm Sexy Diet isn't just a short-term wonder; it's a diet for the long haul. The antioxidant-rich foods, whole grains, and healthy fats and proteins will all boost your lifespan. Even the fiber is powerful.

A large-scale study from the National Institutes of Health, which involved following 388,000 people for a 9-year period, found that eating a diet high in fiber from whole plant food results in greater longevity. Women who ate the most fiber—about 25.8 grams a day, but still below the U.S. dietary guideline recommendations of about 28—were 19 percent less likely to die from any reason during the course of the study. And yep, you'll get more than that on the Slim Calm Sexy Diet: usually more than 30 grams per day. Combine that with the heart-healthy, anticancer benefits of the foods you'll be eating, and you'd better start buying stock in birthday cake candles.

I hope you are excited about starting this plan and finding an easier way to achieve the goals that will make you slimmer, calmer, and sexier.

Find Your Benchmarks

• • •   You may not like this part, but I promise, you'll thank me later: I want you to document your current weight and health as carefully as possible, and to do it right now.

One of the best ways to make a weight loss plan stick, and to make success so much sweeter, is to know where you started. Ideally, you should see a doctor if you haven't had a checkup for a while. Ask your doctor to check your blood pressure, cholesterol levels, and blood sugar and to write it down for you. On the same piece of paper, write your weight and some key measurements—not just your waist and hips but also your chest, biceps, thighs, and calves. If you're joining a gym or already belong to one, ask to have your body-fat percentage calculated.

I know that you probably bought this book because you're not loving the way you look now, but take a few pictures of yourself, maybe even in a bathing suit. (You can ask a friend, or do it yourself using a full-length mirror.) Do it. Once you accomplish your amazing "after" self, these "before" pictures will be more meaningful than you can imagine.

before

DATE ☐☐ / ☐☐ / ☐☐

HERE'S MY "BEFORE" ON THE SLIM CALM SEXY DIET:

JEANS SIZE	WAIST	UPPER THIGH*
WEIGHT	HIPS	BICEP*
BMI	CHEST	CALVES

OTHER

_____

_____

_____

BEFORE
PHOTO

psych up to slim down

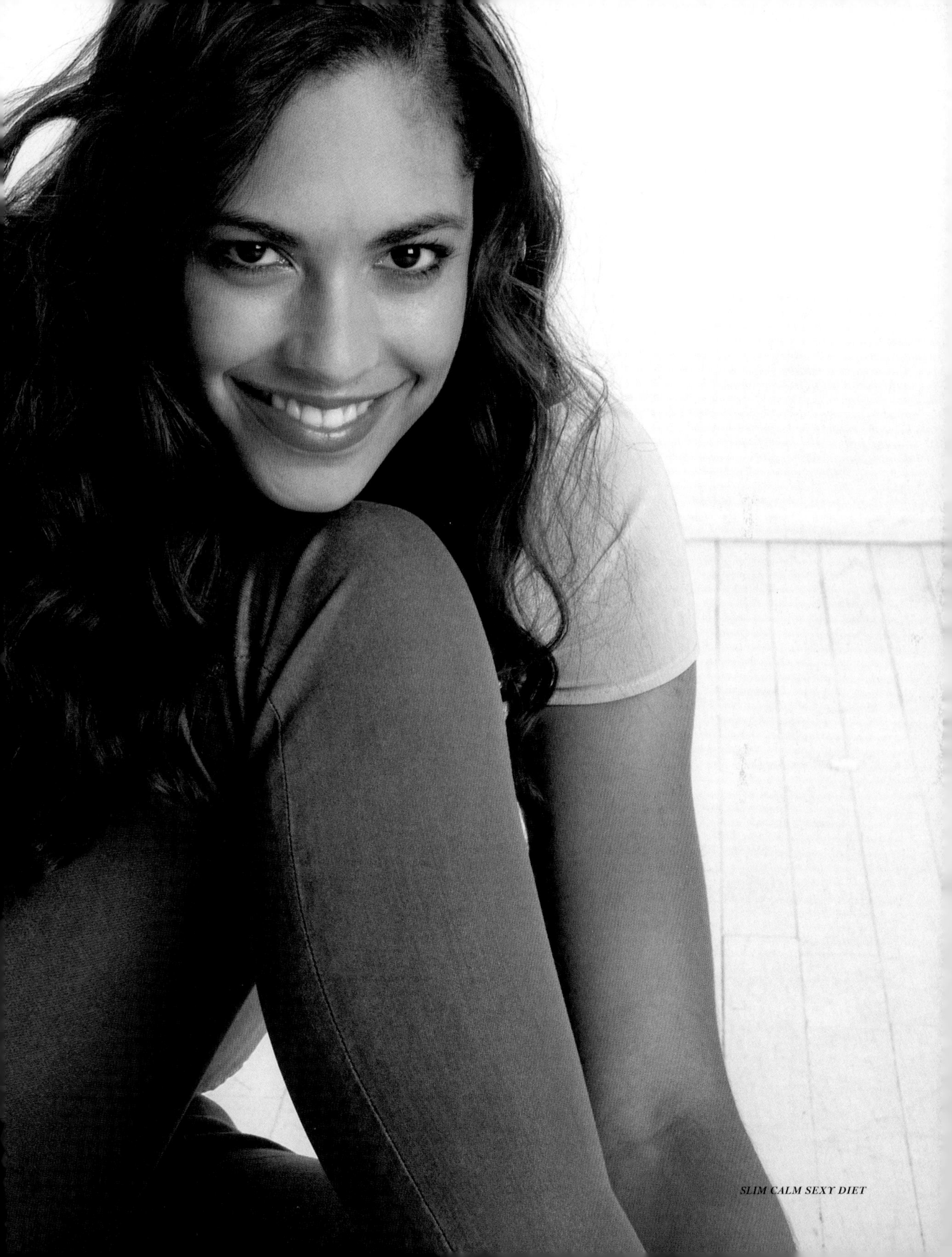

Before

I start talking about the delicious foods you'll be eating for the next 6 weeks, and how they'll help you reclaim your slimmest, calmest, sexiest self, I want to get you in the right frame of mind. While it's true that the foods you eat are what will power your weight loss, your attitude toward the plan is everything.

If you've dieted before, you know exactly what I mean. Some diets make you feel like a weight loss martyr, whimpering and watching the clock until it's time for the next serving of rabbit food. On the Slim Calm Sexy Diet, you'll feel like you're totally in the zone. So before you start the plan, I want to give you the very best, latest information about the psychology of losing weight.

We've already talked about stress, and I hope you're sold on the idea of learning to eat in a way that adds calm to your life, not chaos. But what I really want you to know is that learning how to handle that stress is a proven weight loss tool. When researchers at Kings College in London tracked 71 women through stressful times, they found that those who were the most stressed, as measured by cortisol in their bloodstream, gained the most weight. But they also found that what kept the women from gaining even more weight was a skill they called mastery—learning tricks and techniques for managing stress, eating, and cravings and for developing a healthier attitude about food and weight loss.

So while it's no fun to dwell on past setbacks, it does help to take a look at why so many people fail in their weight loss efforts. Everyone has their own diet history. That way, you can learn the methods that work instead, making you a master of weight loss, too.

You're probably thinking that sounds pretty obvious. Problem Solving 101, right? And it is. But many people who struggle with their weight can't quite see it that way, and here's why: Their relationship with food— something that started out as pure biology and chemistry—has turned into an emotional minefield. It's even a moral battleground for some people, where Good and Evil play a constant tug-of-war for their waist-lines. (Seriously, when some of my clients explain these epic battles against buffalo chicken wings or Ben & Jerry's, I feel like I'm talking to my 8-year-old son about Ninjago!)

When people are in that moment—when they make a destructive eating choice, one they know will sabotage their weight loss or maintenance efforts, as well as their frame of mind—they're not quite thinking, let alone using basic problem-solving skills. Thinking requires the rational part of our brain, and when we're stressed, that's the first thing to go. Instead, we begin to make decisions with what experts call the limbic brain, the lower, more reptilian parts that focus on our basic needs, like sex, self preservation, and ... eating. (Remember, eating is first and foremost a survival skill. That's why hunger urges are so powerful.)

After we have one of these stress-triggered eating events, whether it's an epic ice-cream binge or a few extra servings of a whole wheat pasta dish, guilt kicks in. And all of a sudden, what started as straightforward biology and primal urges—hey, you were hungry and so you ate—turns into an emotional swamp, with more drama than an episode of *Real Housewives*.

In many circumstances in life, bad feelings like that discourage the behavior that caused them. When people discover they hate hot yoga, do they buy a year's worth of classes? No way! But when women feel bad because they've eaten too much, they often respond by eating too much again. No, you're not psycho. And no, it doesn't mean you have an eating disorder. Researchers believe that women who do this see eating as a form of comforting themselves. So when they feel bad—even if it's about overeating—they reward themselves with more food, which makes them feel bad. ... You get the idea.

When clients talk to me about this, they often describe it as an emotional seesaw. But it's not: It's basic science. The brain has its own kind of reward system that secretes chemicals like dopamine and serotonin, which make us feel good. For some people, the craving for that good feeling is bigger than common sense or portion control. In fact, some of the foods that are the worst for us are most likely to trigger that response. "The opioids produced by eating high-sugar, high-fat foods can relieve pain or stress and calm us down," writes David A. Kessler, MD, in his great book, *The End of Overeating.* (Kessler is the former commissioner of the U.S. Food and Drug Administration and has struggled with overeating himself.) "At least in the short run, they make us feel better."

The resulting change in brain circuitry, he says, isn't much different from what happens when people use drugs like cocaine or heroin. The substance—whether it's chocolate or crack—triggers a short-term burst of pleasure. The bad news, of course, is that the good feeling is quickly replaced by a bad feeling. "Oh no," we say to ourselves. Or, à la Britney Spears: "Oops, I did it again."

Does this kind of negative cycle mean you have an eating disorder? No. But it very likely means you have a problematic relationship with food, something experts call "disordered eating." One study by the University of North Carolina at Chapel Hill found that while only about 10 percent of American women between the ages of 25 and 45 have behaviors extreme enough to be classified as true eating disorders, such as anorexia, bulimia, or binge eating, an additional 65 percent have disordered eating behaviors. Some 67 percent of the more than 4,000 women who participated are currently trying to lose weight and have used all kinds of unhealthy tricks to do it—skipping meals, taking laxatives, purging, ditching entire food groups, even smoking. It's such a big problem that 39 percent of women say concerns about what they eat or weigh interfere with their happiness. Overall, three out of four women have an unhealthy relationship with food. And contrary to other studies, this research found that the insanity cuts across all ethnic, educational, and income levels.

Take Your Daily Dose of Kindness

● ● ●   My job is to do two things. First, I need to let you off the hook and coach you in having a little compassion for yourself. (Please trust me on this. Kindness is very calming.) I think the reason we resist compassion is that it feels somehow like giving up. It's as if being nice to ourselves about eating our boyfriend's french fries at dinner last night means we're really giving ourselves permission to go hog wild and eat anything we want, anytime we want. Talk about rigid and unforgiving. Some of my clients sound so puritanical that you'd think they were ready to throw themselves in the stocks because they didn't use a measuring cup for their morning cereal. I find myself sometimes saying things like, "Don't worry, you really won't gain weight because you used creamer in your coffee at that business meeting yesterday." Sometimes, the weight loss process can make women that brittle and rigid. It's just no fun.

Beating yourself up like that isn't just unkind; it's also counterproductive. Here's one of my favorite experiments that proves it. Researchers at Wake Forest University asked a group of women to eat doughnuts while watching TV. (The women thought the experiment was study- ing their reactions to television and eating.) Then they were left alone with three bowls of candy and told it was a taste test. The women who felt bad about eating the doughnuts—the ones who were bashing themselves for their loss of control—ate significantly more candy. Those who had been coached in self-compassion just before the experiment ate significantly less. The compassion instructions were so easy: "I hope you won't be hard on yourself," the researchers simply told the women. "Everyone in this study eats this stuff, so I don't think there's any reason to feel bad."

How great is that? It doesn't need to be the Gettysburg Address or a Shakespearean sonnet. Simply say to yourself, "Oops, overdid it there. Happens to the best of us. I will try to do better, starting right now."

Therefore, kindness is the first ingredient on the Slim Calm Sexy Diet.

What's Your Major Diet Downfall?

● ● ●   It's also a good idea to think about what struggles might lie ahead. That way, they'll cause less stress if and when they happen to you, and you'll have a handful of coping strategies prepared in advance. That's how you'll build your sense of mastery, every step of the way.

Skim through the following list of common stumbling blocks. These are the things that trip up most dieters at one time or another, so it's pretty likely that two or three will have your name written all over them. (Me? I'm sensitive to smell. I know my friends' different types of

HONOR YOUR CRAVING CYCLE

Food cravings are influenced by your menstrual cycle. A University of Hawaii study tracked a group of women over 2 years and found that they were least likely to have food cravings—and most likely to resist them— when they were ovulating, usually 14 days after a period ends. They were most likely to crave, and eat, during their premenstrual phase.

perfumes, and I think I could pick my kids out of a lineup just by using my nose. I'm especially prone to cravings triggered by my senses. The smell of chocolate chip cookies in the oven can usually derail me.)

PROBLEM: **YOU STARVE YOURSELF.** "I don't know what happened," a client will say. "I ate a very small breakfast, and at lunch I went to the salad bar and had a mountain of lettuce, carrots, and some grilled shrimp. I munched celery sticks in between appointments. And even though I was planning on going home and eating a plain grilled chicken breast, a friend called and asked me out for pizza, and before I knew it, I was on my fifth slice." I wish I had a dollar for every time I heard a story like this.

While the person trying to lose weight often sees this as a baffling personality problem—"Why don't I have any willpower?"—this one is pure biology. Hate is a word I almost never use, but I absolutely hate the word willpower. It creates tremendous negative energy.

Eating too little food throughout the day almost always backfires this way. That's because, physiologically, your body is screaming for energy. And psychologically, you're feeling deprived. Both create measurable physical stress, which in turn makes you more vulnerable to overeating as the day wears on.

The problem is that super-restrained eating throughout the day means that our blood sugar, energy levels, and ability to focus are all over the map, making us oh-so-vulnerable to poor food choices. Then we overeat and we gain weight. The result is demoralizing, right? "I suffered all day and then ruined it in 15 minutes," clients tell me. "Why am I so weak?" Being so "good" is almost always bad and results in late-night noshing that sabotages everything.

THE SLIM CALM SEXY SOLUTION: The first skill I teach clients is about learning their hunger quotient—or HQ, for short. Throughout the day, I'd like you to ask yourself: How hungry am I? On a scale of 1 to 10—with 1 meaning you couldn't eat a bite, even if I paid you, the way some people feel after a Thanksgiving dinner; and 10 being so hungry that anything (tablecloths, small dogs, pigeons) looks tasty. Your goal for the next month is to never get hungrier than a 7; preferably even a 6. Any higher than that and you're not being virtuous; you're just setting yourself up to fail.

On this plan, you'll eat plenty of nourishing food throughout the day, including two between-meal snacks and a Happy Hour snack (I'll explain this in a minute). Snacks! You heard me. That's because you need a steady supply of feel-good foods, eaten throughout the day—all providing just the right combination of carbs, fats, and protein. (Protein promotes thermogenesis, the fancy word for fat burning, and is more satisfying than carbs or fats.) This way, when you sit down to dinner, even if you're wiped out from a long day, your blood sugar will be stable enough that you can eat calmly. And you'll be more satisfied, so even if you do have the urge to storm the kitchen after dinner, it will be in a much less reckless way.

In a study at the University of Washington in Seattle, overweight people switched to a diet that was 30 percent protein (roughly what you'll consume on the Slim Calm Sexy Diet). Researchers found that the greater satiety that came from the increased level of protein powered "rapid losses of weight and body fat," due to a decrease in appetite—and a lower caloric intake when the study subjects were given the chance to eat whatever they wanted. Now there's satiety hard at work!

PROBLEM: **YOU GET BORED WITH A RESTRICTED LIST OF FOODS.** Because most diets you've been on likely offer a limited amount of food, each day starts to feel just like the one before—like that old movie *Groundhog Day.* At first, the diet feels easy to follow because the foods are novel to you. (Plus, if you've been eating poorly, a switch to a healthy diet usually makes you feel great.) And as soon as the pounds start to slip off, it's very motivating.

But soon—usually after about 2 weeks, which is the key "induction phase" of popular diets like Atkins and South Beach—those same 5 or 10 foods are more likely to make you yawn than salivate. And the deeper that food rut gets, the more likely you are to crave the tastes, flavors, and textures that are missing. Because you've spent 14 days categorizing foods as either "allowed" or "off-limits," suddenly the forbidden foods are everywhere. "Seriously," a client confided, "I never noticed that there's a Dunkin' Donuts on every block in this town."

THE SLIM CALM SEXY SOLUTION: In the next 6 weeks, you will eat a much wider variety of food than you'd imagine—for many of you, probably more new foods than you've had in the last year. While there is a suggested meal plan for the Slim Calm Sexy Diet, this is not a restrictive eating plan. (The cleanse portion, which you're free to skip, is quite limited. That's why you should do it only for a few days.) And of course, you'll also learn how to stay on the diet when you eat out.

While there is a certain amount of repetition to the way each meal is constructed and to the rhythm of the meals and snacks, my goal is to empower you to eat all kinds of foods—including some you've never tried and some you never thought you would like. I encourage you to switch up the meal plan whenever you please. Go crazy with nonstarchy vegetables, which you can eat freely, and feel free to substitute fruits, grains, fats, and proteins as you move along.

TAKE IT FROM
Keri

THINK THIN

Feeling the urge to eat, and not sure if you should? For the next week, when you find yourself reaching for food, I want you to think THIN:

T *Are you thirsty?*

H *Are you hungry? On a scale of 1 to 10, what's your HQ?*

I *In the mood for something you can't put your finger on? Is it salty, crunchy, sweet, or creamy? Reward yourself with the precise flavor—10 salted almonds, or yogurt drizzled with a teaspoon of chocolate syrup.*

N *Not sure how you feel? Are you stressed? Upset? Imagine putting that feeling on a conveyer belt and sending it away before you reach for a snack.*

Doing so doesn't mean you're cheating. It means you're improvising. Like a good musician, you're interpreting the meal plan and making it your own. If the meals I've laid out start to feel dull to you, dare yourself to walk through the supermarket and buy three new things—whether kumquats, lemongrass, fresh sage, fig vinegar, or red quinoa. (I hope you'll flip through the food chapters or even bring this book to the grocery store with you for inspiration.) By taking charge and adding something new and exciting, you will make the next 6 weels more about building a healthier body and less about slavishly following a restricted meal plan.

PROBLEM: YOU THINK YOU'RE DIETING, BUT YOU ARE REALLY ON A SEMI-HUNGER STRIKE. As you weigh less, you will need to eat less. That's just physics: An itty-bitty Honda needs less gas than a Cadillac Escalade. But when you cut back too much on calories, you actually slow down your metabolism. It's as if you tricked your body into thinking, "Uh oh, we might be heading into a famine—better hang on to each little fat cell with all my might." So not only do you feel crummy because you're not consuming enough food, but you also get discouraged because weight loss slows. It varies, but for most women that threshold is 1,200 calories a day. However, I don't want you to think about calories very often. Counting calories doesn't work for most people, especially since all calories are not created equal. I've done all the math for you. You just need to follow the plan and listen to your body.

There's something else that often comes into play. When I find out a client is consuming too little food, and I look at her food journal, I usually see she's especially skimping on protein. That slows weight loss, since protein takes longer to digest than carbs, according to the National Institute of Diabetes and Digestive and Kidney Disease. Too little protein also means you aren't getting the maximum benefit of protein in building lean muscle.

THE SLIM CALM SEXY SOLUTION: *MORE FOOD!* The meals and snacks I've developed will provide more than enough energy to go to work, live your life, have fun with friends and family, and still lose weight. And because of the way I've constructed the plan, you never even have to think about whether you're getting enough protein, carbs, or fat—I've already balanced it for you. Just follow the plan, listen to your body, and your metabolism will find its perfect level.

Part of what makes this plan work is that I'll suggest certain meals at certain times, in order to help your metabolism run most efficiently. Midmorning and midafternoon snacks are key, and so is this diet's secret weapon: the Happy Hour snack—a generous serving of nutrient-dense foods, eaten about a half hour before your evening meal. I created a special soup and other snacks to make sure your nutrition needs are fully met—and your belly is nicely full—before you head to the dinner table.

PROBLEM: **YOU THINK SHORT-TERM.** I'll often hear diet warriors say things like, "I can do anything for a week." And taking things day by day is an absolutely brilliant approach to life and eating. But the truth is, in order to make a meaningful change in your body, you have to make a meaningful change in the way you live. Following the Slim Calm Sexy Diet (or any plan, for that matter) for 6 weeks and then going right back to the same old "normal" eating won't work. "Normal" is what got you here in the first place.

THE SLIM CALM SEXY SOLUTION: I'm not asking you to go on a diet, really—I'm asking you to create a new normal. Many people rush to get "off" a diet as soon as they've lost a little weight, likely because they really feel they're missing something. Maybe it's a specific food, or maybe it's just the "freedom" to eat what they want, when they want. Either way, it's a decision based on some kind of deprivation. Because we've got 6 weeks to tame your stress and create brand-new reservoirs of calm, the odds of that happening now will be much less. Sure, you may occasionally be tempted to eat a food that doesn't fit with this new way of thinking. But the more empowered an eater you become, the more you'll appreciate the peace of mind that comes from this mastery. Believe it or not, it's not something you'll be willing to trade for any ordinary junk food.

PROBLEM: **YOU THINK YOU CAN EAT YOUR WAY OUT OF EXERCISING.** Some people just hate to work out, and despite my own passion for exercise, I really do get that. But I'm sorry to tell you (as if you haven't heard it a million times from friends, family, the media, and probably your doctor) that you really do have to be more active if you want to find and keep your healthy weight.

Notice I didn't say that you need to work out to lose weight. You don't, and exercise is not the magic ingredient of any weight loss program. In fact, studies have shown that people who diet but don't exercise are somewhat more likely to lose weight than people who exercise more but don't modify their diet. But I'd be kidding you if I didn't tell you that people who exercise have all kinds of health and weight loss advantages over those who don't. What works best? Combining diet and exercise— exactly what you'll be doing for the next 6 weeks.

STEP AWAY FROM YOUR COMPUTER

What if I told you that eating in front of your computer made you eat twice as much? It does! New research published in the American Journal of Clinical Nutrition *shows that when participants were left in front of a computer video game with snacks for a 30-minute period, they ate twice as much as those who weren't at a computer. What's more, they remembered less about what they ate and were more likely to eat excessively as the day wore on.*

Step away from your computer, phone, or TV to really savor what you're eating, and stop when you're truly full.

The world's most successful dieters—whose results have been tabulated in the National Weight Control Registry, maintained by researchers at Brown University—are like weight loss Olympians. They are men and women from all over the country who have been chosen to be part of this database because they've successfully lost a lot of weight: an average of 66 pounds. More remarkably, they've kept the weight off for an average of 5 years. While they don't all work out, most of them do, and they work out hard. They tend to exercise an hour a day, five to six times a week. While you certainly don't need to train like an Olympian, you can find simple, effective exercises that help you maintain a healthy weight.

THE SLIM CALM SEXY SOLUTION: In Chapter 9, you'll find some easy-to-do, easy-to-modify routines that are bound to suit any workout style. Start slowly, but *start*. The latest guidelines from the government note that in order to lose weight, you need to be physically active for 60 minutes a day, most days of the week. If it sounds like a lot, well, it is. And you don't necessarily need to go from zero to 60 like that. The wonderful workouts you'll find in Chapter 9 are 30 minutes each, enough to get you burning calories and maintaining your health.

PROBLEM: YOU EAT WITHOUT THINKING. Sometimes when I use the phrase "emotional eating" with my clients, I can see them balk a little. It makes sense. Who likes to think of themselves as emotionally out of control? And when I ask them to describe a recent overeating experience, they'll say, "I don't know why I ate that. I wasn't even thinking." But if I push a little harder, I often get them to explain that something was happening—they were bored, frustrated, angry, or maybe even a little lonely. And rather than taking the time to acknowledge their feelings, they were just eating to avoid them.

THE SLIM CALM SEXY SOLUTION: Because this type of eating is so tricky for people to deal with, researchers are working all the time to find the most effective ways to fight it. To me, it all comes back to recognizing when stress is in the driver's seat. So whenever you find a forkful of Chinese takeout or a candy bar in your hand—freeze! Physically put your hand around your wrist and pull that hand back. Take a breath or two, step away from the food for a moment, and ask yourself: How hungry am I right now? What's my HQ?

If you're hungry, think back through your day. Did you skip a meal? If so, by all means, eat, but if what's in your hand isn't the right choice, put it down and go fix yourself a meal or a snack that is on the plan. (When this happens to me, I always grab the almonds in my purse. It's my no-fail food solution.)

Your next question: Am I thirsty? Again, it seems like you should know the answer right off the bat, but there are days when I am running so fast that I somehow get knocked off my usual hydration routine. Maybe I left my water bottle at home when I went to the gym, or I skipped my afternoon tea break. Thirst often fools us into thinking we're hungry when we aren't.

Not hungry or thirsty? Take a few more deep breaths and try to figure out what's going on. What's your stress level? Is there anything specific on your mind? A work deadline? A conflict with someone you love? Once you understand how those feelings make you uncomfortable, you'll start to see that eating just to distract yourself is no fun. You're not really enjoying the food. And you certainly aren't looking forward to gaining weight, are you? Didn't think so.

The funny thing is that researchers in the Netherlands have proven that it's not the difficult feelings themselves that make us eat. It's the act of trying to suppress them that sends us scrambling for these so-called comfort foods.

Try something new. A group of women enrolled in an ongoing study at Temple University have had a lot of success using a simple visualization method called the conveyer belt. They visualize putting whatever feeling they've got on a conveyer belt and watching it move away from them.

Also, write down how you feel when you eat. That's why I've included a 1 to 10 stress scale in the food journal (yes, I want you to keep a food journal—I've posted one for you at www.nutritiouslife.com). But please, don't just use the number scale. Jot down a few words like "Stressed" or "Wanna strangle my boss." The Temple research has shown that writing something that simple can "un-stuff" your feelings and help you curb emotional eating.

PROBLEM: **WHEN YOU CRAVE, YOU CAVE.** There are often times you just want something. For many women, it's chocolate; for others, ice cream. And, perhaps more commonly, it's a food you can't quite put your finger on. Pretzels? Nachos? Peanut butter?

That, my friend, is a food craving and nothing to be ashamed of. We all have 'em, and in fact if we didn't, we might never eat. A new study from Tufts University tracked women dieters over a 1-year period and found that 94 percent reported experiencing cravings. Research from the University of Calgary in Alberta, Canada, puts the stat even higher—at 97 percent. And we give in to the cravings about 50 percent of the time.

THE SLIM CALM SEXY SOLUTION: Years of hands-on practice has taught me that dealing with cravings is a key to weight loss. Sure, you can fight cravings off for a little while. But eventually, one will sneak up on you when you're tired and suck you into a big diet detour. Show

DON'T EAT AROUND A CRAVING

I've seen women who are craving something, maybe chocolate or a crunchy-salty fix, do far more damage trying to eat around the desire than if they had embraced their craving and had what they wanted. They'll eat this, they'll eat that, all in an effort to avoid the "bad" thing. Honestly, no food is that bad. Take a small serving of the best option whatever it is, grab a spoon, and sit down and enjoy every bite.

me a woman who just scarfed down an entire box of Girl Scout cookies, and I'll show you someone who was wrestling with a craving for hours before it happened.

When you get that feeling, take a few deep breaths and sit down to really think about your craving. Again, what's your HQ? Usually, when we're hungry, just about anything sounds good. Cravings, on the other hand, are usually super specific.

One tactic is to try to put your finger on what you're yearning for and find the best food to satisfy it. It's a great way to see how smart your body is. Investigating a craving for something crunchy and sweet might make you realize you skimped on protein and fat that day, and a handful of pecans is just what you need. Reward your craving with the right match for it.

But if you're craving a food that's not on the plan, spend a few minutes fantasizing about it. It will feel strange at first, especially if you've never done any visualization or meditation. Imagine yourself eating the thing you crave—holding it, putting it in your mouth, and actually chewing it. It will make you feel almost as satisfied as eating the real thing. A study done at Carnegie Mellon University found that people who imagined eating 30 M&M's, one at a time, were able to eat less of the real thing. (I know from experience that M&M's are very high on many people's cravings list.) Interestingly, behavioral researchers have found this helps people who are trying to quit smoking, too.

The Science of Cravings

• • •   People have been trying to understand food cravings for thousands of years. Like dreams, cravings sometimes seem impossible to understand. They have that same random quality—"Whoa, Fig Newtons … where did that come from?" And they're subject to amateur interpretations, as anyone who's been pregnant knows—"Ooh, you're craving something sweet? You must be having a girl!"

Sometimes, these cravings seem to have mystical powers. "Honestly, Keri, I don't know how it happened," a client will tell me. "I was at the mall shoe shopping, and then—boom—all of a sudden, I was eating a cinnamon bun the size of a cabbage!"

It would be nice to believe that our cravings are linked to a genuine nutritional need. Sometimes they are. Often, when a client tells me she's longing for something sweet and creamy, we'll check her food journal and realize she's inadvertently slacked off on dairy for a few days. Or someone with a cold will jones for fresh fruit—that acidic tang of a pineapple or grapefruit is just what the doctor ordered. Many women crave red meat when they're having their period, which makes sense since beef is such a good source of iron and many women struggle with low-level anemia, especially during their period.

The reverse is certainly true as well. Researchers from Cornell University have discovered that the kinds of foods women are most averse to in pregnancy are those that are most potentially harmful to a developing fetus, including alcoholic drinks, caffeine, and strong-tasting vegetables, for example, or meat and eggs, which are more likely than some other foods to cause food-borne illnesses. And it's a kind of evolutionary brilliance that toddlers start to hate new foods around 18 months, just when they're old enough to find their way into things that might be poisonous.

But for the most part, there's no reason to presume that a food we crave is actually something we need. Case in point: Many of us often crave something salty, even though the typical American consumes way more salt than is healthy. In fact, the latest polling from Cornell University reveals that only about 40 percent of foods people crave are good for them. Women say their top three comfort foods are ice cream, chocolate, and cookies.

There's even some evidence that people who aren't getting enough of what they need have opposite—or contradictory—cravings. In my practice, it's often the woman craving the jumbo turquoise cupcake who's also craving tortilla chips. Her cravings are a red flag that she's missing out on all kinds of tastes and textures.

There are gender differences, too. The Cornell University poll found that men's top comfort foods include soup, pizza, and pasta, along with ice cream. Guys are much more likely to salivate over a steak than a cupcake. But they get fewer cravings. And researchers at Brookhaven National Laboratory, using very high-tech scanners to measure brain activity, have found that men are better able to resist their favorite foods. Researchers think that might explain why it is tougher for women to lose weight.

So if a craving doesn't come from a nutritional need or from actual hunger, where does it come from? While researchers have long known that cravings can be triggered by smells (hot pizza, freshly baked sweets) and associations (hot dogs at baseball games), a team of Australian researchers thinks mental imagery may be one of the strongest triggers. In fact, the Australian researchers found that when people in their study imagined a food they craved, they couldn't concentrate on much else and performed poorly on cognitive tests.

In my experience, most underlying cravings have a subconscious cause. I have a client who eats beautifully all day long. She is the model citizen for a Slim Calm Sexy life. But the minute she heads for home, she starts to eat all kinds of food that aren't right for her—big, fatty cinnamon twists from the bakery near her house or yogurt-covered pretzels from the convenience store. It's taken her some time, but she now realizes that this kind of eating isn't about food cravings at all. It's about the way her current job—being trapped in a cubicle she doesn't like very much all day long—makes her feel. As soon as she leaves the office, she feels like she has to celebrate her "freedom" somehow. It's proof that keeping a good food journal can help us see what we really need. It goes well beyond the food itself. My client really needed to update her résumé and find a more satisfying job.

Increasingly, it seems that once we're really in the mood to indulge that craving, it's hard to stop us. At the University of Chicago, scientists tracked chronic dieters—people who have had a fair amount of experience with gaining and losing weight. They found that once the dieters are in that "hot" state, when their desire for a certain food has been primed beforehand (maybe by staring at a display case of pastries), managing those cravings becomes more difficult.

Remember: Grab your hand and pull it away from the food. Think about what you are reaching for, and do something about it. Giving in will slow your weight loss, and ignoring cravings just isn't effective.

A team of researchers at St. George's University in London recently divided women into three groups. Some were told not to think about chocolate, some were told to think about nothing but chocolate, and some were told to think about anything they wanted. If you've ever heard of Adam and Eve, you've probably already guessed that the women who were told chocolate was off-limits ate significantly more as soon as they had a chance.

So what else works? Own the craving. Take a few minutes to really appreciate what it feels like, and accept it for what it is. Researchers in the Netherlands have found that very simple mindfulness techniques— as basic as accepting a craving—significantly lowered the number of cravings people had. The experts think it has something to do with being able to stop the obsessive thinking, the tug-of-war as you wonder, "Should I eat the pie, or should I resist?"

Not a mindfulness kind of gal? Then once you realize you've got a craving, by all means acknowledge it to yourself and get moving. Another study from England found that a brisk 15-minute walk helped bust a chocolate bar craving.

What Are Your Main Food "Triggers"?

• • •   It's fascinating the way all of us have slightly different hot buttons when it comes to overeating. For me, it's often that I'm just beat, and something happened with my schedule to make me skip a meal or a snack. But everyone is different. At Nutritious Life, I ask my clients to select the two things that are their biggest triggers. Why only two, when most of us have more than that? Because it's always better to start with smaller changes on a new eating plan. Otherwise, it gets too over-whelming, and many people just give up entirely.

||||||||||||||||||||||||||||||||||||||||||||||||||||||||||||||||||||||||||||||||||||||||||||||||||||||||||||||||||||||||||||||||||||||||||||||

END YOUR FOOD TRIGGERS

Pick from the list below, or jot down your specific triggers. And promise yourself that for the next 6 weeks, you will pay special attention to protecting yourself from them (I'll show you how on page 107):

- ☐ Skipping breakfast
- ☐ Eating too fast
- ☐ Always finishing a meal with a sweet
- ☐ Shopping without a grocery list or when you're hungry
- ☐ Not shopping at all, so when you're hungry you have to go out or order in
- ☐ Eating in front of the TV or computer
- ☐ Picking off your kid's plate
- ☐ Snacking on empty calories
- ☐ Grazing (eating all day long without listening to your HQ)
- ☐ Eating too large of a starch or fat serving at a meal
- ☐ Going too long between meals

||||||||||||||||||||||||||||||||||||||||||||||||||||||||||||||||||||||||||||||||||||||||||||||||||||||||||||||||||||||||||||||||||||||||||||||

Is Food Addictive?

• • •   Every so often, someone who is struggling to take off extra pounds will ask me, "Am I addicted to food?"

Even a decade ago, that phrase made a lot of experts scoff. "Addiction" was a word usually applied to drugs or alcohol, not food, which everyone needs to survive. But while the idea of food addiction is still controversial, more and more evidence suggests that some people with weight problems are genuinely addicted.

For one thing, technology has advanced enough that neuroscientists can document, through brain imaging, that the pleasure some people

TAKE IT FROM
Keri

FIND A GYM CLOSE TO HOME

Sometimes the biggest barrier to working out is just getting there. So if you're gym shopping, don't overlook your friendly YMCA. There are more than 2,700 YMCAs across the country, and 57 percent of American households live within 3 miles of one. Many now offer a wide variety of yoga, Pilates, and dance classes as well as cardio machines. Memberships are reasonably priced compared with those at fancier health clubs.

get from overeating and from certain "high reward" foods makes their brain light up in the same way that drugs like cocaine and opiates light up the brain of others. And, according to research from Rush University Medical Center in Chicago, sweets, carbohydrates, fats, sweet-fat combinations, and possibly processed and/or high salt foods all seem to have this potential, too, There's also a chemical component: Eating these foods creates a rush of dopamine, just as drug use does.

It isn't that these highly palatable foods are addictive, exactly, according to nutrition researchers at Penn State University. It's that people become addicted to them following a restriction/binge pattern of eating. And of course, it's no surprise that this addictive behavior leads to weight gain and obesity. But it also leads to depression, anxiety, and even substance abuse.

Dr. Kessler made big news with the publication of *The End of Overeating*, which details the many sneaky ways the food industry has encouraged addictive eating, including layering these sweet and salty tastes on top of one another to make their products irresistible. (Turns out, this combo of sugar and salt is linked to intense cravings.) What's more, these foods are everywhere. Drive down any road in the country, and you'll find far greater access to unhealthy foods than to the good stuff. It's crazy that most of us live within a few miles of dozens of different ginormous cheeseburgers and brownie-blast sundaes, but hardly any great fresh salads. And adding insult to injury, these carb-, sugar-, and salt-laden foods are usually cheaper than healthier alternatives.

But does just being overweight mean you are a food addict? I don't think so, and neither do most experts. If you worry that you might have a problem that goes deeper, please check it out. While there isn't a foolproof way to diagnose a food addiction—whether it's compulsive overeating, binge eating, or a whole range of eating disorders—you may need help from an addiction specialist, as well as a registered dietitian.

Two places to start: Overeaters Anonymous, which is based on the same ideas as Alcoholics Anonymous (go to www.oa.org). Meetings aren't your bag? I urge you to find a counselor who can help you decide if you need treatment. The American Psychological Association has a Web site for such referrals, http://locator.apa.org.

the eyes definitely have it

"I'm on the see-food diet," my clients sometimes say. "If I see food, I eat it!" I always laugh, because it is so true. Seeing high-calorie food—in any amount—definitely primes us to want to eat it, and our eyes fool us about how to control portions.

Often, we are unaware of how much the appearance of food can trigger us to eat. Brian Wansink, PhD, an economist who runs the prestigious Food and Brand Lab at Cornell University, has spent years researching eating behavior and has proven that our eyes constantly fool us. Among his findings:

+

People who use short, wide glasses think they contain less liquid than tall, slender glasses. (Turns out we think shorter glasses contain less, no matter how wide they are.) In one experiment, people poured 76 percent more juice when using shorter glasses.

+

Moviegoers given popcorn in big containers will scarf down 34 percent more than those given the same popcorn in medium-size containers —even when it's yucky and stale.

+

When dishing up ice cream, people given larger bowls typically serve themselves 31 percent more than people given smaller bowls. And if the serving spoon is bigger, the servings increased another 14.5 percent.

So always, always use smaller dishes, glasses, and silverware when you can. Then you will feel better about eating everything you see.

bring on the food

slim calm sexy diet essentials

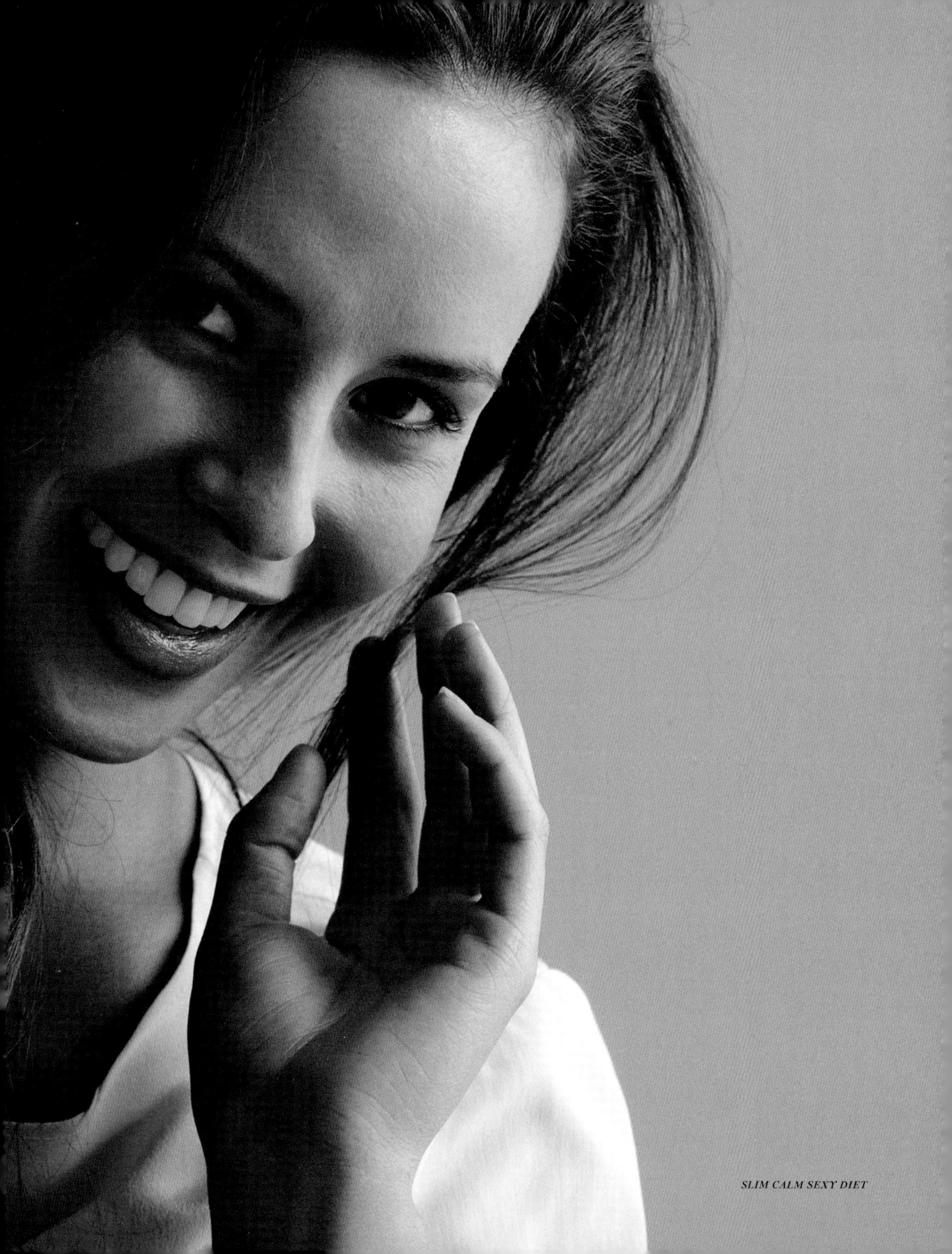

Sometimes

people ask me if I became a nutritionist because I like to help people lose weight, and of course, I do. But the real reason is because I *love* food. And it's fun to watch what happens when I teach others that it's okay for them to love food, too. You might even say I'm a bit of a matchmaker. My job is essentially to hook you up with foods you're crazy about—high-performance chow that will help you burn off that excess fat, boost your mood, and put the vroom back in your libido.

Once I make the introductions, the ball is in your court. Many of the Slim Calm Sexy Diet meals will become instant classics, and the ingredients will be on your go-to list for years. You'll treasure them for how they taste, of course, and how satisfied they leave you. But most of all, you'll love how confident you feel. These foods fuel your healthiest self, knocking off pounds while keeping you energetic and happy.

It's what I call empowered eating, and it's my mantra. It's the most important skill I teach my clients—and now you. Most of us live in a world where we can get just about anything we want to eat, whether it's from a delivery service or a nearby drive-thru. But why eat just anything when you can sink your teeth into delicious foods that have the power to change your body, your mood, your health, and your life?

On the Slim Calm Sexy Diet, you'll learn that eating real food—not the absence of food—is what losing weight is all about. I'm not going to convert you into a nutrition nut who knows exactly how many grams of vitamin C are in your kiwifruit. Nor will I try and turn you into an over-the-top foodie. There are some who take great pleasure in knowing the smoke point of grapeseed oil, or can differentiate between fresh thyme and marjoram at 50 paces, or have 365 recipes for a fennel bulb. I say, more power to you. You're welcome here, and you'll find plenty to eat that meets your high standards.

But if you're like most people, and you're not sure about what you can and can't eat to lose weight, you've come to the right place. Remember: Eat Empowered. I think you're going to like those two words so much you'll write them on sticky notes and post them around your house.

Empowered eating is when you let your nutrition know-how—that's the thinking part of your brain—be the boss of cravings, which are the more primitive side of your brain. The more you know about your foods, the more savvy an eater you will become. You know that old joke about how if all you have is a hammer, every problem starts to look like a nail? Well, with the Slim Calm Sexy Diet, you'll have a toolbox fully stocked with hundreds of power-packed foods.

Think in Threes

• • •   Over the course of a day you will be eating roughly equal proportions of carbs, proteins, and fats. A moderate-protein diet with a reasonable amount of good carbohydrates and the appropriate amount of healthy fats is the best way to lose weight—and the most effective way to maintain your weight loss.

The First Third: Satisfying Proteins

• • •   Protein is essential to the way our bodies function. We need it to build and repair all tissues in the body, especially muscles; to form enzymes and hormones; and even to build the antibodies that keep us safe from infection. There's a reason I talk about it first: Researchers now know that protein is the most satisfying type of food, meaning it makes you feel the fullest and fuels you best for longer periods. Experts once believed that fat was more satisfying, and some argue that carbs are really what keep them going. But overall, the *American Journal of Clinical Nutrition* reports, protein reigns supreme.

While there's never been a debate about why we need protein, there have been decades of arguing about how much is enough. You'll notice the Slim Calm Sexy Diet is roughly one-third protein, and that's a very deliberate decision. First, this amount, which falls within the guidelines of the National Institutes of Health's Dietary Reference Intakes, is proven to be the most slimming. Researchers from the University of Washington School of Medicine in Seattle found that when people increased the amount of protein they consumed from 15 to 30 percent—roughly what you'll do on the Slim Calm Sexy plan—they lost significantly more weight in a 12-week period. They also reported a "markedly" increased level of satisfaction.

Second, this amount of protein will support your efforts to build muscle, which in turn helps you burn fat, according to research from the University of Texas. The greater your muscle mass, the higher your metabolic rate. There's also plenty of evidence that more intense workouts may require a bit more protein, eaten just before, during, or after your workout. This protein not only makes you exercise more efficiently; it also allows you to exercise more intensely, report exercise physiologists at Texas A&M.

On this plan, you'll eat the healthiest kinds of slimming proteins: turkey, chicken, grass-fed beef, and even pork. You'll also munch on plenty of dairy protein, fish, nuts, seeds, and eggs (one of my favorites). Here's a rundown of some of my favorite ways to get protein (see the appendix for a full list).

LOTS OF DAIRY.

This includes creamy Greek yogurt, fat-free milk, cottage cheese, and low-fat cheeses. That's because a recent study in the *Journal of Nutrition* has shown that a combination of dairy protein and dietary calcium produces a greater lean body mass and lower fat mass than either nutrient alone. And, while it's controversial, a University of Tennessee study found that dieters who added three servings of yogurt a day to their diets lost 81 percent more belly fat over 12 weeks than those who didn't eat yogurt.

Not only is yogurt slimming, but it's also satisfying, portable, sold in many places, and fits in your purse. What's not to love?

If you don't love yogurt, are lactose intolerant, or vegan, there are other options. Try almond milk, rice milk, or hemp milk.

FISH, FISH, AND MORE FISH.

I've loaded these menus with fish because I've found that once people get the hang of cooking it, they love the health benefits— whether it's the slimming protein kick that comes from cod and flounder or the healthy-fat perks of omega-3 in salmon.

It's also more satisfying than other protein foods. Researchers in Sweden studied a group of people who had eaten a lunch of either fish or beef. Four hours later, the subjects sat down to dinner. While both groups rated their hunger at an equal level before their evening meal, the fish-for-lunch crowd ate an average of 11 percent fewer calories, yet reported being just as satisfied after dinner as the other group. Remember, highly satisfying foods are inherently slimming. You won't be tempted to eat something not in the plan or to overeat.

EGGS-CELLENT PROTEIN.

Eggs are cheap, versatile, easy to cook, and they're even sold in single portions. And they're powerfully slimming. In a recent study at St. Louis University, participants who ate eggs for breakfast lost 65 percent more weight than those who didn't. (One warning: If you have diabetes or heart disease, it's best to limit your intake to three egg yolks per week, according to researchers at Harvard University.)

Don't be shy about eating those sunny yellow yolks. They're packed with healthy nutrients, including choline, a structural element in cell membranes.

TAKE IT FROM
Keri

ISN'T WHOLE MILK HEALTHIER?

Wait a minute, you may be thinking, haven't I been hearing that whole milk is actually healthier than reduced fat varieties? It may be: New and very compelling research suggests that after years of getting labeled as a bad guy, linked to higher rates of heart disease, the fats in dairy may actually reduce the risk of developing heart disease, as well as colon cancer. And other studies suggest organic whole milk may be even healthier.

That's why I do recommend working small amounts of whole-milk products into your diet, once you've reached your goal weight. For the best weight loss results, though, you'll need to stick with the low-fat and fat-free recommendations I've made throughout the plan.

WRITE IT DOWN, WATCH IT HAPPEN

Want to maximize your weight loss results? Take a few minutes to write down your goals for the month ahead. How much do you plan to lose? What major eating changes do you plan to make so that it happens?

Researchers at McGill University in Montreal recently asked 177 students to make a goal of eating more fruit in the next 7 days. While all the students did so, the group that had made a concrete plan, written it down, and then visualized it—right down to where they would buy the fruit and prepare it—ate twice as much fruit as those who didn't.

The Second Third: Hearty Carbs

• • •   Whether it's comforting oatmeal, robust barley, or wonderfully crunchy-chewy quinoa, this diet is full of healthy whole grains, even bread. Sometimes, clients are surprised when I explain that these foods are slimming. After all, consumers have been bombarded by "carbs are evil" messages over the last 20 years. It's easy to see why people are confused.

In fact, I do think some carbs are evil, and that's why you won't find sugars, white flours, or any refined, overly processed foods on this plan. These foods increasingly have been shown to lead to insulin resistance, also called metabolic syndrome. It works like this: Insulin helps blood sugar (glucose) enter cells. If you have insulin resistance, your body doesn't respond to insulin, and blood sugar can't get where it's supposed to go. As a result, the body has to produce more and more insulin. As insulin and blood sugar levels rise, it affects function and raises the level of blood fats, such as triglycerides. Your blood pressure rises. Fat accumulates around your middle, and you are in a danger zone, inching your way toward a diabetes diagnosis and at a much higher risk for heart disease.

In his book *Why We Get Fat,* health reporter Gary Taubes makes a compelling case for just how closely refined carbs are linked to insulin resistance, altering the body's own regulatory system so that it becomes almost impossible to lose weight. He argues that the basic calories-in, calories-out approach to weight loss—a way of looking at obesity that has shaped many nutritionists and experts—is missing the point by not focusing more on this dangerous connection. We begin to secrete insulin as soon as we even start thinking about eating carbs, he points out, and our insulin levels are effectively determined by the carbohydrates we eat. "The more carbohydrates we eat, and the easier they are to digest and the sweeter they are, the more insulin we will ultimately secrete. . . . We do not get fat because we overeat," he insists. "We get fat because the carbohydrates in our diet make us fat."

While Taubes takes his argument to warn people away from all carbs, I'm not willing to do that. Healthy carbs, like the ones found in vegetables, fruit, and whole grains, provide us with the energy we need to get through our day. Carbs that come from whole grains are full of fiber, which means we digest them slowly to get a nice, steady supply of energy—not that quick, sugary rush that comes from white carbs (followed by that depressing crash after it wears off).

Whole grain and other complex carbs also cause our brain to make serotonin, a chemical that is soothing and makes us happy. (It's the chemical targeted by many of the leading antidepressant drugs, by the way.) In fact, researchers at the Massachusetts Institute of Technology have proven that when we eat too few carbohydrates, our brain actually stops making serotonin. So if you ever found that swearing off carbs made you grouchy, there's your explanation. And because women have less serotonin in their brains than men, we're particularly vulnerable. People who crave carbs, these researchers found, are especially likely to notice a mood shift in the late afternoon or mid-evening, which is why you'll always have a Happy Hour snack then!

The Final Third: Friendly Fats

• • •   The fat controversy keeps getting louder—and it should be center stage. After all, heart disease continues to be the biggest killer in the United States, and the wrong fats bear some of the blame.

That's why monounsaturated fats, like nuts and olive oil, are such a big part of the Slim Calm Sexy Diet. But I'd like you to develop more than a passing acquaintance with polyunsaturated fats, as well. These include safflower, sesame, soy, corn, and sunflower oils, nuts, and seeds. Unsure of the difference? Polyunsaturated oils are liquid at both room temperature and in the refrigerator. Monounsaturated oils start to solidify in the fridge. Both deserve a place in your diet because they may help lower your blood cholesterol level when used in place of saturated fats, reports the American Heart Association. And while they need to be used sparingly—oils are usually about twice as caloric as a protein or a carb—they're also critical in your weight loss plan.

While there's no doubt that naturally lower-fat foods are key for weight loss (veggies, for example), eliminating all fat is a bad idea. It's found in, and essential to, many protein-rich foods. Our bodies need fat to function, and they can't manufacture it from scratch. It's used in cells, and it's the only way we can stockpile certain nutrients, like the fat-soluble vitamins A, D, E, and K. On a cellular level, triglycerides are the types of fats best suited for energy use, and they pack twice as much energy as a carb or a protein. So when we need a little extra energy—for finishing a workout or running for a bus—we use enzymes called lipases to break down these stored triglycerides, reports the National Institutes of Health. Then our mitochondria convert those triglycerides into the body's main energy source, a substance called adenosine triphosphate.

That was a pretty technical explanation (I lose most people as soon as I say "enzymes"). But here's what I love about nutrition research. Even though scientists know all this, they still don't fully know how it all happens. Right now, food geeks in lab coats are peering at silkworms, fruit flies, and mosquitoes, all in the name of helping us get a better handle on fat consumption.

Fat is also vital for mental health. It helps us feel calm and, believe it or not, even boosts libido. (Studies have linked both nuts and fish to higher levels of testosterone, a hormone men and women need in the sack.)

What fats won't you find in my plan? The level of saturated fats, the kind that come from animal products, is very low. There are some—from dairy, meats, and the egg yolks—but not many. And there are no trans fats. Not a smidgen. Trans fats are also unsaturated, but they are the result of adding hydrogen to vegetable oils used in commercial baked goods and for cooking in most restaurants and fast-food chains. They're harmful because they can raise total and LDL ("bad") cholesterol and lower HDL ("good") cholesterol.

While I've made selecting fats foolproof in this plan, I invite you to make a habit of checking out food labels. Now that companies are aware of how many consumers want to avoid saturated and trans fats, they're creating healthier options all the time. You just have to be careful. Not all of them are any healthier. I've even seen candy—pure sugar—labeled as "trans fat free," like it's a health food.

NUTS EVERY DAY.

Wondering why I'm so nuts about nuts? There are so many things to love about them that sometimes I don't know where to start.

From a health standpoint, nuts are loaded with antioxidants and good-for-your heart fats. Second, they combine protein and fat, with few carbohydrates, in a way that's uniquely satisfying. And they're a known weapon in your weight loss arsenal.

A study at the City of Hope National Medical Center found that including them in a 24-week diet for overweight and obese people resulted in a much bigger weight loss. And blood pressure decreased most for the almond eaters, as did insulin resistance—so much so that many participants had their diabetes medications reduced.

Shower All Three with Antioxidant Power

• • • Now that you know how solid the protein-carb-fat portion of the plan is, let's add on the fun stuff: the mountains of produce you'll eat in the next month. Eat as much and as many types of nonstarchy vegetables as you please. The more the better! And savor the fruits, as well. Because they're higher in natural, healthy sugars, I've calculated fruits toward your carbohydrate levels for the day. These plant-based foods—the ones Mother Nature is cranking out for our benefit all the time—are the ones that will likely add the most joy, zest, and zing, all while slimming your body, thrilling your tastebuds, and satisfying your spirit.

Whenever possible, I've made selections that contain the highest levels of antioxidants. I know you've heard the term before, and I won't bore you with a molecular lecture, but antioxidants are powerful nutrients. If you'd like to read more, my book, *The O2 Diet*, focuses on this. They work to contain the damage caused by free-roaming oxygen in our bodies, the free radicals that have been linked to disease, fatigue, and overweight. Some amount of oxidation—the same thing that causes an apple to turn brown after it's cut—is normal, of course. But too much of it is powerfully damaging, whether it's caused by stress, diet, or our environment. The plant foods I've included here, from green tea to asparagus to blueberries, made the cut because they offer more of this antioxidant power than others. I'm a big believer in antioxidants, and I'm thrilled to see that many people are trying to increase their antioxidant consumption whenever they can, in order to lose weight and improve their health.

How to Stock Up on Omega-3s

These fatty acids aren't just important to help you achieve a blissfully calm weight loss experience. They have a huge impact on your long-term health. And by now, everyone knows that salmon and walnuts are great sources, but there are many other options. Here are some I love:

FOOD	SERVING SIZE	OMEGA-3 CONTENT
Flaxseed Oil	2 Tbsp	15.4 g
Health Warrior Chia Seeds	2 Tbsp	6 g
Naturally More Flax & Omega-3 Peanut Butter	2 Tbsp	4.1 g
Ground Flaxseed	2 Tbsp	3.2 g
Salmon	4 oz	3 g
Walnuts	14 halves	2.5 g
Canned Salmon	4 oz	2.2 g
Grass-Fed Beef	4 oz	2 g
Canned Sardines	4 oz	1.7 g
Atlantic Mackerel	4 oz	1.4 g
Canned Tuna	4 oz	1.1 g
Living Harvest Tempt Hempmilk	1 c	1.1 g
Uncle Sam Cereal	4 oz	1 g
Gold Circle Farms DHA Omega-3 Eggs	1 egg	150 mg
Organic Valley Omega-3 Milk	1 c	75 mg
Silk DHA Omega-3 & Calcium Soymilk	1 c	32 mg

Power Produce List

These 20 foods are here because they're both delicious, and uniquely powerful. They rank very high in both nutrient density (meaning there's all kinds of nourishing stuff in there) and water density (which means they are a powerful diet food). What makes them amazing is that they're top of the charts on both lists—iceberg lettuce, for example, gets high marks for its water content but not for its nutrients; the reverse could be said of an avocado. I hope you'll fall in love with all 20 and constantly find new ways to work them in to your repertoire.

FOOD	SERVING SIZE	TOTAL FIBER (G)	WATER CONTENT
Artichoke	1 medium (cooked)	10.3	82%
Broccoli	1 cup (boiled)	5.1	91%
Apple (with skin)	1 medium	4.4	84%
Peas	½ cup (cooked)	4.4	79%
Raspberries	½ cup	4	87%
Blackberries	½ cup	3.8	88%
Brussels Sprouts	½ cup (cooked)	3.2	87%
Orange	1 medium	3.1	87%
Mango	½ small	2.9	82%
Kale	½ cup (fresh, chopped)	2.5	90%
Spinach	½ cup (cooked)	2	92%
Yellow Squash	½ cup (cooked)	1.8	94%
Asparagus	6 spears	1.8	91%
Celery	1 cup (chopped)	1.7	95%
Carrot	1 medium (raw)	1.7	87%
Blueberries	½ cup	1.7	85%
Tomato	1 small	1.6	94%
Strawberries	½ cup	1.5	92%
Red Cabbage	1 cup	1.5	92%
Cauliflower	½ cup (cooked)	1.4	92%

Commonly Asked Questions

What do I need to do to prepare for the Slim Calm Sexy Diet?
In addition to the food shopping lists (the cleanse list is on page 57, and the regular meal plan list starts on page 274), you might find it helpful to spend a little time reorganizing the kitchen. There's no need to do major housekeeping, but try to clear some space in the fridge and pantry so that you'll see the Slim Calm Sexy foods front and center. Make space on your counter to set up your blender, because there are smoothies and shakes ahead. And make room in an easy-to-reach drawer for your measuring cups and spoons, to make cooking and portion control easier. It also helps to invest in three or four pieces of glass containers with lids, so you can make extra and store it. And get out your prettiest dessert plates—the ones that are slightly smaller than dinner plates. Try using them to help with portion control over the next 6 weeks. Researchers at Cornell University found that when people eat from bigger plates, they typically pile on between 25 and 28 percent more food.

I'm not hungry when I wake up. Can I eat my "breakfast" later in the day?
Your brain may think you're not hungry, but your body knows better. It's been fasting since before bedtime, and in order to kick that metabolism in gear, it needs energy. My suggestion is that you start with a nice big glass of lemon water when you get up, then have your coffee or green tea and get ready for your day. Eat at least part of your breakfast— maybe the fruit portion or perhaps just the nuts. Then head to work. Once you settle into your day's routine, check your hunger quotient (HQ): I bet you're ready for the rest of your breakfast now.

Remember the weight loss Olympians I mentioned earlier—the ones who lost all that weight and have kept it off for 5 years, and who share their wisdom in the National Weight Control Registry? About 78 percent of them say they eat breakfast every single day. Keep in mind that I'm not asking you to eat a lumberjack platter. When you're trying to lose

TAKE IT FROM Keri

EVERY MEAL IS MONDAY MORNING

Did you get off track today? Stop the slide right now. I've heard people joke that if they fell halfway down a flight of stairs, they wouldn't turn around and say, "Oh well, I screwed up—might as well throw myself all the way down." So why overeat at dinner because you overate at lunch? Remember, every snack and every meal is a total do-over. So don't criticize yourself for the last "bad" thing you ate. Celebrate the good decisions you're making right now.

weight, a right-size breakfast is your first opportunity to make sure you're getting the energy and nutrients you need to feel even-keeled, and to be master of your own diet destiny.

How quickly will I see results?

Within a day! Drinking plenty of water and green tea and eliminating hard-to-digest bad-for-you foods make an impact early on. My clients tell me that their eyes seem clearer, their face is a little less puffy, and their skin seems smoother. They usually feel calmer, and that changes their appearance, too. And in just a few days, you'll notice your clothes fit you a little better. Most people will lose 5 to 6 pounds in the cleanse period, another 5 pounds in the first 2 weeks, and then about 2 pounds each week after that.

How often should I weigh myself?

Believe it or not, this is one of the most loaded, complex questions in the diet business. The problem is that even though you want to lose weight—and you will, I promise—weight itself is a very imprecise measure. Everyone's weight fluctuates during the day by as much as 3 to 5 pounds. It depends on things like how much fluid and sodium you've consumed and, ahem, the contents of your digestive tract. It can be very damaging for someone who has been impeccable about following the plan to step on a scale and see practically no results, even though they may truly be losing weight. It just isn't evident on the scale yet. Some people get so overly focused on those numbers that it can trigger a diet meltdown. They'll throw in the towel just because the scale isn't moving the way they expected it to. But in truth, weight loss always makes a jagged little downward line. It looks more like the ever-fluctuating stock market than a straight progression.

So here's my best advice for getting used to the down-a-little, up-a-little nature of the weight loss process. Weigh yourself once a day, at the same time, without any clothes on. Researchers have found that this daily weigh-in not only helps with weight loss, but it also prevents weight gain. Cornell University researchers have found that daily weigh-ins even help fight the dreaded "freshman 15."

Let's say you do come up with a number you don't like. Suppose a client starts with a weight of 150, goes down to 147 in Week 1, then back to 150 in Week 2. She is often practically devastated. "All this effort," she'll say, "and I haven't lost any weight?"

"No," I'll insist, handing her a tissue. (I'm not kidding—this scale thing really messes with some women's minds.) "It's not the same 150 pounds." Here's what I mean: Since we typically have a 3-pound range, I'm betting that the first weigh-in of 150 might just as easily have been

153. And the last 150 could have been 147, which would mean a weight loss of up to 6 pounds. That's great! The key is to eat consistently and weigh yourself consistently. And on those days when the scale just seems stuck or even inches up a bit, despite your best efforts? Please don't worry—it's normal. You will soon see a steady downward trend.

If a daily weigh-in is too nerve-racking, find your own schedule. Just promise me you won't weigh yourself more than once a day. That road leads to its own kind of insanity, including fooling yourself into believing you "gained" 2 pounds at lunch and "lost" 2 pounds after dinner. On the flip side, even if you're a scale-o-phobe (which so many people are), push yourself to get on the scale at least once a week. Imprecise or not—and as telling as your favorite pair of skinny jeans can be in this regard—body weight is the best ongoing measure of how well the plan is working and whether you need to make any adjustments.

If you're really afraid of the numbers, just be kind to yourself and avoid the scale if it upsets you. But find some other measure, so you can track your progress. Many gyms offer a body-fat analysis, which is another viable way, albeit not perfect, to track your progress on the plan.

I'm on a pretty strict budget these days, and many of the foods you suggest are expensive—especially all the organic produce and salmon. How can I do it on the cheap?
You're right—and personally, I think it's a shame that we live in a world where fast food is super affordable, and fresh organic food can break the bank. While it takes a little effort, you can follow this plan and spare your wallet. Here are a few simple tricks:
• Shop seasonally by touring the produce aisle before filling your basket. Market prices fluctuate from week to week, and something is always cheaper than it was last week. Done this way, you'll find fresh is often more affordable than you think. One recent government study found, in fact, that produce averages 12 to 18 cents per serving.
• Visit farmers' markets and food co-ops, and join a community-supported agriculture program (where you typically buy a share or a half share per season). All are generally cheaper than supermarkets.
• Don't turn up your nose at canned and frozen fruits and vegetables. They are often well priced, just as nutritious, and very convenient. Canned wild salmon (look for "boneless" and "skinless" on the label) is affordable, tastes great in salads, and is among the healthiest choices you can make, since it's made from wild salmon.
• Eat eggs. They're a wonderfully affordable, healthy protein.
• Buy yogurt in bulk, or even make your own. (I know, I'd never do it either. But I have friends who insist their homemade yogurt is the easiest, yummiest, cheapest, and healthiest.)

Sexy in a **FLASH**

BALSAMIC BERRIES

Set a romantic mood by making dessert look special. Slice strawberries very thinly, arrange them in a fan shape, and then drizzle them with a little balsamic vinegar, which provides an unexpected tangy twist. Classic, slimming, pretty on the plate, and very sexy.

Do I have to exercise?

I could tell you that you'll lose weight on the Slim Calm Sexy Diet if you choose not to exercise. It's not a lie—you will. But you won't be as slim. People who cut down on the amount of energy they consume and increase the amount of energy they expend lose weight faster. They also feel better. Their health improves, their stress levels drop, and they smile more. And their sex lives get way hotter!

I know that plenty of people loathe working out. But I have to be honest, just as I would if you were asking me, "Is it okay if I smoke?" Not exercising may be killing you. Between 25 and 35 percent of American adults, as many as 50 million, are basically sedentary. Thanks to the Aerobics Center Longitudinal Study, researchers know that these folks are at risk for any number of diseases and early death. Early death. In fact, researchers have shown, people who are overweight but active are healthier and live longer than thin people who don't exercise.

So the short answer is no, you don't have to exercise. But trust me, it's well worth a try. Please turn to page 148 for three unique workouts I think you'll really like. They're designed for people who aren't fans of the gym.

"But I can't eat _____ [fill in a food from our plan]!"

No worries. Please don't choke down any food on the plan if you really don't like it. If it's a vegetable, replace it with one that you do like. See the appendix for options. The same goes for a fruit, protein, or starch. (It still boggles my mind that there are people who don't like oatmeal, but I hear that many of you had bad experiences as a child. I'm sorry to hear that! Oatmeal is a fabulous source of fiber, as well as vitamins B12 and E.) The same goes for foods that you're either allergic to or that don't agree with you. I've already mentioned almond milk, rice milk, and hemp milk as good substitutes for those who are avoiding dairy. Going gluten free? Rice and sweet potatoes are good choices. Have a nut allergy? Keep plenty of avocados and olives on hand.

I travel a lot. Can I still do the Slim Calm Sexy Diet?

Yep! While the whole question of carrying food and drinks (not to mention mascara and tweezers) on planes has gotten very complicated, arm yourself with a good travel plan and you'll be fine. Resealable plastic bags of nuts, turkey jerky, and individual nut butters are all good bets. Carefully wrapped food is allowed to travel through security. (Uneaten fruit doesn't have to be wrapped, though, so why not toss an orange and an apple in your carry-on? If you get stuck circling Cleveland for hours, you'll thank me.) Staying prepared with easy, healthy options will prevent you from heading toward that disastrous fast food line.

Can I have any food labeled "low-fat"? How about sugar substitutes, like Splenda?

Please don't. While I'm a believer in plain low-fat yogurt, there's a world of difference between that and the many poor choices out there with a "low-fat" or "fat-free" sticker on them. Many of these "fake" foods are full of all kinds of chemicals and often sugars that you just don't need. And they don't help you lose weight. For example, in an experiment at Cornell University's Food and Brand Lab, dieters were given low-fat granola. (For the record, it has only about 12 percent fewer calories than the real thing.) But people ate 32 percent more than when they were given the higher-fat version. Is it that lower-fat foods are inherently less satisfying? Maybe, to a degree. But it's just as likely that the "low-fat" buzzword triggers some sort of spring break free-for-all in our heads—"Woohoo! I can eat more, way more."

My suggestion? When you crave "forbidden" foods, like ice cream or french fries, allow yourself to have them as your "conscious indulgence." Measure out a portion, sit down, pay attention, and enjoy every bite. I bet when you do that, you won't need to keep eating and eating and eating.

Another example: Much of the low-fat flavored yogurt Americans eat, believing they are making a really healthy food choice, is actually a trick. Manufacturers take out the fat (which isn't all that much or all that unhealthy), and then load it back up with high-fructose corn syrup and other sugars. Instead of a good protein choice, like the low-fat plain yogurt I recommend, it's a carb and sugar disaster.

Artificial sweeteners are also more of a problem than a solution. They keep you craving unnaturally sweet foods. I'm going to teach you to appreciate the natural sweetness of fruits. Dumping yellow, pink, or blue packets on everything will undermine that—not to mention, those uninvited chemicals are worrisome. That goes for diet soda, too. There's no solid evidence it helps people lose weight. And how's this for scary? One recent joint study by Columbia University and Miami's Miller School of Medicine found that diet soda drinkers are 61 percent more likely to have vascular problems, including stroke, than those who don't drink it.

In the first 2 weeks, I lost 7 pounds; this week, only 1.5. What am I doing wrong?

Nothing! On the Slim Calm Sexy Diet—as on most weight loss plans—people typically drop more in the first 2 weeks. There's a simple explanation: Cutting back on the amount of food you eat creates an energy imbalance, which your body solves by releasing glycogen, a carbohydrate stored in your muscles and liver. Glycogen holds on to a lot of water, so when you burn it up, water is released. That water is what accounts for a lot of early weight loss. After the excess glycogen is used, your body then has to work at using excess fat for energy. That's still weight loss, but since fat doesn't store water the same way, it happens more slowly and therefore feels like you're shedding fewer pounds.

In fact, as a general rule, I don't want you to lose more than 2 pounds per week. Don't be disappointed. Losing more than 2 pounds per week may mean you are breaking down the lean protein in your body, and we don't want that. You want to keep (and build) muscle, not starve it away.

Most dieters will lose between 1 and 2 pounds per week as they follow a healthy eating plan like this one, and they'll continue to lose weight until they reach their goal. In the long run, more realistic weight loss goals result in better long-term success. If you're more concerned about dropping a dress size before your high school reunion next month, relax. This diet is proven to help you shed 17 pounds in 6 weeks.

I don't feel calm. I'm snapping at everyone I talk to. What gives? Can I please have more carbs to sweeten my mood?
Changing the way we eat does affect our moods, but my guess is that you don't need more carbs—you need a nap. (Sorry, my kids hate it when I say that, too.) Often, people don't realize that they are chronically tired because they have "cured" their fatigue with food—usually a late-afternoon sugar- or carb-rich snack, or coffee—or with pure adrenaline. For the next week, make sure you track your sleep in your food journal, and see if going to bed an hour earlier makes a difference. If you still feel grouchy, add a little more protein to your lunch and dinner (maybe you are light in calories).

Okay, I screwed up. I went out to lunch and had a cheeseburger and fries. I felt terrible and drowned my sorrows in a big bowl of pasta later that night. Should I start over with the cleanse?
You didn't "screw up." Decades of behavioral research tells me that you are not failing—you're learning. The important thing is, what's the lesson? Since I wasn't there, I can only guess, but my first question is, what was your HQ? Did you let yourself get too hungry? If you don't think it was a splurge borne out of hunger, what was it? Have you been eating the full variety of the plan? It's okay if you aren't. Many people follow the Slim Calm Sexy Diet by picking a few favorite meals and sticking with them. That's great for some people. But for others, it starts a food rut and creates an unconscious yearning for something different, and makes little food benders like yours inevitable.

If you think that's what happened to you, try to work a little harder on food variety. Go to a different supermarket, for example, or perhaps explore a new produce aisle. It's also interesting that you craved beef. I'm a meat lover, too, and the smell of a sizzling steak gets me drooling.

Some women crave iron-rich beef during their periods, when they might be anemic. Have you been cheating yourself on protein servings? Maybe experiment with a slight increase in protein each day, and see if that makes you feel more satisfied.

And nope, no need to go back to the cleanse—you didn't sin, and the cleanse isn't penance. Just get back on track with your next meal.

It's bedtime, and I just realized that I had such a hectic day that I didn't eat all the food I was supposed to. I missed lunch and my afternoon snack. Should I eat them now?

No. However, think of moments like these as great learning opportunities. Be extra attentive to your HQ tomorrow. How do you feel, energy-wise? How is your concentration? If you work out, what's your stamina like? Forgetting to eat—not something that happens to me very often— can be a symptom of being too busy. If that goes on too long, it sets you up for a major eat-athon, so be extra careful about how you're managing your schedule and stress load. A useful tip if you're on the computer all day is to set reminders for yourself in Outlook, or do it on your cell phone—especially for those between-meal snacks that are easy to forget.

the slim calm sexy cleanse

|||||||||||||||||||||||||||||||||||||||||||||||||||||||||||||||

Lose 5 Pounds in This 3-Day Jump-Start

• • •   It's possible that at this moment, you're not feeling so great. You haven't been eating right, sleeping enough, or working out the way you want. You might even be avoiding sex more often than not. Blecchhh! And it may be because you're so upset about that bulge around your middle that you're talking all kinds of trash to yourself and beating yourself up even more for feeling terrible.

If so, I suggest you start here: a 3-day cleanse that will catapult you right into the healthy benefits of the Slim Calm Sexy Diet. You'll likely lose about 5 pounds in the cleanse period, and by the fourth day, when you start the diet plan, you'll be in prime position to keep that weight loss momentum going. You'll also feel, well, cleansed. Rejuvenated.

I promise, this isn't an extreme cleanse or anything close to it. I don't think they usually work, and most people find them very difficult to follow. Instead, these pure, simple foods provide the most natural type of "detox."

People often throw the word "detox" around when it comes to a cleanse, and it's become such a part of our dieting slang that we don't think about what it really means. But that's a mistake. It's not that your body is so filled with toxins or that eating well for 3 days can work some sort of cellular miracle. (And to be fair, many mainstream docs sort of roll their eyes when people use the term.)

But here is what can and does happen. Your digestive system has a chance to get rid of all the processed foods and fats, and to rest a little.

Your stomach has a chance to reset to what a true portion feels like it. Eating right-size meals for a few days is the best way to cure the chronic portion distortion so many people live with. Your palate has a chance to reawaken to the goodness of natural flavors. And perhaps most important, your mind and spirit get the opportunity to enjoy a mini-retreat. In a perfect world, of course, we'd be able to do this cleanse at some kind of wonderful, cell phone–free spa, with a massage every day. But you can adapt that idea right here at home: For 3 days, take as much time to pamper yourself as you can. You're on the verge of losing weight—one of the healthiest gifts you can give yourself. Make it special.

As your body gets a break from all the hard-to-digest processed foods you've been eating, you'll find yourself feeling more relaxed, more in control, and more energetic, starting on the very first day. Here's what I'd like you to eat:

▶ *Breakfast*

1	cup green tea
1	egg plus 2 additional egg whites (scrambled or hard-cooked)

▶ *Snack*

½	grapefruit
½	teaspoon cinnamon

▶ *Lunch*

2	cups greens or greens juice
4	ounces lean protein of your choice
¼	avocado
1	cup green tea

▶ *Snack*

2	tablespoons sunflower seeds or 10 almonds

▶ *Happy Hour Snack*

1	cup sliced cucumbers
1–2	tablespoons rice vinegar

▶ *Dinner*

2	cups steamed spinach or kale
4	ounces grilled fish or lean protein of your choice
1	cup Slim Slaw (page 76)

Calm in a FLASH

LAZE INTO YOGA

Here's a pose that my hard-core yoga pals swear is one of the most restorative positions ever. It's easy, and for each day of the cleanse, I'd like you to try it for 15 minutes (or 5 minutes at the very least!). Take a folded blanket and roll it into a cylinder shape like a bolster pillow. Now lie down on the floor and scoot your butt near the wall, about 5 or 6 inches away. Put your legs straight up the wall with the pillow under your lower back. Let your arms fall naturally to your sides, and let all the tension release from your legs, hips, and back. Breathe deeply and enjoy!

Make sure you drink plenty of water, more than you think you might need. I know it's hard, especially when you're just starting out. Often, when we've been eating poorly, our thirst and hunger signals get all tangled up. Drinking plenty of water will allow your body to cleanse itself and also prevent you from feeling hungry.

I'd like you to actually mix up your water by choosing from the three "recipes" below. That way, you're not just drinking mindlessly, but you'll be sure to drink enough. You'll be thinking more about how certain flavors make you feel and how that affects your hunger quotient (HQ). Try to drink 10 glasses on each of the 3 days, including one when you first wake up. Mix up a pitcher of each of these waters and leave them in the fridge, so they're easy to grab throughout the day.

SLIMMING WATER:

Add a dash of cayenne pepper for a kick of energy.

CALMING WATER:

Add a few slices of cucumber for a soothing effect.

SEXY WATER:

Add a little cinnamon, clove, and cardamom for an exotic flavor.

TAKE IT FROM Keri

MINTY FRESH, BUT NOT SO SEXY

Some people love water with mint in it—me included. It's a little more refreshing on a hot day. But some researchers believe that mint may actually lower libido—nice for a nap, but not so nice for a Saturday night.

CLEANSE GROCERY LIST
(3 DAYS):

PRODUCE

- ☐ 2   grapefruit
- ☐ 6   cups greens of your choice or green juice
- ☐ 6   cups spinach or kale
- ☐ 1   avocado
- ☐ 2   red cabbages
- ☐ 2   green cabbages
- ☐ 3   cucumbers

EGGS

- ☐ 9   DHA-fortified eggs

NUTS, NUT BUTTERS, AND SEEDS

- ☐ 6   tablespoons sunflower seeds or ⅓ cup almonds
- ☐ ¾   cup almonds (for Slim Slaw)

MEAT AND SEAFOOD

- ☐ 24 ounces lean protein of your choice
  (such as sliced turkey, shrimp, and fish)

CONDIMENTS AND TEAS

- ☐ Green tea (enough for 6 servings)
- ☐ Cinnamon
- ☐ Dijon mustard
- ☐ Rice vinegar

slim calm sexy

the eating plan

SLIM CALM SEXY DIET

Now

that I've explained the science behind the Slim Calm Sexy Diet, you probably have two really big questions for me: What can I eat? And when can I start? I've already given you the very basic structure of the plan, but let me go over it again. You'll be eating three meals a day, each of them centered on:

The perfect balance. No worrying about how much carbs, protein, or fat to eat. I've created each day to include roughly a third each of carbs, protein, and fat: the most nourishing whole grains; lean and satisfying meat, chicken, and fish; delicious dairy foods; and the types of fats your body needs most, mainly from antioxidant-rich plant sources such as olives, nuts, and avocados.

100 percent real foods. These foods are the real thing, with an emphasis on fiber-rich starches, fruits, and vegetables. As much as possible, I've chosen unprocessed organic items, because they're better for you and for the planet. You'll be getting plenty of antioxidants and omega-3 fatty acids. You'll also be eating lots of herbs and spices, which don't just add flavor, but also increase the range of antivoxidants and other nutrients you need for healthy weight loss.

Slimming science. I've chosen the perfect combination of these foods—and the timing of when you eat them—as well as included special ingredients with added slimming power. Whether it's cinnamon or sunflower seeds or pears, each meal and snack combines the right amount of nutrients for extra weight loss oomph!

DON'T FORGET TO WEIGH IN

I know, you bought this book because you're dreading looking at those numbers. But I hope you will take the brave step to get a good, honest weigh-in before you start. It's not the only way to measure your success on the Slim Calm Sexy Diet, but it's an important first step. As the weeks go by, you'll be able to gauge your progress and to see whether you need to make any adjustments.

But there's more. You'll also have a morning snack, an afternoon snack, and you'll enjoy a little trick I call the Slim Calm Sexy Happy Hour: a perfectly engineered cocktail of 100-proof nutrition, specifically designed to help speed your weight loss four ways. These Happy Hour snacks are:

• **TIMED PERFECTLY.** Over and over, clients tells me the same story: "I was perfect all day. I had a great breakfast and a really healthy lunch. But then I went out to dinner and ruined it all." It's not an accident—as we get closer to dinner, we're more likely to be tired and low on energy. And even if we manage to avoid tempting foods during the day, it's tougher at dinner. Research from the University of Texas at El Paso has found that we tend to eat about 42 percent of a day's calories—close to half—during and after dinner. And the meals typically served in the evening are likely to be higher in the less-healthy types of fat. My Happy Hour snacks will protect you, making it easier to go into the dinner hour with a calm, in-control feeling.

• **A HAPPY RITUAL.** There's something a little personal about each of these snacks—a hint of mint, a crunch of walnuts, a little extra zing from rice vinegar. Even if you're cooking for a crowd or meeting friends for a late dinner, you can find a private moment to sit down and really enjoy these foods. It's a great time to hit "pause" on your day and think back on what you've done right or enjoyed. Take a few deep breaths between bites, and think about what's ahead in the next few hours. What triggers might be at the restaurant or in your fridge? How will you control them? Think of these Happy Hour snacks as your own private moment to regain that sense of control.

• **HIGH WATER VOLUME.** I've already primed you for afternoon sucess with a satisfying snack, like the Slim Shake or the crunchy Slim Slaw. But these Happy Hour treats—a special salad or vegetable-dense soup—that I'd like you to eat about a half hour before your dinner are designed to really fill you up. A sensation of fullness is built-in protection against overdoing it. While nutritionists have always known that fullness helps people control eating, research from Penn State has shown that eating these high-volume foods before a meal help people consume as much as 20 percent fewer calories. If possible, I'd like you to have your Happy Hour snack a half hour or so before dinner.

• **NUTRIENT DENSE.** While all the foods in the plan are nutrient dense—a fancy way of saying they have more good stuff per calorie than many other foods—the ingredients in the Happy Hour snacks are especially so because they're low in calories but loaded with nutrients. And they also include a high percentage of water, making them even more potent weight loss weapons.

The 6-Week Plan

✛ Every day, drink at least two cups of green tea. The antioxidants are great for your health and also speed weight loss. Also, drink at least 8 glasses of water.

✛ Every night with dinner, have a salad of at least 1 cup of greens—spinach, kale, and mesclun are all great—in addition to the veggie you're having. If you have prepared your evening meal with an oil, eat your salad greens with vinegar, herbs, spices, or lemon juice. For example, on your Portobello Burger night, you won't need to add a fat. But if you skip the cheese, go ahead and get your fat serving either by having a tablespoon of oil-based dressing, a portion of nuts, or 2 teaspoons of oil.

✛ Add as many herbs and spices as you like. I didn't want to intimidate you by using so many different ingredients in each meal, but these really ratchet up the flavor and nutrition level of everything you eat. Cinnamon, nutmeg, cloves, oregano, thyme, rosemary, basil, and parsley are always on my countertop. Experiment with parsley on your cucumber salad and nutmeg in your cottage cheese. Aim to add some to every meal and snack!

Slim Calm Sexy Cooking Tips

BAKING In general, whole cuts of meat such as beef and pork should be cooked until a food thermometer inserted in the thickest part of the meat reaches an internal temperature of at least 145 degrees, or 160 degrees for ground meat. All poultry items should reach 165 degrees. All meat should rest for 3 minutes after cooking to ensure doneness. Fish should be baked until it is opaque throughout, reaches 145 degrees, and flakes easily with a fork. Whole potatoes should be pierced with a fork and baked at 400 degrees for 45 minutes or until tender, depending on size.

BOILING Generally, grains can be simmered covered, until water is absorbed and grains are softened, using a 1:2 grains to water ratio and a dash of salt. Turn off the heat and let rest, covered, for a few minutes before stirring.

GRILLING Coat a nonstick pan with canola oil spray and place over medium-high heat. Season meat and seafood with sea salt and pepper before grilling.

ROASTING For no-fuss roasting, mist veggies with 3 sprays canola oil spray, toss and spread in a single layer on a baking sheet. Roast at 400 degrees for 15 minutes, turning once. For chicken and most meats, coat on all sides with 1 tsp olive oil, and season with sea salt and pepper. Place in baking pan and roast at 400 degrees for 20 minutes or until cooked through (see temperatures above for baking).

SAUTEING AND STIR FRYING Coat a nonstick skillet with canola oil spray and cook meat first, then remove from skillet. Coat the pan once more with spray and add veggies. Cook veggies until fork-tender, then add meat and mix with a dash of soy sauce or seasoning as indicated. (Remember to peel and devein shrimp!)

	MONDAY	TUESDAY	WEDNESDAY
breakfast	**Pumpkin-Pear and Milk** 1 small pear, cubed 1 Tbsp pumpkin seeds 1 cup almond milk Pour milk over pear and pumpkin seeds. Sprinkle ¼ tsp cinnamon.	**Nutty Oats** 1 cup fat-free milk ½ cup steel-cut oats Prepare oats with milk and top with 7 chopped walnut halves.	**Power Yogurt** 1 cup açai-flavored Oikos Greek yogurt ¾ cup Smart Bran cereal 2 Tbsp ground flaxseed Top yogurt with cereal and flaxseeds.
snack	15 raw almonds	2 ribs celery with 2 tsp natural peanut butter	1 hard-cooked egg
lunch	**Spinach Turkey Salad** 2 cups baby spinach 1 Tbsp chopped red onion ¼ cup cherry tomatoes 4 oz sliced turkey Toss with 2 tsp cold-pressed olive oil, 2 tsp grated parmesan cheese and ¼ tsp dried basil.	**Open Faced Veggie Sandwich** 1 slice whole grain bread 2 Tbsp guacamole or ⅛ avocado 4 Tbsp hummus ¼ cup alfalfa sprouts 1 slice tomato Layer on bread and sprinkle with sea salt and pepper to taste.	**Wild Salmon Salad** 4 oz canned wild salmon 2 cups chopped romaine ¼ cup sliced cucumbers 8 chopped olives Toss all with lemon juice and sea salt to taste.
snack	Slim Shake	Slim Slaw	Slim On-the-Go
dinner	**Portobello Stack** 1 portobello mushroom 2 oz reduced-fat Cheddar 1 slice tomato Small baked sweet potato Season mushroom with sea salt and pepper. Add cheese and broil until melted. Top with the tomato before serving.	**Simple Salmon** 4 oz salmon 1 cup brussels sprouts Season fish with gomashio (sesame salt) and broil. Roast brussels sprouts and serve on the side.	**Beef Stir Fry** 4 oz lean beef ⅓ cup brown rice 1 cup snow peas, water chestnuts, carrots Stir fry beef and vegetables, and serve over brown rice.

see page 76

See page 274 for the grocery list!

THURSDAY	FRIDAY	SATURDAY	SUNDAY
Colorful Cottage Cheese ½ cup fat-free cottage cheese ⅛ cup dried mango 18 pistachios Top cottage cheese with mango and nuts.	**Cereal Gone Nuts** 1 cup fat-free milk ¾ cup Smart Bran cereal 10 raw, chopped almonds Top cereal and milk with almonds. Sprinkle ¼ tsp cinnamon.	**Chocolate Peanut Butter Smoothie** 1 cup fat-free chocolate milk 1 small banana 2 tsp natural peanut butter Blend all with 1 cup ice until smooth.	**Egg and Cheese Melt** 1 oz low-fat Swiss cheese 2 fiber crackers 1 hard-cooked egg, halved Top each cracker with half an egg and ½ oz cheese. Broil for 1 minute or until the cheese melts.

THURSDAY	FRIDAY	SATURDAY	SUNDAY
2 Tbsp sunflower seeds	15 raw almonds	1 hard-cooked egg	2 ribs celery with 2 tsp natural peanut butter

THURSDAY	FRIDAY	SATURDAY	SUNDAY
Yogurt Chicken Salad 4 oz chunked white meat chicken (mixed with 2 Tbsp plain fat-free yogurt, 1 Tbsp balsamic vinegar, 2 tsp cold-pressed olive oil, ½ tsp Dijon mustard) ⅓ cup cold, cooked bulgur 2 cups chopped romaine Serve chicken and bulgur over lettuce.	**Greek Salad** 2 cups chopped romaine ½ cup sliced cucumber ¼ cup canned or frozen (thawed) artichoke hearts ¼ cup sliced tomato 2 oz reduced-fat feta cheese ½ cup lentils Toss all with 2 tsp cold-pressed olive oil and ½ tsp oregano.	**Quinoa Pistachio Salad** ⅓ cup cooked quinoa 18 pistachios ½ cup chickpeas ½ cup cold-pressed olive oil, ¼ fresh lemon juice, ½ tsp salt, ¼ tsp pepper 2 cups spinach Toss with 1 Tbsp lemon vinaigrette dressing and serve over spinach.	**Burger to Bite** 4 oz 85% lean organic ground beef burger 1 oz reduced-fat Cheddar cheese 1 cup steamed string beans Broil burger and top with cheese. Serve with string beans on the side.

THURSDAY	FRIDAY	SATURDAY	SUNDAY
Slim Shake	Slim Yo	Slim Slaw	Slim On-the-Go

THURSDAY	FRIDAY	SATURDAY	SUNDAY
Tofu Kebabs 4 oz cubed firm tofu alternated on kebabs with red and yellow peppers, red onions, mushrooms 1 cup steamed spinach Season kebabs with sea salt and pepper. Broil and serve with spinach on the side.	**Foil-Baked Cod** 4 oz cod filet 1 steamed artichoke 2 tsp cold-pressed olive oil mixed with 2 tsp lemon juice and herbs of choice (dipping sauce) Coat cod with 1 tsp olive oil, squeeze of lemon, herbs of choice, and bake. Serve with artichoke and dipping sauce.	**Spicy Shrimp Marinara** 4 oz shrimp (peeled and deveined) ⅓ cup marinara sauce 1 cup steamed spinach Sprinkle shrimp with red pepper flakes before sautéing. Toss with sauce and serve with spinach on the side.	**Rotisserie Chicken** 4 oz white meat skinless chicken 1 cup roasted asparagus topped with 2 Tbsp shredded parmesan cheese ⅓ cup cooked wild rice Roast chicken and serve over rice with asparagus on the side.

	MONDAY	TUESDAY	WEDNESDAY
breakfast	**Warm Quinoa** 1 cup soy milk ⅓ cup cooked quinoa 2 Tbsp chia seeds Add soy milk to quinoa and top with chia seeds.	**Cherry Yogurt** 1 cup Oikos Greek Yogurt ½ cup fresh, pitted cherries 2 Brazil nuts, chopped Top yogurt with cherries and nuts.	**Almond Butter Toast** 1 cup fat-free milk 1 slice whole wheat toast 2 tsp almond butter Spread almond butter on toast. Sprinkle ¼ tsp cinnamon, and serve with glass of milk.
snack	15 raw almonds	2 stalks celery with 2 tsp natural peanut butter	1 hard-cooked egg
lunch	**Caprese Lite** 1 slice whole grain toast 2 oz fresh mozzarella 1 slice tomato 2 tsp cold-pressed olive oil 1 cup crudite(red and yellow bell peppers, celery, mushrooms) Layer mozzarella and tomato on toast, drizzle with olive oil, and season to taste. Serve with side of veggies.	**ORAC Omelet** 1 whole DHA- fortified egg/2 egg whites ¼ cup spinach ¼ cup chopped tomatoes ¼ red onions ⅛ avocado Prepare omelet with veggies and avocado, and top with 1 tsp dried oregano.	**Art-Tuna Salad** ½ cup artichoke hearts (canned or jarred in water) 4 oz water-packed chunk light tuna 2 tsp cold-pressed olive oil 2 cups baby spinach 4 high-fiber crackers Mix tuna with olive oil, toss with spinach and artichokes, and drizzle with 1 Tbsp balsamic vinegar.
snack	Slim On-the-Go	Slim Shake	Slim On-the-Go
dinner	**Roasted Pork Tenderloin** 4 oz pork tenderloin 1 cup cauliflower Roast pork and serve with steamed cauliflower on the side.	**Grilled Scallops** 4 oz scallops 1 cup steamed broccoli ⅓ cup cooked quinoa Grill scallops and serve with quinoa and broccoli on the side.	**Vegetarian Chili** 1 cup Amy's Organic Black Bean Chili 1 cup steamed bok choy Prepare chili according to package and serve with bok choy on the side. (An easy, healthy prepared meal for those super-busy days!)

THURSDAY	FRIDAY	SATURDAY	SUNDAY
Feta Scramble 1 whole DHA-fortified egg/2 egg whites 1 oz reduced-fat feta cheese ½ grapefruit Scramble eggs with cheese, and serve with grapefruit on the side.	**Cottage Cheese Melon Cup** ½ cup fat-free cottage cheese ½ cantaloupe, cubed 2 Tbsp ground flaxseed Serve cottage cheese with cantaloupe and top with flaxseeds.	**Mozzarella Melt** 1 oz fresh mozzarella 1 slice whole wheat toast 2 tsp cold-pressed olive oil Top toast with cheese, and drizzle with olive oil.	**Almond Avocado Smoothie** 1 cup almond milk ¼ avocado 1 small banana Blend all with 1 cup ice.
2 Tbsp sunflower seeds	15 raw almonds	1 hard-cooked egg	2 stalks celery with 2 tsp natural peanut butter
Easy Kale Salad 2 cups chopped kale 1 Tbsp pine nuts 2 oz goat cheese ½ cup cherry tomatoes Balsamic vinegar Toss ingredients together and drizzle with balsamic vinegar.	**Hearty Roasted Veggie Salad** 2 cups chopped romaine 2 cups roasted carrots, zucchini, mushrooms, onions, red peppers ½ cup chickpeas ½ cup cold-pressed olive oil, ¼ fresh lemon juice, ½ tsp salt, ¼ tsp pepper Toss vegetables and chickpeas together and serve with 1 Tbsp dressing.	**Med Platter** 4 Tbsp hummus 8 olives 1 cup sliced cucumber and tomatoes tossed with balsamic vinegar ½ cup artichoke hearts (canned or jarred in water) 4 high-fiber crackers Plate all together and serve with crackers on the side.	**Traditional Turkey Unsandwich** 4 oz sliced turkey ¼ sliced avocado 1 slice tomato 1 cup sugar snap peas Layer turkey with avocado and tomato, with sea salt and pepper to taste. Serve with sugar snap peas on the side.
Slim Yo	Slim Shake	Slim On-the-Go	Slim Slaw
Chicken Sausage 4 oz chicken sausage 1 steamed artichoke ½ cup cooked wild rice Grill and slice sausage and toss with rice. Serve artichoke on the side.	**Grilled Lemon Chicken** 4 oz chicken breast 2 tsp cold-pressed olive oil 1 tsp thyme 2 lemon slices 1 cup steamed spinach ½ cup mashed butternut squash Brush chicken with olive oil and grill. Layer lemon slices on top and sprinkle with thyme. Serve with spinach and squash on the side.	**Roasted Filet** 4 oz beef filet 1 cup steamed bok choy or broccoli Roast meat and serve with vegetable of choice on the side.	**Fish Tacos** 4 oz cod 2 small corn tortillas 2 Tbsp guacamole 1 Tbsp fat-free Greek yogurt 2 Tbsp salsa ½ cup shredded romaine 1 cup red and yellow bell peppers, chopped Grill fish and layer on tortillas with veggies, guacamole, yogurt and salsa as desired!

	MONDAY	TUESDAY	WEDNESDAY
breakfast	**Power Yogurt** 1 cup açai-flavored Oikos Greek yogurt ¾ cup Smart Bran cereal 2 Tbsp ground flaxseed Top yogurt with cereal and flaxseeds.	**Nutty Oats** 1 cup fat-free milk ½ cup steel-cut oats Prepare oats with milk and top with 7 chopped walnut halves.	**Pumpkin-Pear and Milk** 1 small pear, cubed 1 Tbsp pumpkin seeds 1 cup almond milk Pour milk over pear and pumpkin seeds. Sprinkle ¼ tsp cinnamon.
snack	1 hard-cooked egg	2 ribs celery with 2 tsp natural peanut butter	15 raw almonds
lunch	**Wild Salmon Salad** 4 oz canned wild salmon 2 cups chopped romaine ¼ cup sliced cucumbers 8 chopped olives Toss all with lemon juice and sea salt to taste.	**Open Faced Veggie Sandwich** 1 slice whole grain bread 2 Tbsp guacamole or ⅛ avocado 4 Tbsp hummus ¼ cup alfalfa sprouts 1 slice tomato Layer on bread and sprinkle with sea salt and pepper to taste.	**Spinach Turkey Salad** 2 cups baby spinach 1 Tbsp chopped red onion ¼ cup cherry tomatoes 4 oz sliced turkey Toss with 2 tsp cold-pressed olive oil, 2 tsp grated parmesan cheese and ¼ tsp dried basil
snack	Slim On-the-Go	Slim Slaw	Slim Shake
dinner	**Rotisserie Chicken** 4 oz white meat skinless chicken 1 cup roasted asparagus topped with 2 Tbsp shredded parmesan cheese ⅓ cup cooked wild rice Roast chicken and serve over rice with asparagus on the side.	**Simple Salmon** 4 oz salmon 1 cup brussels sprouts Season fish with gomashio (sesame salt) and broil. Roast brussels sprouts and serve on the side.	**Portobello Stack** 1 portobello mushroom 2 oz reduced-fat cheddar 1 slice tomato Small baked sweet potato Season mushroom with sea salt and pepper. Add cheese and broil until melted. Top with the tomato before serving.

THURSDAY	FRIDAY	SATURDAY	SUNDAY
Colorful Cottage Cheese ½ cup fat-free cottage cheese ⅛ cup dried mango 18 pistachios Top cottage cheese with mango and nuts.	**Egg and Cheese Melt** 1 oz low-fat Swiss cheese 2 fiber crackers 1 hard-cooked egg, halved Top each cracker with half an egg and ½ oz cheese. Broil for 1 minute or until cheese melts.	**Chocolate Peanut Butter Smoothie** 1 cup fat-free chocolate milk 1 small banana 2 tsp natural peanut butter. Blend with 1 cup ice until smooth.	**Cereal Gone Nuts** 1 cup fat-free milk ¾ cup Smart Bran cereal 10 raw, chopped almonds Top cereal and milk with almonds. Sprinkle ¼ tsp cinnamon.
2 Tbsp sunflower seeds	2 ribs celery with 2 tsp natural peanut butter	1 hard-cooked egg	15 raw almonds
Yogurt Chicken Salad 4 oz chunked white meat chicken (mixed with 2 Tbsp plain fat-free yogurt, 1 Tbsp balsamic vinegar, 2 tsp cold-pressed olive oil, ½ tsp Dijon mustard) ⅓ cup cold, cooked bulgur 2 cups chopped romaine Serve chicken and bulgur over lettuce.	**Burger to Bite** 4 oz 85% lean organic ground beef burger 1 oz reduced-fat Cheddar cheese 1 cup steamed string beans Broil burger and top with cheese. Serve with string beans on the side.	**Quinoa Pistachio Salad** ⅓ cup cooked quinoa 18 pistachios ½ cup chickpeas ½ cup cold-pressed olive oil, ¼ fresh lemon juice, ½ tsp salt, ¼ tsp pepper 2 cups spinach Toss with 1 Tbsp lemon vinaigrette dressing and serve over spinach.	**Greek Salad** 2 cups chopped romaine ½ cup sliced cucumber ¼ cup canned or frozen (thawed) artichoke hearts ¼ cup sliced tomato 2 oz reduced-fat feta cheese ½ cup lentils Toss all with 2 tsp cold-pressed olive oil and ½ tsp oregano.
Slim Shake	Slim On-the-Go	Slim Slaw	Slim Yo
Tofu Kebabs 4 oz cubed firm tofu alternated on kebabs with red and yellow peppers, red onions, mushrooms 2 cups steamed spinach Season kebabs with sea salt and pepper. Broil and serve with spinach on the side.	**Beef Stir-Fry** 4 oz lean beef ⅓ cup brown rice 1 cup snow peas, water chestnuts, and carrots Stir fry beef and vegetables, and serve over brown rice.	**Spicy Shrimp Marinara** 4 oz shrimp (peeled and deveined) ⅓ cup marinara sauce 1 cup steamed spinach Sprinkle shrimp with red pepper flakes before sauteing. Toss with sauce and serve with spinach on the side.	**Foil-Baked Cod** 4 oz cod filet 1 steamed artichoke 2 tsp cold-pressed olive oil mixed with 2 tsp lemon juice and herbs of choice (dipping sauce) Coat cod with 1 tsp olive oil, squeeze of lemon, and herbs of choice, and bake. Serve with artichoke and dipping sauce.

	MONDAY	TUESDAY	WEDNESDAY
breakfast	**Cottage Cheese Melon Cup** ½ cup fat-free cottage cheese ½ cantaloupe, cubed 2 Tbsp ground flaxseed Serve cottage cheese with cantaloupe and top with flaxseeds.	**Cherry Yogurt** 1 cup Oikos Greek Yogurt ½ cup fresh, pitted cherries 2 Brazil nuts, chopped Top yogurt with cherries and nuts.	**Mozzarella Melt** 1 oz fresh mozzarella 1 slice whole wheat toast 2 tsp cold-pressed olive oil Top toast with cheese, and drizzle with olive oil.
snack	15 raw almonds	2 stalks celery with 2 tsp natural peanut butter	1 hard-cooked egg
lunch	**Hearty Roasted Veggie Salad** 2 cup chopped romaine 2 cup roasted carrots, zucchini, mushrooms, onions, red peppers ½ cup chickpeas ½ cup cold-pressed olive oil, ¼ fresh lemon juice, ½ tsp salt, ¼ tsp pepper Toss vegetables and chickpeas together and serve with 1 Tbsp dressing.	**ORAC Omelet** 1 whole DHA- fortified egg/2 egg whites ¼ cup spinach ¼ cup chopped tomatoes ¼ red onions ⅛ avocado Prepare omelet with veggies and avocado, and top with 1 tsp dried oregano.	**Med Platter** 4 Tbsp hummus 8 olives 1 cup sliced cucumber and tomatoes tossed with balsamic vinegar ½ cup artichoke hearts (canned or jarred in water) 4 high-fiber crackers Plate all together and serve with crackers on the side.
snack	Slim Shake	Slim Shake	Slim On-the-Go
dinner	**Grilled Lemon Chicken** 4 oz chicken breast 2 tsp cold-pressed olive oil 1 tsp thyme 2 lemon slices 1 cup steamed spinach ½ cup mashed butternut squash Brush chicken with olive oil and grill. Layer lemon slices on top and sprinkle with thyme. Serve with spinach and squash on the side.	**Grilled Scallops** 4 oz scallops 1 cup steamed broccoli ⅓ cup cooked quinoa Grill scallops and serve with quinoa and broccoli on the side.	**Roasted Filet** 4 oz beef filet 1 cup steamed bok choy or broccoli Roast meat and serve with vegetable of choice on the side.

THURSDAY	FRIDAY	SATURDAY	SUNDAY
Feta Scramble 1 whole DHA-fortified scrambled egg/2 whites 1 oz reduced-fat feta cheese ½ grapefruit Scramble eggs with cheese, and serve with grapefruit on the side.	**Warm Quinoa** 1 cup soy milk ⅓ cup quinoa 2 Tbsp chia seeds Add soy milk to quinoa and top with chia seeds.	**Almond Butter Toast** 1 cup fat-free milk 1 slice whole wheat toast 2 tsp almond butter Spread almond butter on toast. Sprinkle ¼ tsp cinnamon, and serve with glass of milk.	**Almond Avocado Smoothie** 1 cup almond milk ¼ avocado 1 small banana Blend all with 1 cup ice
2 Tbsp sunflower seeds	15 raw almonds	1 hard-cooked egg	2 stalks celery with 2 tsp natural peanut butter
Easy Kale Salad 2 cups chopped kale 1 Tbsp pine nuts 2 oz goat cheese ½ cup cherry tomatoes Balsamic vinegar Toss ingredients together and drizzle with balsamic vinegar.	**Caprese Lite** 1 slice whole grain toast 2 oz fresh mozzarella 1 slice tomato 2 tsp cold-pressed olive oil 1 cup crudite (red and yellow bell peppers, celery, mushrooms) Layer mozzarella and tomato on toast, drizzle with olive oil, and season to taste. Serve with side of veggies.	**Art-Tuna Salad** ½ cup artichoke hearts (canned or jarred in water) 4 oz water-packed chunk light tuna 2 tsp cold-pressed olive oil 2 cups baby spinach 4 high-fiber crackers Mix tuna with olive oil, toss with spinach and artichokes, and drizzle with 1 Tbsp balsamic vinegar.	**Traditional Turkey Unsandwich** 4 oz turkey ¼ sliced avocado 1 slice tomato 1 cup sugar snap peas Layer turkey with avocado and tomato, with sea salt and pepper to taste. Serve with sugar snap peas on the side.
Slim Yo	Slim On-the-Go	Slim On-the-Go	Slim Slaw
Chicken Sausage 4 oz chicken sausage 1 steamed artichoke ⅓ cup cooked wild rice Grill and slice sausage and toss with rice. Serve artichoke on the side.	**Roasted Pork Tenderloin** 4 oz pork tenderloin 1 cup cauliflower Roast pork and serve with steamed cauliflower on the side.	**Vegetarian Chili** 1 cup Amy's Organic Black Bean Chili 1 cup steamed bok choy Prepare chili according to package and serve with bok choy on the side.	**Fish Tacos** 4 oz cod 2 small corn tortillas 2 Tbsp guacamole 1 Tbsp fat-free Greek yogurt 2 Tbsp salsa ½ cup shredded romaine 1 cup red and yellow bell peppers, chopped Grill fish and layer on tortillas with veggies, guacamole, yogurt and salsa as desired!

	MONDAY	TUESDAY	WEDNESDAY
breakfast	**Pumpkin-Pear and Milk** 1 small pear, cubed 1 Tbsp pumpkin seeds 1 cup almond milk Pour milk over pear and pumpkin seeds. Sprinkle ¼ tsp cinnamon.	**Colorful Cottage Cheese** ½ cup fat-free cottage cheese ⅛ cup dried mango 18 pistachios Top cottage cheese with mango and nuts.	**Chocolate Peanut Butter Smoothie** 1 cup fat-free chocolate milk 1 small banana 2 tsp natural peanut butter Blend all with 1 cup of ice until smooth.
snack	15 raw almonds	2 Tbsp sunflower seeds	1 hard-cooked egg
lunch	**Spinach Turkey Salad** 2 cups baby spinach 1 Tbsp chopped red onion ¼ cup cherry tomatoes 4 oz sliced turkey Toss with 2 tsp cold-pressed olive oil, 2 tsp grated parmesan cheese, and ¼ tsp dried basil	**Yogurt Chicken Salad** 4 oz chunked white meat chicken (mixed with 2 Tbsp plain fat-free yogurt, 1 Tbsp balsamic vinegar, 2 tsp olive oil, ½ tsp Dijon mustard) ⅓ cup cold, cooked bulgur 2 cups chopped romaine Serve chicken and bulgur over lettuce.	**Quinoa Pistachio Salad** ⅓ cup cooked quinoa 18 pistachios ½ cup chickpeas ½ cup cold-pressed olive oil, ¼ fresh lemon juice, ½ tsp salt, ¼ tsp pepper 2 cups spinach Toss with 1 Tbsp lemon vinaigrette dressing and serve over spinach.
snack	Slim Shake	Slim Shake	Slim Slaw
dinner	**Portobello Stack** 1 portobello mushroom 2 oz reduced-fat Cheddar 1 slice tomato Small baked sweet potato Season mushroom with sea salt and pepper. Add cheese and broil until melted. Top with the tomato before serving.	**Tofu Kebabs** 4 oz cubed firm tofu alternated on skewers with red and yellow peppers, red onions, mushrooms 2 cups steamed spinach Season kebabs with sea salt and black pepper. Broil and serve with spinach on the side.	**Spicy Shrimp Marinara** 4 oz shrimp (peeled and deveined) ⅓ cup marinara sauce 1 cup steamed spinach Sprinkle shrimp with red pepper flakes before sauteing. Toss with sauce and serve with spinach on the side.

THURSDAY	FRIDAY	SATURDAY	SUNDAY
Nutty Oats 1 cup fat-free milk ½ cup steel-cut oats Prepare oats with milk and top with 7 chopped walnut halves.	**Egg and Cheese Melt** 1 oz low-fat Swiss cheese 2 fiber crackers 1 hard-cooked egg, halved Top each cracker with half an egg and ½ oz cheese. Broil for 1 minute or until cheese melts.	**Power Yogurt** 1 cup açai-flavored Oikos Greek yogurt ¾ cup Smart Bran cereal 2 Tbsp ground flaxseed Top yogurt with cereal and flaxseeds.	**Cereal Gone Nuts** 1 cup fat-free milk ¾ cup Smart Bran cereal 10 raw, chopped almonds Top cereal and milk with almonds. Sprinkle ¼ tsp cinnamon.
2 ribs celery with 2 tsp natural peanut butter	2 ribs celery with 2 tsp natural peanut butter	1 hard-cooked egg	15 raw almonds
Open Faced Veggie Sandwich 1 slice whole grain bread 2 Tbsp guacamole or ⅛ avocado 4 Tbsp hummus ¼ cup alfalfa sprouts 1 slice tomato Layer on bread and sprinkle with sea salt and pepper to taste.	**Burger to Bite** 4 oz 85% lean organic ground beef burger 1 oz reduced-fat Cheddar cheese 1 cup steamed string beans Broil burger and top with cheese. Serve with string beans on the side.	**Wild Salmon Salad** 4 oz canned wild salmon 2 cups chopped romaine ¼ cup sliced cucumbers 8 chopped olives Toss all with lemon juice and sea salt to taste.	**Greek Salad** 2 cups chopped romaine ½ cup sliced cucumber ¼ cup canned or frozen (thawed) artichoke hearts ¼ cup sliced tomato 2 oz reduced-fat feta cheese ½ cup lentils Toss all with 2 tsp cold-pressed olive oil and ½ tsp oregano.
Slim Slaw	Slim On-the-Go	Slim On-the-Go	Slim Yo
Simple Salmon 4 oz salmon 1 cup brussels sprouts Season fish with gomashio (sesame salt) and broil. Roast brussels sprouts and serve on the side.	**Rotisserie Chicken** 4 oz white meat skinless chicken 1 cup roasted asparagus topped with 2 Tbsp shredded parmesan cheese ⅓ cup cooked wild rice Roast chicken and serve over rice with asparagus on the side.	**Beef Stir Fry** 4 oz lean beef ⅓ cup brown rice 1 cup snow peas, water chestnuts, and carrots Stir fry beef and vegetables, and serve over brown rice.	**Foil-Baked Cod** 4 oz cod filet 1 steamed artichoke 2 tsp cold-pressed olive oil mixed with 2 tsp lemon juice and herbs of choice (dipping sauce) Coat cod with 1 tsp olive oil, squeeze of lemon, herbs of choice, and bake. Serve with artichoke and dipping sauce.

	MONDAY	TUESDAY	WEDNESDAY
breakfast	**Feta Scramble** 1 whole DHA- fortified scrambled egg/2 whites 1 oz reduced-fat feta cheese ½ grapefruit Scramble eggs with cheese, and serve with grapefruit on the side.	**Mozzarella Melt** 1 oz fresh mozzarella 1 slice whole wheat toast 2 tsp cold-pressed olive oil Top toast with cheese, and drizzle with olive oil.	**Almond Butter Toast** 1 cup fat-free milk 1 slice whole wheat toast 2 tsp almond butter Spread almond butter on toast. Sprinkle ¼ tsp cinnamon, and serve with glass of milk.
snack	2 Tbsp sunflower seeds	1 hard-cooked egg	1 hard-cooked egg
lunch	**Easy Kale Salad** 2 cups chopped kale 1 Tbsp pine nuts 2 oz goat cheese ½ cup cherry tomatoes Balsamic vinegar Toss ingredients together and drizzle with balsamic vinegar.	**Med Platter** 4 Tbsp hummus 8 olives 1 cup sliced cucumber and tomatoes with balsamic vinegar ½ cup artichoke hearts (canned or jarred in water) 4 high-fiber crackers Plate all together and serve with crackers on the side.	**Art-Tuna Salad** ½ cup artichoke hearts (canned or jarred in water) 4 oz water-packed chunk light tuna 2 tsp cold-pressed olive oil 2 cups baby spinach 4 high-fiber crackers Mix tuna with olive oil, toss with spinach and artichokes, and drizzle with 1 Tbsp balsamic vinegar.
snack	Slim Yo	Slim On-the-Go	Slim On-the-Go
dinner	**Chicken Sausage** 4 oz chicken sausage 1 steamed artichoke ⅓ cup cooked wild rice Grill and slice sausage and toss with rice. Serve artichoke on the side.	**Roasted Filet** 4 oz beef filet 1 cup steamed bok choy or broccoli Roast meat and serve with vegetable of choice on the side.	**Vegetarian Chili** 1 cup Amy's Organic Black Bean Chili 1 cup steamed bok choy Prepare chili according to package and serve with bok choy on the side.

THURSDAY

Warm Quinoa
1 cup soy milk
⅓ cup quinoa
2 Tbsp chia seeds
Add soy milk to quinoa and top with chia seeds.

15 raw almonds

Caprese Lite
1 slice whole grain toast
2 oz fresh mozzarella
1 slice tomato
2 tsp cold-pressed olive oil
1 cup crudite(red and yellow bell peppers, celery, mushrooms)
Layer mozzarella and tomato on toast, drizzle with olive oil, and season to taste. Serve with side of veggies.

Slim On-the-Go

Roasted Pork Tenderloin
4 oz pork tenderloin
1 cup cauliflower
Roast pork and serve with steamed cauliflower on the side.

FRIDAY

Almond Avocado Smoothie
1 cup almond milk
¼ avocado
1 small banana
Blend all with 1 cup ice.

2 stalks celery with 2 tsp natural peanut butter

Traditional Turkey Unsandwich
4 oz turkey
¼ sliced avocado
1 slice tomato
1 cup sugar snap peas
Layer turkey with avocado and tomato, with sea salt and pepper to taste. Serve with sugar snap peas on the side.

Slim Slaw

Fish Tacos
4 oz cod
2 small corn tortillas
2 Tbsp guacamole
1 Tbsp fat-free Greek yogurt
2 Tbsp salsa
½ cup shredded romaine
1 cup red and yellow bell peppers, chopped
Grill fish and layer on tortillas with veggies, guacamole, yogurt and salsa as desired!

SATURDAY

Cherry Yogurt
1 cup Oikos Greek Yogurt
½ cup fresh, pitted cherries
2 Brazil nuts, chopped
Top yogurt with cherries and nuts.

2 stalks celery with 2 tsp natural peanut butter

ORAC Omelet
1 whole DHA-fortified egg/2 egg whites
¼ cup spinach
¼ cup chopped tomatoes
¼ red onions
⅛ avocado
Prepare omelet with veggies and avocado, and top with 1 tsp dried oregano.

Slim Shake

Grilled Scallops
4 oz scallops
1 cup steamed broccoli
⅓ cup cooked quinoa
Grill scallops and serve with quinoa and broccoli on the side.

SUNDAY

Cottage Cheese Melon Cup
½ cup fat-free cottage cheese
½ cantaloupe, cubed
2 Tbsp ground flaxseed
Serve cottage cheese with cantaloupe and top with flaxseeds.

15 raw almonds

Hearty Roasted Veggie Salad
2 cup chopped romaine
2 cup roasted carrots, zucchini, mushrooms, onions, red peppers
½ cup chickpeas
½ cup cold-pressed olive oil,
¼ fresh lemon juice,
½ tsp salt, ¼ tsp pepper
Toss vegetables and chickpeas together and serve with 1 Tbsp dressing.

Slim Shake

Grilled Lemon Chicken
4 oz chicken breast
2 tsp cold-pressed olive oil
1 tsp thyme
2 lemon slices
1 cup steamed spinach
½ cup mashed butternut squash
Brush chicken with olive oil and grill. Layer lemon slices on top with sprinkle with thyme. Serve with spinach and squash on the side.

Snacks

■ Slim Snacks Whether you're in the mood for sweet or savory (or both!) a great snack is one that has between 120 and 160 calories, and includes either a healthy fat, protein, and/or fiber. The following are my go-to snack options!

+ **SLIM SHAKE**
 1 cup fat-free milk
 ¼ avocado
 ½ squeezed lime
 1 teaspoon mint

+ **SLIM SLAW**
 ½ cup sliced red cabbage
 ½ cup sliced green cabbage
 ¼ cup sliced almonds
 1 tablespoon rice vinegar
 1 teaspoon Dijon mustard

+ **SLIM ON-THE-GO**
 1 cup organic fat-free Greek yogurt
 1 tablespoon chopped walnuts
 ½ teaspoon vanilla extract
 1 pinch cinnamon

+ **SLIM YO**
 1 cup organic fat-free Greek yogurt
 1 tablespoon matcha powder or ground coffee, or 2 tablespoons peanut butter

MORNING

These are usually a fat or protein, and a vegetable. Don't be afraid to make up your own combos—olives and celery, or cashews and radishes do the trick for me sometimes.

+ 15 raw almonds and sliced carrots
+ 2 ribs celery with 2 teaspoons natural peanut butter
+ 1 hard-cooked egg with endive
+ 2 tablespoons sunflower seeds and sliced red peppers
+ 1 large tomato slice with 1 thin slice fresh mozzarella
+ 2 tablespoons pumpkin seeds and sugar-snap peas
+ 1 (4 ounces) individual Light n' Lively Lowfat Cottage Cheese and 2 celery stalks
+ ¼ avocado and sliced yellow peppers

AFTERNOON

These are usually milk or a milk substitute, or milk and a fat if you're very hungry. Medium hungry? Go for the vegetable and fat snacks. Let your HQ be your guide. Choose from the Slim Snacks listed above, or try one of these satisfying combos:

+ 1 cup Greek yogurt with 2 teaspoons natural peanut butter and a dash of cinnamon
+ 1 cup fat-free milk with 2 teaspoons natural almond butter and ½ cup ice (blend)
+ 1 cup almond milk with 1 tablespoon cocoa powder and 1 cup ice (blend)
+ ½ cup nonfat cottage cheese and 10 pistachios
+ 1 apple and 2 teaspoons natural peanut butter
+ 2 ounces turkey jerky

▪ Happy Hour Snacks

I already talked about how this special snack works on page 62. Here they are! Each is a perfect "cocktail" designed to speed your weight loss by filling you up right on time to prevent those late-day cravings. (Please note that these snacks are not included in the grocery list for each week because it is up to you to choose! Don't forget to add the ingredients to your shopping list.)

+ Cucumber Salad
cucumber slices tossed with lemon juice and rice vinegar, to taste

+ Asparagus Spears
canned or fresh asparagus sprinkled with sea salt and pepper

+ Jicama Salad
sliced jicama and carrots mixed with brown rice vinegar and 1 teaspoon Dijon mustard

+ Mini Chopped Salad
chopped celery, carrots, artichoke hearts, and cucumber sprinkled with lemon juice and sea salt, to taste

+ Seaweed Wrap
sliced red and green cabbage rolled in a nori sheet

+ Vegetable Soup
Think of this as your Happy Hour all-star dish. Make a big pot on a Sunday and refrigerate for the week ahead. Feel free to vary it with as many vegetables and herbs as you like:

1   can (14.5 ounces) diced or petite diced organic tomatoes
1   small carrot, peeled and cut into $1/8$"-thick rounds
1   rib celery, cut into $1/4$"-thick slices
2   teaspoons minced garlic (about 2 large cloves)
    Salt
    Freshly ground black pepper
$1/2$ cup thinly sliced button mushrooms (about 2 large)
1   cup baby spinach
$1/4$ cup finely chopped fresh basil, or 1 teaspoon dried
2   teaspoons balsamic vinegar

1. Add the tomatoes and $1/2$ cup water to a small saucepan over medium heat. Stir in the carrot, celery, and garlic and season with salt and pepper. Cover and bring to a slow boil, then reduce the heat to low and simmer, covered, for 15 minutes, or until the vegetables are tender. Halfway through the cooking time, stir in the mushrooms.
2. Add the spinach and basil, stir, and cook 1 minute longer, or until the spinach wilts.
3. Stir in the vinegar and serve.

MAKES 2 SERVINGS

QUICK PICK-ME-UPS

When I need a slimming snack—maybe I know I'll eat a richer-than-usual meal that night, or I feel a little bloated— here are the three foods I go to again and again:

+ Artichoke with squeezed lemon (this is also a great Happy Hour snack)

+ Half a grapefruit sprinkled with cinnamon and a tablespoon of chopped pecans

+ $1/4$ cup of fat-free cottage cheese with a little black pepper (a great afternoon snack)

Swaps

◼ Quick Swap Menu

There are going to be plenty of times when it's just not practical to follow the plan exactly as I've laid it out. Maybe you hate a certain food or know you'll be on the run all day or don't have time to head to the store. No problem! You can make these Slim Swaps absolutely any time and not worry about going off track. And I've chosen them because you can find them anywhere— at almost any gas station, airport, or convenience store. That's why I think of them as my "when all else fails" options. My only caution is to not over-rely on them. There's a chance of growing bored of the same foods without realizing it. And that's risky, because if you suddenly feel you might scream if you eat one more almond, you're more likely to reach for something far less nutritious. So swap away when you have to, but make sure you're getting lots of food variety.

BREAKFAST	LUNCH	DINNER
1 packet plain oatmeal or ½ cup quick cooked oats	*4 ounces grilled lean protein (your choice)*	*Mixed green salad with 2 teaspoons cold-pressed olive oil*
1 cup fat-free or almond milk	*Chopped romaine*	*Steamed green vegetable*
Hard-cooked egg	*1 tablespoon vinaigrette dressing*	*4 ounces roasted or grilled lean protein (your choice)*

Remember to practice portion control. Whether you're following the 6-week meal plan I've created for you or the following do-it-yourself versions, you will have to make adjustments to suit your body—everyone is a little different. Feel free to eat as many non-starchy vegetables as you'd like, and if you feel hungry, add in small amounts of protein, too. But please stick to my suggested portions of fats and starches. While you need these foods to be healthy, they are easy to overeat. Your success on the plan will depend on how well you control them.

◼ Do it Yourself Menu

If the menus I've created don't appeal to you, by all means, do the Slim Calm Sexy Diet *your* way. This next section will make it easy for you to do so and still stay on track with your weight loss.

I've created the diet along these basic lines. Read through them, and go ahead and interpret them your own way. You'll be fine as long as you follow the framework for each meal, choosing the building blocks from the lists that follow, and in the right proportions.

Build a breakfast that includes:

Starch or fruit
Milk or milk substitute
Fat or protein

Build a morning snack that includes:

Fat or protein
Veggie

Build a lunch that includes:

Veggie
Protein
Fat
Starch
(if you aren't having starch at dinner)

Build an afternoon snack that includes:

Milk or milk substitute
Fat

Choose a Happy Hour snack that includes:

Any vegetables. My favorite is veggie soup, but even a cup of crudités works. These add water, volume, and crunch satisfaction at the time of day you need it most.

Build a dinner that includes:

Veggie
Protein
Fat
Starch
(if you didn't have starch at lunch)

✦ see the appendix for a list of Keri's favorite foods

SPICE IT UP

These foods may not make me feel like Cleopatra right away (especially if I'm feeling like an overworked mom), but they are known to support sexual health:

✦ *A cup of cubed watermelon topped with 15 crushed peanuts*

✦ *½ ounce of dark chocolate sprinkled with a little cayenne pepper*

✦ *A cup of edamame sprinkled with gomashio*

Making It Easier

The Packaged Factor

• • •   In a perfect world, none of us would ever eat packaged foods. We'd have time to cook everything from scratch and not have to worry about preservatives and additives. But no one I know has time to live like that—and you don't have to, either. These days, there are so many terrific, conscientious food companies out there, producing high-quality, healthy options that make eating right easy. I've listed some of my favorites in the Appendix.

Heavy Up on Herbs and Spices

• • •   The reason I've added so many fresh herbs and spices to the plan is that I love the way they can transform a meal. It's amazing to me that something as simple as a teaspoon of curry can turn a chicken breast into something completely different from the one you made with oregano last week. But most people don't realize that herbs and spices also contain a crazy—I mean, *crazy*—level of nutrition. Bet you didn't know that cloves, oregano, basil, thyme, and cinnamon are among the most antioxidant-rich foods.

Toss spices that are more than 2 years old, and store spices in a dark cupboard. Being too near the stove or sunlight will weaken their nutritional power. (Not sure how old they are? If they're McCormick spices, go to www.mccormick.com, click on Spices 101, and type in the product code to find out when each was bottled.)

Wondering what to do with the big bunches of fresh herbs you're buying for the plan? Freeze 'em—they won't look very nice afterward, but they'll be just as flavorful and nutritious. The cooks at Purdue University say it's this easy:

+ Rinse herbs
+ Blanch for a few seconds using the following method:
>   Hold the herbs by their stems with tongs.
>   Dip them in boiling water briefly and swish around a bit.
>   When their color brightens, remove them from the water.
+ Cool, either by holding them under running water and then blotting dry with paper towels, or by placing them on towels after taking them from the boiling water to let them air-dry.
+ Remove stems and chop, if desired, or leave whole to chop later.
+ Freeze by placing them in plastic freezer bags in portion-size amounts.

I Want to Cheat! What Should I Do?

There are bound to be some days when you feel like the plan—generous as it is—is too confining. There are times when you just have a strong craving. It's important to me that you heed your Inner Wild Child and listen to your body. That craving is telling you to take a break and indulge yourself somehow.

What works for most of my clients is finding an indulgence they can trust. In other words, it will satisfy them enough so that they feel they've had a special treat, but not so much that they feel guilty, which might set them up for a major bender. In fact, I'm such a big believer in eating empowered and making these "conscious indulgences" that I actually recommend them. Ideally, you should avoid them for the first 6 weeks, but then allow yourself one a week. If you can continue to lose or maintain, by all means go for it.

Here are some of my favorite little splurges:

Slim indulgence:	Calm indulgence:	Sexy indulgence:
Mix 1 cup frozen mixed berries with ¼ cup full-fat yogurt and a drizzle of chocolate syrup. It's a little more decadent.	Melt ½ ounce chocolate with ¼ teaspoon lavender extract. Dip 8 cashews in and freeze. Enjoy!	Melt ½ ounce chocolate with a dash of nutmeg. Then dip 1 table-spoon of pickled ginger in it. Sounds weird, but yes, it is sexy.

The Slim Calm Sexy Way to Party

Feel free to have a drink now and then on the Slim Calm Sexy Diet. During the 6-week plan I recommend one drink per week. Just be aware that cocktails (and mocktails) have calories—and too many will stop you from losing weight. If you're not careful, it will wreck your mood, too. Most people don't realize that booze is a depressant, and who needs that?

Here are my favorites:

Slim cocktail	Calm cocktail	Sexy cocktail
1 ounce vodka with a splash of grapefruit juice and a lemon twist	Hot Toddy—combine 1 cup hot chamomile tea with 1/2 tablespoon honey, a shot of bourbon or brandy, and a lemon slice	2 ounces club soda with 1 ounce vodka, and a pinch of cayenne pepper, over ice

at goal weight?

I bet you're wondering what comes next, once you've achieved your "magic number." At this point, I'm guessing that following the Slim Calm Sexy meal plan probably feels both effortless and familiar—it's easy to get used to feeling this good! And while lots of diet books think achieving goal weight is the time to introduce a maintenance plan, I disagree. You've done so well on this plan that you've turned it into a true lifestyle, not a diet—why mess with success, right?

Let your body (and perhaps the scale, as well as your best pair of jeans) be your guide, slowly adding in the following:

+

A splurge, or conscious indulgence, per week—including alcohol. You've earned it! Just be mindful that tiptoeing back toward some of those "forbidden" foods may act as a trigger, so be extra attentive about keeping your food journal.

+

One more fruit per day. Yes, fruits do contain carbohydrates in the form of simple sugar, but they're also loaded with water, fiber, and amazing antioxidants. Pop one in your daily plan wherever you choose.

+

When you're dining out or faced with a meal that is far less healthy than the ones you've been eating for the last six weeks, don't panic. Instead, use whatever vegetables are available as the basic architecture of your meal, and then choose the best possible protein and fat serving to round it out. As long as you follow the basic building blocks of the plan, you won't do any serious damage.

+

Focus on keeping 18 of your meals each week as on track as possible. There will always be the occasional dinner party where you're not in control of the meal. Remember to Eat Empowered and stop when you are slightly satisfied.

slim & healthy foods

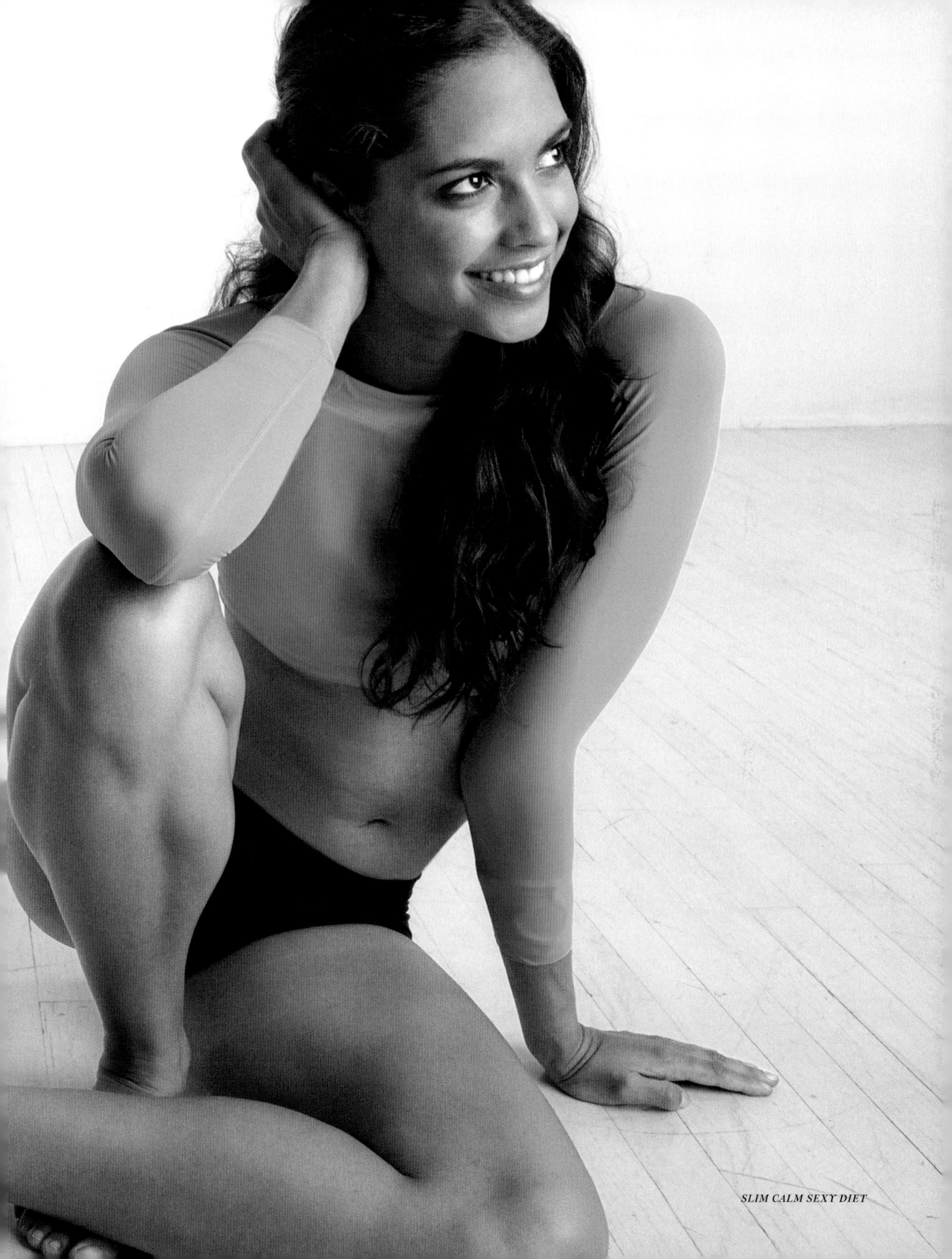

There's

not a food I've mentioned to you so far that doesn't have the potential to transform your health. But in this chapter, I'm going to single out the foods that not only have the power to slim you down, but also are the best for your health. I'm talking about the foods that are relatively high in nutrient density, meaning that the ratio of nutrients they provide per calories is very high. They are the fundamental opposite of foods that are energy dense, or full of "empty calories."

I'm looking far beyond 5 pounds, 10 pounds, and even your goal weight. I've got your back for the long haul. These foods will protect you from heart disease, diabetes, and cancer. They're that powerful. I know that many health problems and diseases are genetically determined, but it doesn't mean you can't build up a strong line of defense. Did you know nearly one-third of all cancer deaths in the United States can be attributed to a poor diet?

What makes thes foods go beyond just plain healthy to healthy and slimming is their nutrient density. Let me explain a little more about what makes a food like cabbage soar to the top of nutrient-density charts and another, let's say jelly beans, bounce to the bottom. Among the factors:

• • •   WATER adds volume but no calories to food, automatically making high-water-content foods a good choice. For example, a 100-calorie serving of grapes—a low-energy-density, high-water-content food—contains 1⅔ cups water, while a 100-calorie serving of raisins, a high-energy-density food, contains only ¼ cup. Over a decade ago, researchers at Penn State showed that eating foods with a high water content helps people lose weight. The researchers served a group of women a first course before lunch, of either a chicken rice casserole, the same casserole with a glass of water, or a bowl of chicken rice soup. (The soup and the casserole contained exactly the same ingredients.) Women who had the soup ate fewer calories when they sat down to lunch. This is one of the reasons I recommend the Slim Calm Sexy Diet's Vegetable Soup (page 77) as a satisfying Happy Hour snack.

• • •   FIBER affects the rate of nutrient absorption. There are two types of fiber. Soluble fiber—found in oat bran, barley, nuts, seeds, beans, lentils, and some fruits and vegetables—attracts even more water and turns to gel during digestion. It also helps lower cholesterol, which can prevent heart disease. Insoluble fiber is found in foods such as wheat bran, vegetables, and whole grains. We need plenty of both, and the richer a food is in fiber, the more slowly it will be processed. And it is frequently less calorie dense and lower in fat and added sugars.

• • •   FATS tend to be high in calories and among the most energy-dense foods. But many fats, especially the ones I'm asking you to eat, are also nutrient rich. That's why nuts, avocados, and olive oil are featured so prominently in the Slim Calm Sexy Diet. Even though they are higher in calories than some other foods, they compensate with more than enough nutritional value. The omega-3s I've discussed that are found in flax, fish, and even hemp are healthy fats that have also been linked to burning fat. Fat feels yummy and is really satisfying.

Keri's

3

FAVORITE
SLIMMING
FOODS

*Artichokes,
grapefruit,
and
green teas*

A note about sugar: Sugar usually pushes foods to the bottom of the nutrient-density charts. Sugars bring plenty of calories to the party, but usually not much else. While some foods, such as bananas, are relatively high in sugar, it's because they pack some additional power, making the trade-off worth it (if using portion control).

The Reality of Nutrition Research

• • •   I'd like to make a point about much of the nutritional data you're reading. All research is very expensive. Who pays for it? Sometimes the government funds it; sometimes universities, hospitals, or medical centers do. But often, entities with a vested interest—like the Dairy Council, the Egg Board, or even companies like General Mills—pay for these studies. And that can create controversy. For example, about a decade ago, several studies demonstrated the ability of low-fat dairy to speed weight loss. The studies were funded by "special interest" groups, one spearheaded by a University of Tennessee researcher who held dairy-related patents. Of course they wanted to promote dairy! Other studies found dairy consumption had no impact on weight loss, and a real firestorm broke out.

The Physicians Committee for Responsible Medicine, a group devoted to promoting higher standards in research, filed a petition asking the Dairy Council, which by then was spending hundreds of millions of dollars advertising milk's weight loss powers, to knock it off. In 2007, the Dairy Council agreed to stop making those weight loss claims.

Where does that leave us now? While full-fat dairy does have its place in a healthy diet, I still recommend low-fat dairy for the majority of people trying to lose weight. I accept that the data is inconclusive, not just because subsequent studies have shown dairy's benefit for weight loss, but also because of its more proven impact on lowering insulin resistance in people with diabetes. (One big study, for example, found that for each additional dairy serving consumed, the risk of insulin resistance declined 21 percent.) And like many experts, I think research on insulin resistance in people with diabetes may yield important weight loss insights for everyone.

So while I pay close attention to how any given study is funded (and hope you will, too), there's no point in automatically dismissing the information, either. It would be like throwing the baby out with the bathwater to disregard important news about blueberries, for example, just because a blueberry council funded the findings. Researchers are required to reveal their own conflicts of interest, as well as funding sources, and in order to be published in peer-reviewed scientific journals—the sources I trust the most—the data has to be solid. So you can feel confident that the Slim Calm Sexy Diet is based on the most comprehensive, proven research available.

Eat Your Way Slim (and Healthy)

• • •   I've chosen the following foods based their high nutrient density and ability to slim as well as give you good health. So go on—eat up!

ALMONDS Like all nuts, these are high in the healthy fats that leave us feeling super satisfied and are the best whole-food source of vitamin E. One itty-bitty ounce—about a handful—gives you 12 percent of your daily allowance of protein and 35 percent of your daily vitamin E, as well as magnesium, phosphorus, zinc, fiber, and even calcium. Best of all, they're a proven weight loss tool. One 24-week study found that dieters eating many complex carbs with almonds lost 62 percent more than those eating the same meals without almonds. I like to buy raw organic almonds in bulk. Here's an easy way to measure a serving (because who has time to count out 23 nuts?): Use either a shot glass or an ice-cream scoop.

ARTICHOKES There's nothing boring about artichokes. I think peeling the leaves back one by one is more interesting than tossing a salad any day. At only 60 calories each, they're filling, so if you eat an artichoke as an appetizer, you may end up consuming fewer calories overall in the main course. Artichokes are one of the most antioxidant-rich foods we know of and contain phytochemicals that may lower cholesterol levels. And they act as an anti-inflammatory in the skin, making them a beauty food as well. I love them steamed, but it's nice to always have a few cans of artichoke hearts on hand. Puree them in the food processor with a little olive oil and fresh rosemary for a simple veggie dip.

AVOCADO While high in calories, these provide glutathione, a substance that specifically blocks intestinal absorption of certain fats that cause oxidative damage. Avocados also contain beta-carotene, lutein, vitamin E, and more folate than any other fruit. A single serving (about one-quarter of an avocado) has plenty of B vitamins, too. Because it is so satisfying, it's a slimming food I couldn't live without. Try it as an old-fashioned 1950s treat: Toss chopped avocado with shrimp for a refreshing lunch.

MAKE YOUR OWN HEALTHY DESTINY

While anywhere from 30 to 70 percent of body weight may be linked to genetics, the rest is up to you and what you eat. Food is power!

BANANAS Yes, they're a slimming food. They contain something called resistant starch, an indigestible fiber that blocks the absorption of some carbohydrates as fuel. A University of Colorado study says that as a result, bananas can decrease long-term fat accumulation. I also love that they've got plenty of B vitamins and potassium. Be like Elvis—eat them with organic peanut butter.

BARLEY This pearly little grain is one of the most overlooked foods out there. Like oatmeal, it has plenty of beta-glucan soluble fiber, so it's known to promote healthier cholesterol levels, and the carbs it provides are absorbed slowly into the bloodstream, making for a nice, steady sort of energy. In several studies of people with diabetes, it's been shown to significantly reduce glucose and insulin responses. It's also a good source of niacin, selenium, iron, magnesium, zinc, phosphorus, and copper. Have it in soups, as a side dish, in stir-fries, even for breakfast. One study showed that it kept blood sugar levels 20 to 30 percent lower than whole wheat grains were able to do. While most of us are accustomed to eating it in soups, stews, and other dinnertime dishes, it's a really nice breakfast grain, too. Add a little cinnamon and some almonds.

BULGUR This is a form of wheat that includes both the germ and the bran, giving it a nutty flavor. I use it as an alternative to brown rice, and I love that it's loaded with fiber, lutein, niacin, and zinc. Because it's a complex carb, it's a great energy choice. But I've also had clients tell me it quickly turns into one of their new comfort foods, too. As side dishes go, it's a little more unexpected than rice but just as satisfying.

CAULIFLOWER A cousin of broccoli, this vegetable's main charm, I think, is that it tastes a little starchier than it really is. Remember when the South Beach–inspired "mashed cauliflower" was all the rage? Whether you snack on it raw or serve it cooked, it has very high levels of vitamin C—and the more of that we consume, the less likely we are to be overweight, according to research from Arizona State University. If you're looking for new ways to spice it up, think curry. This vegetable is so popular in Indian cuisines because it soaks up those fragrant seasonings perfectly.

CHILE PEPPERS These potent and super-spicy babies have an antioxidant called capsaicin. A new study from the University of California, Los Angeles, found that in the few hours following a meal containing capsaicin, energy expenditure—or calories burned—almost doubled. The substance also significantly increased fat oxidation, pushing the body to use more fat as fuel. While capsaicin gets a lot of attention for its medical applications and is even used as a topical pain reliever, it also seems to have some effect on human appetite. Some studies have found that people who eat meals flavored with plenty of these spices feel less hungry as a result. It also has traces of folate, manganese, potassium, and copper. A fun way to experiment is to buy a variety of premade fresh salsas and read the ingredients carefully. It will give you a sense of which peppers speak your language. Be careful of the super-hot ones.

CHOCOLATE
Yes, you read that right: I'm telling you to eat chocolate—dark chocolate. I do all the time. It's rich in flavonoids and promotes heart health by reducing platelet activation, affecting the relaxation capabilities of blood vessels. And it may also affect the balance of certain hormonelike compounds called eicosanoids, which are thought to play a role in cardiovascular health. But it can also help you shed pounds. Eat it judiciously, and it helps manage cravings. Need help with portion control? Buy individually wrapped servings and keep them in the freezer until you're ready for a treat.

CINNAMON
There's a reason most of us drool when we walk by a bakery. Cinnamon is a big part of it. Just the smell of this heavenly spice is enough to curb fatigue, ease frustration, and increase alertness. Researchers believe that besides managing stress, cinnamon may inhibit certain types of Alzheimer's cells. And for people with diabetes, it helps improve glucose management. Try sprinkling some in your coffee before brewing, for a nice change in the morning. Or try this easy aromatherapy trick: Sprinkle a little on an electric burner, turn on the stove, and keep on a low temperature.

COFFEE
This stimulating beverage used to get a bad rap, but now we recognize that it's a leading source of antioxidants for most Americans. And researchers have found that coffee drinkers have a lower risk of developing type 2 diabetes, as well as Parkinson's disease. Coffee also has been shown to enhance both mental and physical performance. It's been studied extensively in recreational runners and cyclists, and yep, regular coffee drinkers do perform significantly better. Try a cup of coffee about an hour before your next workout. You'll feel the difference.

DRIED FRUIT
Dried papayas, mangos, dates, prunes, and apricots are sweet, almost like candy. And they have many of the nutrients of their fresh counterparts, sometimes more, thanks to the power of concentration. Dried prunes, for example, have a vitamin K kick and lots

of boron, which we need for strong bones. While apricots lose a little vitamin C as they dry, their fiber and iron intensifies. But be careful when you shop: Look for varieties with no added sugar or sulfur. As with all dried fruit, check serving sizes. Calories add up quicker than you would think, because the natural fruit sugars become more concentrated.

EGGS How many foods are not only amazingly nutritious but also look so darn cute? Eggs are affordable, low in calories, and a versatile protein (not to mention a big source of choline, which we need for healthy brain function). They also contain lutein and zeaxanthin, antioxidants that have been linked to healthy eyesight. Research has shown that when eggs are eaten in the morning, people tend to be so satisfied they consume fewer calories throughout the day. For a period of time, eggs got a bad rap because they contain cholesterol. But we now know it's the saturated fat in the diet—not the cholesterol itself—that causes our cholesterol levels to rise. Even the American Heart Association has said it's okay for us to love eggs again. There are so many ways to cook 'em, but I like the classic: scrambled with onions and a few veggies.

FATTY FISH I've talked a lot about lean protein being vital to your weight loss success. But fatty fish, such as salmon, mackerel, and sardines, blast fat, too. With plentiful calcium, vitamin D stores, and omega-3 fatty acids, they provide many health benefits, and have been shown to prevent weight gain in women and to promote weight loss. New research shows that these foods also help us hang on to muscle mass as we age—very good news for our metabolism. If you're shopping for mackerel, pay attention to what type. King mackerel is considered to be dangerously high in mercury, while North Atlantic mackerel— the kind the seals love—is quite low. If you're not brave enough to try cooking it on your own (it has a strong flavor), sample a little the next time you're out for sushi. It's gaining in popularity because it gets high marks for sustainability.

FLAXSEED These powerful little seeds have a nice, nutty flavor. While the whole seed is harder to digest, flax in its ground-up form provides a dynamite dietary source of lignans, plant estrogens that may soothe the monthly mood swings that can lead to emotional overeating. Give some to your guy, too. A new study from Iowa State found that men who sprinkle flax on their food daily lowered their cholesterol by 10 percent. I like the nutty way flax (either the seeds or the meal) tastes when I sprinkle it on cereal. Or add a teaspoon of flax oil to smoothies.

GINGER It's hard not to adore something that, whether powdered or fresh grated, adds so much zing to food. But ginger is also an impressive anti-inflammatory and deserves a front-and-center spot on your spice rack. (It's a nice little treat with your sushi. While pickled ginger is made with a lot of salt and sugar, those few slices really cleanse your palate.) And there's a reason your mom let you sip ginger ale when you felt sick. This spice is a winner for treating car sickness, nausea, and even morning sickness. When added to marinades for meat, it cuts down on cancer-causing chemicals. I keep fresh ginger in a resealable plastic bag in the freezer and grate it right into my recipes.

GRAPEFRUIT This is more than a breakfast food. Packed with vitamin C and fiber, it's a weight loss jump start. One study found that people who ate half a grapefruit with each meal lost 3.6 pounds, while those who drank a serving of grapefruit juice three times a day lost 3.3 pounds. Many people in the study lost more than 10 pounds, without making any other dietary changes. Even if these claims seem too good to be true (I have to confess, I read the study twice to make sure I understood it), I have a soft spot for grapefruit. I grew up eating a half grapefruit before dinner every single night. The pink and red varieties contain lycopene and are extra good for your heart. And all grapefruit contains naringenin, the antioxidant that gives grapefruit its bitter taste, which researchers say can do the same job as two separate drugs currently used to manage type 2 diabetes. Serve grapefruit for dessert: Add a tiny bit of honey, sprinkle on some cardamom, and leave it under the broiler for 2 or 3 minutes.

GRASS-FED BEEF The increasing availability of beef, fed only on grasses, not on grains, is really exciting to me. True, it is expensive. But by buying it, even if it's only an infrequent splurge, you're supporting one of the healthiest movements in American agriculture. Grass-fed beef has all the good things you expect from beef—lots of iron and high-quality protein—and none of the scary hormones and chemicals. It's also a weight loss food. Since this variety of beef is lower in fat, it's lower in calories. Believe it or not, it has even less fat than some cuts of chicken. A study published in the *British Journal of Nutrition* found that eating moderate amounts of grass-fed meat for only 4 weeks will give you healthier levels of essential omega-3 fatty acids. And it's much better for the planet. The simpler the recipe, the more you'll enjoy the flavor.

GREEN TEA Step aside, morning joe—this tea melts fat. While white, black, oolong, and green teas all come from the same plant and have similar amounts of caffeine, green tea leaves are prepared differently.

Green tea leaves aren't fermented before drying, so green tea is richer in antioxidants called catechins, which may trigger weight loss by stimulating the body to burn calories and decrease body fat. Buy tea bags in small quantities, though, and store them in their original packaging and out of the sun. Studies have found that green tea bags can lose up to 32 percent of their antioxidant power in 6 months. Bottled teas have less antioxidant power than steeped teas. Try it iced, with mint.

KEFIR
A fermented dairy product, kefir contains yeast, which gives it a flavor different from yogurt's, as well as a little edge in probiotic value (meaning the amount of healthy bacteria that helps digestion). This drinkable dairy product is a little thicker than milk and a nice change for anyone looking to increase consumption of low-fat dairy. And research from Ohio State University has found that for the many people with lactose intolerance, kefir—which has a wider array of bacteria than yogurt—may be a better choice than yogurt. As with any yogurt, read the ingredients carefully when you shop: Some brands pour in way too many sugars. My favorite brand is Lifeway.

LEAFY GREENS
With their high water content and number of nutrients per ounce, leafy greens are a girl's best friend. Experiment with the different flavors and textures of romaine, mustard greens, beet greens, turnip greens, kale, and Swiss chard. Leafy greens provide a wide range of carotenoids, likely providing protection against cancers of the mouth, pharynx, larynx, and pancreas and slowing the growth of some types of breast, skin, lung, and stomach cancer cells. Experts believe that carotenoids seem to prevent cancer by acting as antioxidants—that is, by scouring potentially dangerous free radicals from the body before they can do harm. Another bonus is that carotenoids have been proven to slow sarcopenia, a fancy name for the natural damage that occurs to our muscles as we age. Eat leafy greens in salads, steam them, or cook them in broth as often as you can.

LENTILS (AND ALL LEGUMES!)
I love these little guys. Like all legumes, lentils provide lean protein, which gives your metabolism a boost as soon as you eat them. (While all foods cause a thermal effect that increases your metabolism, protein has a bit more impact than carbs or fats.) But lentils and chickpeas may have an added advantage: Some research has shown that they contain unique proteins that lower the levels of cholesterol and triglycerides in the bloodstream. They also contain plenty of fiber, which keeps you feeling full, and they have impressive amounts of B vitamins, iron, and zinc. But what makes lentils so much better than other beans, at least

to me, is that they can be prepared quickly. You can have lentils for a delicious meal ready in less than 45 minutes, compared with hours for other legumes. Try black lentils, which are sometimes called beluga because they glisten and shine like caviar once they're cooked. Don't want to cook? Try a prepared lentil soup—365, the private-label brand from Whole Foods Market, makes a yummy organic version.

CHEESES Like other dairy products, cheeses may be useful in weight loss according to some research. But this has also been a little controversial, as other studies found dairy products had no effect. I've seen newer data, including some interesting work with overweight people in Israel, indicating that it is beneficial, which is why I'm recommending dairy so often in this plan. I also like cheeses because they add a different flavor, texture, and character to so many things—fruit, crackers, vegetables, you name it. Even with low-fat varieties, though, watch portion control. It's easy to eat too much. Try crumbled feta in your salad. Because of its strong flavor, you don't need much to take a meal from so-so to special.

MANGOS These are one of the most popular fruits around the world, and I wish more Americans ate them. Like all fruits, of course, mangos pack a strong fiber and antioxidant punch. But they're so high in vitamins C and A that they deserve a special honor. Its smooth texture is different from that of many other fruits, which makes it a creamy contribution to the smoothie blender. Or dice it into a salsa and serve with fish or chicken.

OLIVE OIL It tastes great and performs well, which is the main reason it's the centerpiece of so many different cuisines—Italian, Greek, Spanish, even French. It's high on my list because it's one of the healthiest fats around and teeming with antioxidants. As if that weren't enough, a recent study by a group of cardiologists, which looked at results in more than 534,000 people, confirmed much of what we already knew: A diet that includes olive oil reduces the risk of high blood pressure and heart disease, and increases the odds of a trimmer waist. Your yoga pants will thank you. I recommend that you buy cold-pressed. It has the most antioxidants.

PEANUT BUTTER Natural and organic peanut butters are now offered in almost all mainstream supermarkets these days, as more and more people are discovering why this yummy food is good for you. ("Natural" usually refers to peanut butter that hasn't had any fats added to stabilize it, so it separates and you have to stir it. "Organic" means the peanuts have been grown without any harmful pesticides or fertilizers.) Peanut butter has niacin, a member of the B vitamin family known to promote cell turnover, and even lots of resveratrol (the same as in red wine!) It may prevent Alzheimer's disease and is another proven slimming food. A study in *Obesity* found that over a 28-month period, adults who ate nuts at least twice a week were 31 percent less likely to gain weight than those who didn't. Plain, unsalted peanuts are an especially good choice. A study from Purdue University found that they had high satiety value. I never get tired of peanut butter on apple slices.

PEARS
Like all fruits, pears are a good source of quick energy because of their sweet, natural carbohydrates. But a pear has about 30 percent more potassium than an apple and especially high levels of a kind of fiber called pectin, which is known to help promote weight loss. I like pears because their sweetness feels like a true dessert to me, and they have both a creamy and gritty texture. Try them sliced with an ounce of cheese.

POPCORN
This snack food isn't just delicious—it's also filling. Popcorn's considerable fiber makes it a great snack for someone trying to lose weight. And how convenient that it's also a significant source of antioxidants, with surprisingly large amounts of polyphenols. Air popped and topped with pepper is my favorite.

PUMPKINS
It's time to break this beta-carotene–rich vegetable out of its autumn prison. This wonderful food can do so much more than pies: Add it to muffins and baked goods. It's hearty and filling, and the canned varieties are just as nutritious as making it from scratch. I also use it to thicken stews, soups, and even jarred pasta sauce. It adds flavor and nutrients, and no one but you will know it's there.

RASPBERRIES
Like all berries, these have plenty of fiber and antioxidants. But some studies have shown that raspberries' antioxidant activity is almost 50 percent higher than strawberries', and 10 times the antioxidant activity of tomatoes. Raspberries also have ellagitannins, a family of compounds almost exclusive to the raspberry, which are reported to have anticancer activity. It's also nice that high-quality frozen berries are widely available. I always keep a few bags in my freezer for smoothies. Blackberries, although harder to find fresh, are also widely available frozen and equally packed with anthocyanins. When you get a chance, try boysenberries, a blackberry-raspberry hybrid. Nibble them frozen, right out of the bag—they're a much better snack than gummy candy.

SEAWEED Japanese food fans already know how tasty seaweed can be, but maybe not how healthy—and how slimming. Nori, which is one of my favorites and the type most of us are used to seeing wrapped around a piece of sushi, is especially high in protein, fiber, and nutrients, including vitamins A, B, and more C than a tangerine, as well as iron. And you don't have to become a sushi chef to use it—you can wrap anything in a sheet of this healthy stuff, available in the Asian foods section of most supermarkets. Try a nori wrap with guacamole, chicken, salmon, or tofu.

SHRIMP Because it's so high in protein and low in fat, this is one of the off-the-chart slimming foods. Besides its known heart benefits, shrimp is also a powerful source of vitamin B12. Whether served hot or cold, shrimp are delicious. I love them chilled with slices of avocado.

SOY I know tofu isn't everyone's favorite, and you don't have to eat it if you don't want to. But soy is one of the easiest healthy foods to add to your diet, whether it's tofu, soy milk, or tasty edamame. While soy is not without controversy, it's emerging as a powerful component of a healthy diet, with the American Institute of Cancer Research reporting that its active ingredients—such as isoflavones (which have been studied most), saponins, phenolic acids, phytic acid, and phytosterols—have anticancer properties.

I'm a little skeptical, though, when I hear about people overloading on soy, especially processed soy. While soy is one of the few foods that has gotten a government blessing to market itself as a heart-healthy food, the studies have been inconsistent. In fact, some research has even linked the phytoestrogens in soy to an increased cancer risk. (And they can disrupt the way some anticancer drugs work.)

To me, it makes sense to use soy in moderate amounts, in the least processed, most flavorful forms possible. The most basic form is the nut, and a recent study from Beth Israel Deaconess Medical Center in Boston found that soy nuts may reduce blood pressure in women. Try snacking on soy nuts, which have quite a crunch. Look for low-salt varieties.

SUNFLOWER SEEDS There's a reason baseball players chew these little guys for nine whole innings! Like all nuts, these have healthy oils. And having to bite them out of the shells is a natural way to control portions. Sprinkle them on shakes and salads, too.

SWEET POTATOES Got a sweet tooth? A medium baked sweet potato not only satisfies that craving, but it also contains more than 400 percent of the recommended dietary allowance (RDA) of vitamin A and more eye-healthy beta-carotene than any other vegetable or fruit. They're not just for baking. I like to add diced sweet potatoes to soups.

TOMATOES Whether sliced on your salads or simmering in a sauce on the stove, tomatoes go with everything. No wonder they're the fourth most popular vegetable, even though they're really a fruit. They're loaded with lycopene, and researchers have found that the higher the serum level of this antioxidant in people's blood, the lower their level of heart disease as well as other chronic illnesses. Unlike some other vegetables, cooking actually increases the tomatoes' nutritional power. To me, tomato soup is a true comfort food—especially on a low-energy day.

TURNIPS No, they're not sexy. But they're great vegetables to have on hand. Not only do turnips keep well, but they're always available in supermarkets and are an excellent source of complex carbs, which keep you satisfied longer because they have both soluble and insoluble fiber. Turnips also contain an unexpectedly high amount of vitamin C. If you live in a cooler climate, you can experiment with rutabagas, a close relative of the turnip. I roast them, halved or quartered, in the oven with a little olive oil, whole cloves of garlic, and any fresh herb I have lying around.

WINTER SQUASH While summer squash varieties, such as zucchini and spaghetti squash, are mostly water-based and also nutrient dense, hearty winter squash varieties have a richer flavor and a firmer texture. Winter squash include acorn, buttercup, butternut, hubbard, spaghetti, and turban. They are teeming with complex carbs, beta-carotene, and lutein. Their high levels of both soluble and insoluble fiber mean they are cholesterol fighters, too. Best of all, they are one of the few low-fat sources of vitamin E. I like them pureed, with plenty of cinnamon and fresh black pepper.

YOGURT One of my go-to snacks, yogurt has healthy bacteria that keeps digestion efficient, a must for anyone trying to shed pounds. I'm leery of some of the claims that suggest simply eating more yogurt will help you burn more calories (although wouldn't it be great if it were true?). At least so far, there isn't enough compelling research to convince me. But there is more solid information that any low-fat dairy product is an effective weight loss tool (and that includes fat-free milk, also featured prominently in the plan) regardless of the probiotic benefit. I swear by Greek yogurt, because it's extra creamy, tasty, and more nutritious. It's the perfect snack when I'm on the go.

WHAT YOU CAN'T SEE MAY BE MAKING YOU FAT

Obesogens are chemicals linked to obesity that aren't even necessarily found in foods. Many are used in the packages and plastics that food comes in. Among them are phthalates— chemicals widely used as synthetic fragrance agents, as well as in plastics, and linked to abdominal obesity and insulin resistance. Bisphenol-A (BPA) is a chemical used in food and water containers (even baby bottles). A study published in the Journal of the American Medical Association *found that BPAs are connected to a higher risk of diabetes and cardiovascular disease. Some hypothesize that many other chemicals may be linked to obesity and may be at least partially responsible for the huge upswing in obesity rates in recent decades.*

Experts still aren't clear about how these chemical pollutants promote obesity—whether it's by altering our metabolic "set points," disrupting appetite controls, or upsetting the way fats behave once we've ingested them.

So if we're not sure which chemicals are promoting obesity, or how they do it, what can we do to protect ourselves? First, look for organic goods. A study by Emory University switched grade-school children over to an all-organic diet, and after just 5 days, the level of pesticides found in their urine fell to nearly undetectable levels. Just 5 days!

Second, try to buy food that isn't packaged at all. It's one of the many reasons I love farmers' markets. Of course, that's not always realistic, so when you buy packaged or frozen foods, shop carefully. Some packaged foods are really healthy. Check out my favorites in the appendix.

food fixes

TAKE IT FROM Keri

DABBLE IN COCONUT

Most people think that all saturated fats are unhealthy and that they only come from animal sources. But coconut oil, a plant-derived saturated fat, may actually be good for you. (It's hot among vegans, who can use it in baked goods.) There's even some debate that it may be healthy. The main saturated fat in coconut oil is lauric acid, a fatty acid thought to increase both HDL and LDL without negatively affecting the overall ratio of the two.

My advice if you're a flavor buff? Try this sweet, gentle oil, but as with all fats, use it very sparingly. Try drizzling a little in your oatmeal or using it to sauté some spinach.

WHEN YOU'VE GOT ...

Menstrual bloat	The Blues	Anxiety

MAKE YOUR GO-TO FOOD ...

A monster salad.	Chocolate.	A banana.
It doesn't make sense that high-fiber foods can ease bloating, but they do. And with their high water content and very low sodium level, vegetables will make you feel better fast. (Steer clear of other sodium sources, such as salty dressings.)	Everyone gets down in the dumps sometimes, and for many, a blue mood can trigger a major eating event. Have a little chocolate, whether it's a piece of 70 percent dark chocolate, or chocolate syrup drizzled into your yogurt or milk. A German study gave one group of women an apple as a snack, and another a small serving of chocolate, and then compared their moods. While both groups got happier after their snack, those who had the chocolate had a bigger improvement, and even a sense of joy.	All complex carbohydrates help produce the serotonin that soothes, but because this fruit is low on the glycemic index chart, it'll have a more relaxing effect, with fewer spikes in your blood sugar.

We all know that the right nutrients support your immune system and help prevent disease. That old apple-a-day thing is actually pretty genius. But nutrients can also solve common problems, fast:

WHEN YOU'VE GOT ...

Fatigue	*A cold*	*A hangover*

MAKE YOUR GO-TO FOOD ...

A Granny Smith apple.	Chicken soup.	Whole wheat toast and honey.
All apples provide quick energy (in the form of fructose) along with plenty of fiber. But these green babies have one of the highest levels of antioxidants, making them even more nutrient dense. A sliced Granny Smith with a tablespoon of organic natural nut butter is one of my favorite snacks ever. (And take a nap!)	Chicken soup is known as the Jewish penicillin. But it turns out, according to research at the University of Nebraska, that it's not all about the chicken. The high number of antioxidants that come from the vegetables used in homemade soup may be more beneficial than the chicken. The researchers used a recipe that included chicken, onions, sweet potatoes, parsnips, turnips, carrots, celery, parsley, salt, and pepper and found it prevented some of the upper-respiratory inflammation that comes with colds.	Britain's Royal Society of Chemistry tested this tried-and-true remedy and found that it really works, providing sodium, potassium, and fructose to help the body recover. And drink lots of water—much of your pain comes from dehydration.

calm foods

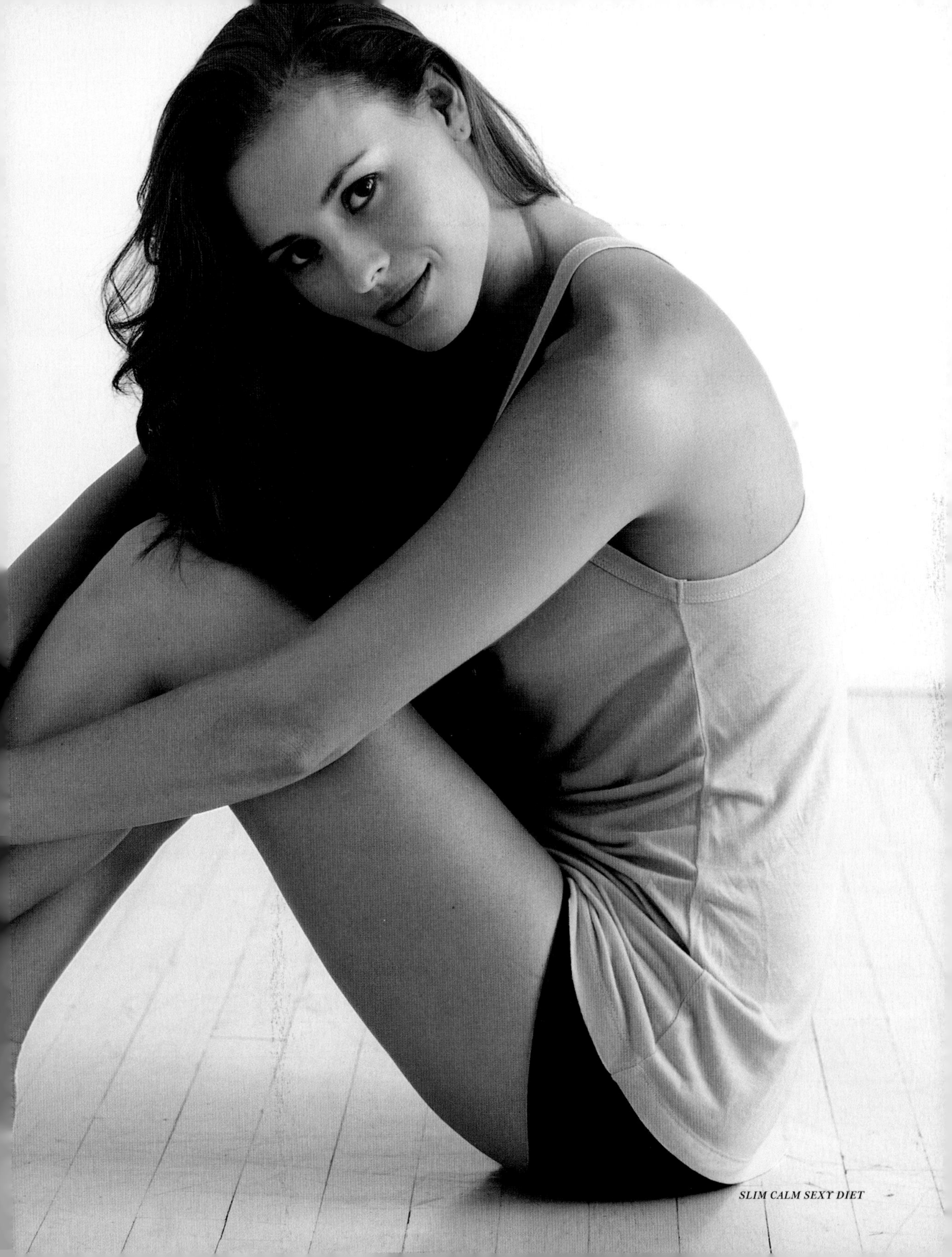

Now

that you're safely launched on what to eat every day on the Slim Calm Sexy Diet, I'd like to take some time to get you better acquainted with specific benefits of certain foods. We'll start with calming foods— nutritional shortcuts to help you feel settled and serene all the time, no matter how much chaos is happening in your life.

What makes a food calming, and what makes it disruptive? Too often, a client will wave me off when I bring up this topic and say, "Oh, Keri, all foods are calming foods. Whenever I'm eating, I feel better." But there's a huge difference between tapping into a food's inherently calming properties and using any food as a kind of emotional anesthesia. That kind of eating may buy you a temporary sense of calm, but it's a quick fix that wears off way too fast. And where does it usually leave you? Weighing more than you'd like and muttering at yourself, "Yuck, how could I have eaten all that?"

There's no point in feeling bad about it. Most of us were raised this way. From the minute we cried when we were infants, someone fed us to make us feel better. Food was used to quiet, calm, and soothe us. And food is often a huge part of cultural traditions and family dynamics. I have plenty of clients who tell me they're constantly offered food by relatives who are really hurt if they don't eat it.

Stress-triggered eating usually leads to the worst foods. They tend to be the high-fat, high-carb combos that are virtually guaranteed to send you into a guilty tailspin even before you've put your plate in the sink. Under normal circumstances, a little bit of some of the most common stress selections—cakes, candy, and ice cream—are tasty. But in large quantities, they are full of unhealthy fats and refined sugars, are hard to digest, and make you feel sluggish and bloated. So let me be clear: Many comfort foods are not calming foods. They turn into stressful foods, practically before you swallow them. When you get a trigger to have those foods, it may help to call them what they really are: foods that will make you gain weight and then feel worse about yourself.

It all comes back to the stress-eating connection we talked about in Chapter 2. Stressful events—and they don't even have to be big, just the daily hassles of life—cause our cortisol levels to rise. Cortisol causes food cravings, and in women those cravings tend to be strongest for carbs, especially sweet foods, according to researchers at the University of California at San Francisco Medical Center. The more of them we eat, the worse our mood gets. As if that weren't bad enough, the cortisol then makes more trouble for us, triggering an enzyme in our fat cells (it converts cortisone to more cortisol). Since our visceral fat cells (the ones in our abdomen, packed around our vital organs) have more of these enzymes than the subcutaneous fat cells (the fat on our thighs and butts, for example), stress causes many women to accumulate more belly fat. The more stress, the more this abdominal, or central, obesity occurs. Some research has found that these belly fat cells, which have been linked to a greater risk for heart disease and diabetes, have four times as many cortisol receptors as regular fat cells.

Keri's

3

FAVORITE
CALMING
FOODS

*Avocado,
chamomile,
and oranges*

So when I talk about calming foods, I don't mean these so-called comfort foods. I mean meals and snacks that will truly soothe and calm you. Whether it's because of the specific nutrients they provide or the steady, reliable source of energy they give you, they'll get you through the day feeling focused, even, and balanced—so you'll have the ability to conquer anything.

Given that definition, I suppose you could argue that every healthy food is also a calming food. What feels better than knowing you're giving your body just what it needs to function well, to perform at its best? When you're eating well—eating empowered—every bite of every meal feels like you're taking a step in a positive direction and taking charge of your health.

Replace Comfort Foods with Secure Foods

• • • Sometimes my clients laugh at me when I introduce the idea of "secure" foods as a way to protect them against those crazy-making "comfort" foods. And I guess the image is kind of funny— as if you'll be clutching spinach and salmon like a security blanket! But "secure" is how I describe munchies that make you feel both safe and nourished.

These are the foods you can count on, over and over, to satisfy your hunger and keep you chugging throughout the day. They protect you from pouncing on a food choice you'll kick yourself for later. Since this is all about how certain foods make you feel, it's entirely subjective.

Maybe the energy bar you've chosen is the right one for you because it always hits the spot and takes the edge off. For one client, it's all about cottage cheese with walnuts and applesauce. When she isn't sure what she wants, she eats her cottage cheese snack, takes a deep breath, and waits 15 minutes. "What can I say?" she jokes. "It settles me down every time." Another client has a fallback of cashew butter on organic whole wheat crackers. She keeps a stash at work, at home, and in her car. In my freezer, you can always find my favorite veggie burger—whether I crumble it in a salad, dice it into a wrap, or eat it on a whole wheat bun, it's always a safe go-to.

These go-to foods are essential to feeling calm and in control about food. You should have at least five of them, and I hope as the weeks go by, many of the Slim Calm Sexy Diet meals will fill at least one of those spots. One of our initial diet testers fell for the Slim Slaw (page 76) so fast that it's become a permanent fixture in her fridge. As soon as it runs low, she whips up another batch.

Safe and Secure: Five Go-To Foods

• • •   Even if you haven't fully immersed yourself in the plan, take a minute to flip through pages 64 to 75 and read through the meals. Pick five foods that sound delicious to you right now, or that you've enjoyed in the past, and write them down here. (They'll probably change over time, which is great. You don't want to get in a rut.)

When I'm starting to feel stressed, I'll reach for:

	FOOD	AMOUNT
Ex.	*Blueberries*	*1 cup*
1.		
2.		
3.		
4.		
5.		

Stock up on these foods, and make sure you've got some wherever you might be—at home, at work, in the car, or on the go.

Rewrite Your Food Rituals

• • •   I'm betting that you can relate to the idea that feeling out of control about eating undermines any sense of calm you have on a given day. Well, get ready to change the way you eat to battle stress. Just as there are certain foods that can trigger cravings—I'll confess, mine are baked goods—there are certain foods that can be eaten in specific ways to soothe us with their calming rituals.

In fact, some cultures demand it. Think of Japanese tea ceremonies, clinking glasses for a toast, or saying a blessing before a meal. These are all ways people use eating as an opportunity to find more meaning in their food, to invest it with some psychological benefit that goes beyond simple nutrition.

You can create your own calming rituals with just about any food. We all know coffee isn't a calming drink, but for millions of people (me included) it's a heavenly morning ritual—and yes, it adds calming structure to the day. I am a morning person, and that first cup is my favorite "me" time. I take my time drinking it, and then I feel ready to start my day.

I have another ritual, in the late afternoon, in between clients, that I call teatime. My current favorite is a big cup of green tea. Yes, green tea has caffeine in it, so it's stimulating, not calming. But because I've built a healthy habit of relaxation with it, it's become a ritual that truly calms me. It's a time for me to inhale, exhale, sip my tea, and get a better grip on what's left of my workday.

I encourage you to create your own food rituals and bask in the good feelings they generate. I have one client who prepares a big kettle of soup on Sunday evenings. To her, the whole process—shopping for the vegetables, slicing them, cooking them slowly so her whole house gets that incredible smell—calms her down. To someone else, it might be just soup or too much work. But to her, it has become symbolic. Not only is it Sunday night's meal, but she also makes enough so that she can have a bowl of homemade soup with dinner every night in the week ahead. It's a big pot of evidence that proves she is taking care of herself.

Three Calming Elements

· · · All three types of nutrients—carbs, fats, and protein—contribute to a healthy mental state, and you can make plenty of choices in each group to dial up your serenity level.

COMPLEX CARBS are probably the most significant group of foods to manage your mood. In fact, after just a few days on the Slim Calm Sexy Diet, you're probably already on a more even keel, thanks to the power of grains like quinoa and oatmeal. All carbohydrates provide quick energy because of the sugars they contain, but complex carbohydrates slow the release of that energy down to a steady, stable supply. That's why a nice quinoa dish, for example, makes you feel wonderful, not only while you're eating it, but a few hours later, too. That's really different from the quick sugar buzz, and then the horrible letdown an hour afterward, that comes from a doughnut. Both types of food provide plenty of glucose, which is what your brain needs to function. (And in fact, it's what all food gets broken down into eventually.) But the difference is the way the speed of

FIND CALMING MOVES

Eating right is just one way to stay calm and feel happy. Exercise is another. Researchers have found that exercise is, in many cases, just as effective in treating depression as medication. And it doesn't have to take long. A study from the University of Texas at Austin found that even 30 minutes on a treadmill is enough to lift the mood of someone with depression. Imagine how well it will work to alleviate the stress of a hectic afternoon. And don't forget about yoga. A single pose, with even just a few minutes of focused breathing, can quickly calm you down.

this process affects your mood—it's like night and day.

Studies have documented how these carbs contribute to our happiness. One recent study, published in the *Archives of Internal Medicine,* followed two groups of dieters for a full year. One group ate a very low level of carbohydrate each day; the other ate a better-balanced diet that, while low in fat, included adequate amounts of whole grains. Both groups lost weight. But the researchers found a significant difference in their mental health. While all remained well within normal mental health ranges, the carb-deprived crowd was more likely to feel depressed, angry, or anxious than those who had eaten whole grains. Kind of explains why the Atkins diet left so many people a little grouchy.

The scientists chalk up the results to serotonin, a neurotransmitter, or a chemical that relays signals from one area of the brain to another. We manufacture serotonin in our brains, where it has an impact on something like 40 million of our brain cells, affecting mood, sexual desire, sexual function, appetite, sleep, memory, and even some social behaviors. Experts believe that serotonin levels play a big role in causing depression, even though they aren't quite sure how. (In fact, antidepressants known as selective serotonin reuptake inhibitors, or SSRIs, like Prozac and Zoloft, are currently among the most commonly prescribed drugs.) Women not only have a little less serotonin than men, but they also seem more vulnerable to a shift in its level, which may explain why depression is much more common in women.

Forty million brain cells can't be wrong! You can give them the serotonin they need by making sure you eat high-quality carbohydrates at every meal. You don't have to worry about this on the Slim Calm Sexy Diet. Each meal and snack includes some of the right kinds of carbs, whether it's in a starch, a vegetable, or a fruit.

FATS Neurologists know that 70 percent of our brain is made of fats, so it shouldn't be shocking that omega-3s, a type of fatty acid, are emerging as critical to brain health. You're already eating plenty, because I've loaded the Slim Calm Sexy Diet with foods like salmon and walnuts. You'll learn more in later chapters about what these can do for your heart. But right now, I want you to know what they can do for your spirits: They've been shown to be beneficial in fighting off depression and other mood disorders. Researchers at Harvard-affiliated McLean Hospital say that some of these foods are so powerful they may act as antidepressants—and they speculate that the omega-3 fatty acids may make membranes more resilient and ease the flow of neurotransmitters within the brain.

nutritious *life-ism*

RISE AND SHINE

Start each day with a glass of water that has 1 ounce of fresh lemon juice in it. Beyond the health benefits (those antioxidants again!), it's a calming ritual that perks you up. You'll be amazed at how energized you feel, even before your shower and morning coffee.

Omega-3s: Under the Sea

• • •   It turns out that omega-3s, which are fatty acids, work all kinds of wonders. While their ability to soothe inflammation inside the body may get the most attention for boosting heart health and possibly preventing cancer, omega-3s are a core component of a calming diet. They've been linked to helping combat both stress and depression. Since our bodies can't make omega-3s on their own, we need to either get them from food or from supplements. If you choose supplements, make sure they bear a certification that they've been tested for safety. Environmental groups have sued some manufacturers whose fish oil supplements were contaminated with PCBs, cancer-causing chemicals found in many parts of the world's oceans.

There are two types of omega-3s, and both are super beneficial. One type is alpha-linolenic acid (ALA), which is found in plant sources such as soybean, canola, and flaxseed. The other is eicosapentaenoic acid (EPA) and docosahexaenoic acid (DHA), found mainly in fatty fish. I've already added plenty of the plant-based types to the plan, but here's something to help you find your way around the fish market. Ideally, it would be great if we were all consuming these types of fish four times per week—all of these options are high in omega-3s, low in mercury, and sustainable.

FISH	Grams of omega-3s per 3-ounce serving
HERRING	1.81
CHINOOK SALMON	1.48
PACIFIC OYSTERS	1.17
FARMED COHO SALMON	1.09
SOCKEYE SALMON	1.05
FARMED TROUT	.98
SARDINES	.98
EASTERN OYSTERS	.95

Eat Ocean-Friendly Fish

Researchers continue to learn more about the healthy benefits of eating seafood, but there's been a downside to its popularity. As fishermen rush to fill their boats to meet the growing worldwide demand, many species have been severely overfished, including my beloved Atlantic salmon. (Alaska wild-caught is now a preferred variety.) Marine populations shift quickly, but you can always find out more

Calm in a **FLASH**

SNIFF YOUR WAY TO SERENITY

Not only does an orange make a great calming snack, thanks to all that vitamin C, but that wonderful whiff of citrus you get when you peel it is instant aromatherapy. Fragrance research-ers have found that citrus smells make people feel happy. Close your eyes as you peel it, put your nose up close, and breathe deeply.

about sustainable fishing practices through programs like Seafood Watch, run by the Monterey Aquarium (www.montereybayaquarium.org; click on "Seafood Watch"). There's even an app with recommendations for buying ocean-friendly seafood that you can download for your phone.

Here's the latest "best of the best" list, meaning best for you and the fish stocks. Seafood Watch has chosen these fish because they have low levels of contaminants (below 216 parts per billion of mercury and 11 parts per billion of PCBs), they have the daily minimum of wonderfully calming omega-3s (at least 250 milligrams per day), and they are classified as the "Best Choices" for sustainability:

+ **Albacore tuna** (troll- or pole-caught, from the United States or British Columbia)
+ **Freshwater coho salmon** (farmed in U.S. tank systems)
+ **Oysters** (farmed)
+ **Pacific sardines** (wild-caught)
+ **Rainbow trout** (farmed)
+ **Salmon** (wild-caught, from Alaska)

But I Don't Eat Fish—What Should I Do?

• • •   Even though fish is a great source of omega-3s, I know plenty of people who won't eat it because they are vegan or vegetarian, or just plain don't like the taste or texture. There's no reason you have to miss out on the calming benefits of omega-3s because of that. Here are the types of omega-3s and their main sources:

ALA	EPA	DHA
found in plants	*found mainly in fish*	*found mainly in fish and seaweed*

The good news is that the body can convert ALA into both DHA and EPA. (This can be a little tricky, though, since it is important to add foods that are high in omega-3s and low in omega-6s, to keep the balance right.) Omega-6 foods include refined oil, such as soy, and is found in many processed foods.

If you don't eat fish, try to incorporate these foods daily:
+ flaxseed oil
+ canola oil
+ ground flaxseeds
+ chia seeds
+ omega-3 DHA-fortified eggs

TAKE IT FROM

Keri

CHANGE COMFORT FOODS TO CALMING FOODS

Researchers at Cornell University found that what we tend to think of as a comfort food has little to do with how it tastes and more to do with a happy memory.

Why not find a new, healthy food memory to savor? For me, it's grapefruit—full of vitamin C and fiber. When I was growing up, my mom often served us half a grapefruit as a first course. It's such a refreshing way to start a meal, and it makes me think of home.

PROTEIN Even though it's toward the end of the list, I'm not dissing the contributions protein can make to keeping you calm, happy, and focused. In fact, protein foods—like the beef, fish, chicken, yogurt, and eggs you're eating on the plan—are ideal sources of vitamin B12, which we need for cognitive functioning, energy, and endurance; without enough of it, we feel exhausted. This can be an especially big problem for vegetarians and vegans since the only sources of B12 are fortified foods, like some breakfast cereals, soy foods, or plant milks. (If that's you, either make sure you eat a fortified food two to three times a day or take a B12 supplement.)

AND DON'T FORGET FRUITS AND VEGGIES Folate, another B vitamin, is strongly linked to mood and cognitive performance. Researchers at Tufts University have found that depressed people often have lower levels of this nutrient in their bodies. And this means that I have another reason to urge all my clients, and you, to eat plenty of foods rich in folate, including most leafy greens (especially spinach), lots of legumes (black-eyed peas and lentils), asparagus, broccoli, avocados, and peanuts.

Folate-Fortified Foods

• • • Since Lucy Wills, a pioneering doctor, discovered that folate could be supplied by a yeast extract in 1930, great strides have been made in fortifying foods with it. Most commercially prepared breads and cereals now contain folate, and that has been a huge boone for Americans. Adequate folate levels are essential in pregnancy, and Wills's discovery has prevented millions of babies from being born with neural-tube defects. So if you normally eat those commercially prepared foods—and most Americans do—you probably get enough folate. But on the Slim Calm Sexy Diet, since I'm often directing you to foods that haven't been fortified, you'll want to make sure you get plenty from other sources. (I'm not a fan of all sources of folate. Chicken and beef livers, for example, just aren't my thing, and besides, organ meats have been shown to raise cholesterol.) While the public health advantages of fortifying breads and breakfast cereals are undeniable, I'd prefer you learn to get all the folate you need from plant sources, which deliver so many other nutrients at the same time. I'm all about multitasking, and these foods deliver plenty of folate plus other important nutrients. The following chart lists my favorites.

FOLATE FOODS

	Serving size	Micrograms of folate per serving	% daily value*
Lentils, cooked	½ cup	180	45
Chickpeas	½ cup	141	35
Asparagus	½ cup	132	35
Spinach, cooked	½ cup	131	33
Black beans	½ cup	128	32
Kidney beans	½ cup	115	29
Tomato juice	1 cup	48	12
Brussels sprouts	½ cup	47	12
Orange	1 medium	47	12
Broccoli, cooked	½ cup	39	10

*From USDA Nutrient Database

TAKE IT FROM Keri

NOT-SO-HAPPY HOUR?

For most people, most of the time, a glass of wine or a cocktail is harmless. Some studies have found health benefits in moderate alcohol use, including protection against heart disease, diabetes, and maybe even Alzheimer's, especially in women who don't smoke. And everyone knows a drink before dinner can make you feel like you're leaving your troubles behind. That's why they call it happy hour, right?

But when it comes to managing your mood via margaritas, the benefits get murky. Even though it feels like it's perking you up, alcohol is technically a depressant. Research from the University of North Carolina at Chapel Hill has shown that even moderate drinking may increase the odds of depression.

My approach? When you want to celebrate, by all means, have a glass of wine or a cocktail with your friends. But when you're truly stressed or feeling low, think before you pour yourself a drink. It will add calories to your day, and it may not be the best coping tool—even after a very long day. Instead, call a pal, take a nap, or toast yourself with a big mug of herbal tea. You'll thank yourself in the morning.

Build Your Calm-Foods Collection

• • •   There are some other foods that can help you stay calm, even beyond the ones I've already outlined. Feel free to work them into your menus as suggested.

ASPARAGUS I know, these slender stalks are known to make your urine smell funny. But they are high in folate, which is essential for keeping your cool. I like them steamed, then added to salads. I also love them broiled until crisp. Go ahead and eat as many as you'd like on the Slim Calm Sexy Diet.

AVOCADOS These creamy fruits stress-proof your body. Rich in glutathione, a substance that specifically blocks intestinal absorption of certain fats that cause oxidative damage, avocados also contain lutein, beta-carotene, vitamin E, and more folate than any other fruit. A single serving (about one-quarter of an avocado) has plenty of B vitamins, too. Remember, this may technically be a fruit, but I count it as a fat on the plan, so use as directed. Thin sliced on sandwiches, it adds a whole new layer of flavor.

BERRIES Blueberries have some of the highest levels of an antioxidant known as anthocyanin, and they've been linked to all kinds of positive health outcomes, including sharper cognition. But all berries, including strawberries, raspberries, and blackberries, are rich in vitamin C, which has been shown to be helpful in combating stress. German researchers tested this by asking 120 people to give a speech, then do hard math problems. Those who had been given vitamin C had lower blood pressure and lower levels of cortisol after the stressfest. Substitute berries for any other fruits on the plan whenever you want. I like to nibble on them frozen, too.

CASHEWS I love all nuts. They're great snacks, and because they are crunchy and a little salty, they cure many cravings. For those trying to lose weight, they're such a potently satisfying combo of protein and fat that it's hard for me not to recommend them at every single meal. (You do have to watch portion size though, since they are high in calories.) Cashews are an especially good source of zinc—a 1-ounce serving has 11 percent of your RDA. Low levels of zinc have been linked to both anxiety and depression. Since our bodies have no way of storing zinc, it's important to get some every day. Trade cashews for other nuts on the plan when you're in the mood. Coarsely chop a handful and toss them into a chicken stir-fry.

CHAMOMILE TEA This is probably one of the most recommended bedtime soothers around. I've always loved it because the flowers are so pretty, like tiny daisies. But now there's more evidence than ever that chamomile calms. A new study from the University of Pennsylvania tested chamomile supplements on 57 participants with generalized anxiety disorder for 8 weeks, and found it led to a significant drop in anxiety symptoms. Of course, I'd much prefer you drink it in tea form—that way, you'll get the warm, wonderfully calming feeling of holding a mug of tea as you sit in a quiet spot before bed. And yes, according to the University of Maryland Medical Center, there is some evidence that, in addition to calming nerves, chamomile promotes sleep. Just pour a cup of boiling water over 2 to 3 heaping tablespoons of the dried flowers (you can buy chamomile either loose or in tea bags at health food stores) and steep for 10 minutes. Try having a cup every night: Turn off the TV, the computer, and your phone, and settle down for a peaceful end to the day. It's nice iced, too.

CHOCOLATE Besides the healthy antioxidants in this treat, which push chocolate to the top of most heart-healthy food lists, it has an undeniable link to mood. A recent study from the University of California, San Diego, School of Medicine reports that both women and men eat more chocolate as depressive symptoms increase. Of course, we've all been there, polishing off an entire package of chocolate after a bad day. But there's evidence that, in moderation, chocolate does actually make you feel better. Dark chocolate, in particular, is known to lower blood pressure, adding to a feeling of calm. It contains more polyphenols and flavonols—two important types of antioxidants—than some fruit juices. You can safely allow yourself dark chocolate as a snack once a week, or as a conscious indulgence, and still stay on track with your weight loss results. I always keep a few squares in my bag.

GARLIC Like many plants, garlic is jam-packed with powerful antioxidants. These chemicals neutralize free radicals (particles that damage our cells, cause diseases, and encourage aging) and may reduce or even help prevent some of the damage the free radicals cause over time. Among the compounds in garlic is allicin, which has been linked to fending off heart disease, cancer, and even the common cold. Because stress weakens our immune system, we need friends like garlic, which can toughen it back up. As long as you sauté it in broth, not oil, you can add it liberally to all the meals on the plan.

GRASS-FED BEEF

This type of beef is not only better for the planet, it's also better for people. It has more antioxidants—including vitamins C and E and beta-carotene—than grain-fed beef, and doesn't have added hormones, antibiotics, or other drugs. And while it's lower in fat overall, it's about two to four times higher in omega-3s. A recent study in the *British Journal of Nutrition* found that healthy volunteers who ate grass-fed meat increased their blood levels of omega-3 fatty acids and decreased their levels of pro-inflammatory omega-6 fatty acids. These changes have been linked with a lower risk of a host of disorders, including cancer, cardio-vascular disease, depression, and inflammatory disease. Grass-fed beef is pricey but well worth the occasional splurge. Use it wherever I've suggested beef. (If you're really gung-ho on the concept, check out local sources for "cowpooling," where you go in with others on shares of grass-fed cattle.)

GREEN TEA

While it does contain caffeine, green tea also has an amino acid called theanine. Researchers at the University of Illinois say that in addition to protecting against some types of cancer, this slimming food is a brain booster as well, enhancing mental performance. Drink two cups each day.

OATMEAL

Talk about comfort food! A complex carbohydrate, oatmeal causes your brain to produce serotonin, a feel-good chemical. Not only does serotonin have antioxidant properties, it also creates a soothing feeling that helps overcome stress. Studies have shown that kids who eat oatmeal for breakfast stay sharper throughout the morning. And beta-glucan, the type of soluble fiber found in oatmeal, has been shown to promote greater satiety scores than other whole grains. Make a batch of the steel-cut variety on the weekend, store it in the fridge, and microwave it on busy mornings. It keeps beautifully, and in fact, that's how restaurants often prepare it.

ORANGES

Another vitamin C powerhouse, oranges have the added benefit of being totally portable. That tough skin keeps them protected while they're bouncing around in your purse or backpack, meaning you can tote them anywhere. Experiment with all the varieties—clementines, tangelos, mineolas.

OYSTERS And you thought you'd only read about oysters in the Sexy Foods chapter! They belong here, too, because they're the Godzilla of zinc: Six oysters, which is what you'd typically be served in a restaurant as an appetizer, have more than half the RDA for this important mineral. I think they're best served on ice with nothing but a lemon wedge.

WALNUTS The sweet flavor of walnuts is so pleasant, and it's nice to know they've been proven to provide a bit of a cognitive edge. They contain alpha-linolenic acid, an essential omega-3 fatty acid, and other polyphenols that have been shown to help prevent memory loss. Researchers at Tufts University found that animals that ingested walnuts even reversed some signs of brain aging. To bring out their flavor, I toast them for 10 minutes, then chop them and add them to salads.

chapter 7

sexy foods

SLIM CALM SEXY DIET

Now

that you're snacking, crunching, and sipping your way toward slim and calm, you're probably wondering when the sexy part of the diet kicks in. Let's bring it on!

I won't be offended if you're rolling your eyes. I'm used to it. My clients are often baffled when I first bring up the subject. "Eating is not sexy," they'll say. "Flat abs in a string bikini—that's sexy. And that means not eating."

Wrong! Men and women have been combining food and friskiness ever since Eve turned Adam on to apples. Food doesn't only nourish us and sustain us for sexual endurance. It can also be a source of delight, pleasure, and even intrigue. And I don't mean things like tying a knot in a cherry stem with your tongue, although I have always wondered how some women learn to do that. I mean the whole deeply sensual aspect of food: tastes, smells, sights, textures, even sounds. (C'mon, are you telling me that bacon sizzling in a pan or whipped cream whooshing out of a container isn't a thrilling noise?)

That's why every culture has so many myths about and recipes for aphrodisiacs. Men and women have always been on the hunt for love potions and male enhancers, well before Viagra hit the market. The good news? As the Slim Calm Sexy Diet reboots your metabolism and shores up your basic level of nutrition, you'll likely see a jump in your energy levels. And as your stress levels decrease, you'll likely see a lift in your libido. In fact, it turns out that slim and calm are the key ingredients in sexy—hence the name of this diet.

American women need to nurture their sexual side more. Some 44 percent suffer from sexual problems, such as low sexual arousal or difficulty reaching orgasm, according to a survey of more than 31,000 women published in the journal *Obstetrics and Gynecology* in 2008. Both stress and being overweight play a key role in some of those problems. (While more women are plagued by being overweight and by obesity—about 68 percent right now, according to federal statistics—44 percent is still a lot.)

The not-so-good news is that when it comes to using food as a way to perk up a woman's desire, there aren't many choices that meet modern scientific standards. Nutrition researchers spend a lot more time trying to figure out what makes men excited than they do worrying about the female libido. In fact, it's only been relatively recent news to many male scientists that we even have one! (Hello? Doesn't "It takes two to tango" mean anything?)

Don't worry, I'm not about to recommend some of the wackier methods women have used through the ages. The idea of deer-penis wine, for example, is hard for me to even think about. And I don't care if Aphrodite ate sparrow brains or that other cultures munch fried skink (an African lizard believed to make anyone who eats it completely irresistible) to get turned on. That's just gross! While there is no single "cure" for female sexual dysfunction, there are plenty of ways to experiment.

So get naked and be your own sex-food researcher! The more sex you have, the better the Slim Calm Sexy Diet works, and I'm not just blowing smoke. Eating empowered makes you feel good about your body, which makes you feel sexy, which makes you crave sex. Orgasm (and even

Keri's

3

FAVORITE
SEXY
FOODS

Coffee, grass-fed beef, and flaxseed

cuddling) releases a beneficial hormone called oxytocin, which has been linked to all kinds of health benefits. It also makes you feel closer to your partner, which makes him more supportive, which makes you even more relaxed, confident, and healthy. A recent study found that women who reported getting it on at least one or two times a week had higher levels of the antibody immunoglobulin A, a defender against the common cold. You see where I'm going with this?

The single decision to eat well is what kicks off this lovely chain of sexual events, making you a more balanced, integrated person. Healthy sexual intimacy gives you that delicious sense of having it all totally together.

I wish more women understood how good sex is for them and how important it is to get enough of it. For years, scientists have known that oxytocin, which they often call the "calm and connection hormone," does a lot to keep us healthy. Oxytocin, secreted in the neurons of the pituitary gland and released in both men and women after orgasm—and even through cuddling or by simply holding hands—acts as a soothing antioxidant for all of our body's systems.

In women, oxytocin also signals when to go into labor and controls milk flow during breast-feeding. (It's such a finely tuned chemical process that the mere sound of a baby crying—even somebody else's baby!—is enough to get a woman's breast milk flowing.) It's also instrumental in establishing maternal behavior, and even how much we trust people.

It's more powerful than some medicines. A University of North Carolina study found that when couples spent just 10 minutes holding hands, oxytocin levels rose enough to significantly lower blood pressure. New research from psychologists at Northern Illinois University has found that higher levels of oxytocin are linked to socializing and keep us from becoming isolated. And since women who breast-feed have lower risks of breast cancer, heart disease, stroke, high blood pressure, and diabetes, some researchers believe that elevated levels of oxytocin may be part of the explanation, offering protection from these serious illnesses.

Sex isn't the only way to trigger oxytocin. Spending time with pets can have a similar effect. Some studies have found that people generate more oxytocin spending time with their pets than with their spouse! The unconditional love of a furry friend might just be what you need. Hugs from good friends and family help, too.

To me, sex and love have health benefits that are more important than those from a chemical perspective. (I admit that chatting about sex is a pretty cool part of my job.) It's about living a healthy, full, nutritious life. When I hear a client talk about spending more time with her guy, it thrills me. Finding more love in our lives is as important as going to the gym or finally getting into that pair of size 6 jeans. It's one more way to say, "I deserve to be slim, calm, and sexy. It's good for me." When that happens, of course, we feel like goddesses. Eating right lets us channel our own sexual inspirations, whether that's Cleopatra, Sophia Loren, or even Lara Croft, "tomb raider."

The No-Sex Epidemic

● ● ●   I must let you in on an ugly little secret. For all we talk about sex, joke about it, dress for it, sing about it, watch it on the Internet, and hunt it down in romantic comedies, we're not getting nearly enough. I've already said that as many as 44 percent of all women suffer from some kind of sexual "issue." A low libido—not caring whether sex happens or not—is the most common. Some studies have shown that as many as 33 percent of all women and 17 percent of all men (despite the stereotypes) suffer from low libido at some point. It's very hard for practitioners like me to address this libido lag, since it so often presents itself in the form of apathy. Women don't bring up not wanting to have sex as a problem, because to them it isn't. (Sadly, I don't always get to interview their husbands and boyfriends, but I'll bet if I did, they would say it's an issue.)

So I have to ask my clients to describe their sex lives. I'd like you to have a quick heart-to-heart with yourself, as well. Think about the last five times you had sex. How was it? Orgasmic or ho-hum? How many times did you initiate it? Are you getting what you need? Do you know what you need?

The average American couple does it about seven times a month, but that's a pretty meaningless definition of "enough." If doing it every night is what you need to feel like a hot tamale, that's great. Less is okay, too. The important thing is that you keep track. Steady sexual frequency is a barometer of your overall health, whether you were raised to think that way or not. (Of course, there can be other problems, such as the inability to have an orgasm or painful intercourse. If that's you, please talk to your doctor—you don't have to suffer in silence.)

Some sexual apathy certainly has to do with stress. When we're worn out and distracted by what's happening at work, for example, it's hard to feel sexy—and easy to pretend to be asleep if we want to avoid it. Relationship problems, kids (boy, do I know about that one!), work demands, and even some medications all play a part.

Body image issues add a stress all their own. Sex (usually) requires getting into your birthday suit or maybe some skimpy lingerie. If that's something you dread, it will drain all the fun out of getting frisky. So it's not surprising that weight is closely linked to sex problems. Up to 30 percent

*Sex, love, friends,
passions, hobbies,
exercise, food—
they're all part of
a balanced life.
And you deserve
it all.*

of people who struggle with their weight also report problems with sex drive, desire, or performance, according to researchers at Duke University. And as many as 50 percent of all people with diabetes, many of whom are also overweight, complain of some level of sexual dysfunction. You don't need to be Dr. Phil to know that low self-esteem is at the root of the problem.

But more and more, researchers are learning that it's chemical, too. The more body fat you have, the more it secretes sex hormone binding globulin (SHBG), which binds to testosterone, the sex hormone found in men and women. Researchers believe that too much SHBG means there is less free testosterone to stimulate libido. Losing as few as 10 pounds is enough to increase sex drive, they've discovered, which is great news. Even on Day 1 of the Slim Calm Sexy Diet, you're well on your way to a livelier libido.

Healthier foods really help. A group of Italian researchers looked at women who suffered from both sexual dysfunction and metabolic syndrome (a catchall term that includes a group of risk factors that occur together and increase the risk for coronary artery disease, stroke, and type 2 diabetes). They divided them into two groups. One continued with their usual diet, while the other switched to a Mediterranean-style diet loaded with fruits, vegetables, nuts, and whole grains for 2 years. The overall sexual function of the Mediterranean diet group improved significantly. These foods are all found in the Slim Calm Sexy Diet and will help maximize your mojo.

Before I dive in to the sex-stoking nutritional properties of specific foods, think about your senses and the way food can affect them:

WHAT FOODS LOOK SEXY? Some experts speculate that the main reason oysters have become the superstars of aphrodisiacs is that they look like female genitalia (as do figs). And foods like celery, carrots, bananas, and asparagus are thought to be turn-ons because they are so phallic-looking.

WHAT FOODS FEEL SEXY? Texture can be very exciting—creamy things can feel so orgasmic in our mouths. My colleagues and I often wonder if the reason many women have a thing for ice cream is because of that sexy-creamy sensation. Me? I love the texture of avocados and probably say "Mmmmm" a little more than most people when I dip into guacamole. That's why I've included so many avocados in the Slim Calm Sexy Diet. But your mouth isn't the only way to thrill your sense of touch. Think of finger foods like shrimp cocktail, artichokes, and pomegranates. They all encourage you to use your fingers, teeth, and tongue in a way that's lots more interesting than eating a soup or a salad. (They're also fun to feed each other, and what's not to love about that?)

WHAT FOODS SMELL SEXY? It's no accident that the word spice has so many sexual connotations. Many of the world's most potent herbs and spices are believed to get men and women all wound up. Curry, cloves, nutmeg, turmeric, and garlic have strong, pungent aromas that stimulate the limbic—or, more primitive—part of our brain. In fact, we have millions of smell receptors in our noses. When they detect a scent, they shoot the information to the olfactory bulb, a pea-size cluster in the brain, which sorts the signals and relays them to the limbic system. This part of the brain governs many memories and emotions; some of our most basic behaviors such as feeding, fighting, or fleeing; and sexual arousal, pleasure, and maybe even addiction. Because of their close proximity, the neurological controls for these behaviors often become entangled. That's why dinner and sex is the peanut butter and jelly of the dating world!

A "Scent-sual" Experiment

• • •   Alan Hirsch, founder and neurological director of the Smell and Taste Treatment and Research Foundation in Chicago, has done fascinating research on men, women, and fragrance. By using devices that measure bloodflow to the penis and vagina, and then asking subjects to wear masks treated with many fragrances, he found that food smells are among the sexiest scents out there.

When he tested men, he discovered that:
+ A combination of lavender and pumpkin pie increased sexual arousal by 40 percent.
+ Doughnut and black licorice increased it by 31.5 percent.
+ Pumpkin pie and doughnut increased it by 20 percent.
+ Orange increased it by 19.5 percent.
+ Lavender and doughnut increased it 18 percent.

He gave women the same test, but with very different results:
+ Good and Plenty candy and cucumber increased sexual arousal by 13 percent.
+ Baby powder increased it by 13 percent.
+ Pumpkin pie and lavender increased it by 11 percent.
+ Baby powder and chocolate increased it by 4 percent.

Of course, you don't need to fill your house with doughnuts and pie to turn on your guy. Look for similarly scented candles to fill the air with the right aroma to get him in the mood.

TAKE IT FROM
Keri

BOOZE CAN BACKFIRE

When it comes to sex, alcohol can definitely help. It's relaxing and known to increase sexual desire. (It's amazing how good some guys can look after you've had just one cocktail, isn't it?) But after going through hundreds of studies, a group of Canadian researchers found that while a drink can increase sexual arousal, it's likely to impede sexual performance.

In fact, drinking causes a problem so common in men that it has a scientific nickname: "brewer's droop." That's no fun for us. And in women, drinking is linked to "inhibited orgasm." That's no fun for us, either!

Fuel-Your-Passion Foods

• • •   Get ready to meet the foods that will really spice things up! I've included choices shown to increase men's sexual performance, too. When it comes to sex, what's good for the gander is definitely good for the goose.

BROCCOLI An excellent source of many antioxidants, broccoli also has a lot of vitamin C, which helps your blood circulation, and it's been linked to an improved female libido—which is why I'm recommending it here. But some people just don't dig it. Researchers have even discovered the gene that makes some of us hate its bitter taste (also found in watercress, mustard greens, turnips, rutabagas, and horseradish). Blanching (briefly cooking it in boiling water) helps tame the bitterness. So does pairing it with something tangy. Try adding a few chopped sun-dried tomatoes.

CAYENNE PEPPER This spice can easily make its way into a pot of chili or a bowl of salsa. It's rich in capsaicin, an antioxidant that I love to talk about since it's a known slimming food. But cayenne pepper also has powerful links to sexual health and has been shown to be effective in combating some types of prostate cancer. Peppers also have anti-inflammatory properties—the hotter the better. But be careful: Those habanero and Scotch bonnets are wild! A simple way to experiment with the intensity? Sprinkle it on plain old chicken breasts.

CELERY Okay, it may not make you feel sexier, but it turns out that when guys crunch this vegetable—loaded with the pheromones androstenone and androstenol—it gives off a subtle odor that turns women on. Serve it to him anytime and feel free to crunch it with him. It may even lead to more memorable sex! Researchers at the University of Illinois have found that the phytonutrient luteolin, found in celery and other vegetables, may reduce brain inflammation and boost memory. Use a stalk or two to stir up a glass of vegetable juice.

CHOCOLATE It's on my list as a sexy food because people describe it in such sensual terms. (I have some clients who may have a deeper connection with chocolate than they do with their significant other!) It also contains a compound called phenylethylamine, which is linked to endorphin release—the same happy-feeling chemicals we get after a good workout. But new research from the University of Guelph in Canada, which examined hundreds of studies on potential aphrodisiacs, found that even though people believe their sexual desire increases after eating chocolate, it's not linked in any way to sexual arousal or satisfaction. In other words, chocolate's sexy powers are likely all in our heads, where it triggers serotonin and endorphins. But that works for me. When I need a little chocolate fix and I'm hungry, I add dark chocolate chips into my Greek yogurt.

CLOVES
This may be my favorite spice to sniff. Its strong odor makes me think of dishes that are sweet, savory, and mysterious all at the same time. A study at a university in India, where cloves have been used to treat male sexual dysfunction for centuries, found clove extracts "produced a significant and sustained increase in the sexual activity of normal male rats." If it can rev up a rodent, I bet it can do the same for you. Add a little to your oatmeal instead of cinnamon.

COFFEE
And to think coffee was once considered a bad thing! A study from Southwestern University found that the female sex drive perks up after a little java, which stimulates the part of the brain that regulates arousal. One caveat: Because getting back to a healthy sleep pattern is so important on the Slim Calm Sexy plan, make sure to pay attention to your afternoon cutoff time. For many people, no caffeine after 2 p.m. is a good rule of thumb.

EGGS
These are a good source of L-arginine, an amino acid that has been shown to be effective in treating some heart ailments and erectile dysfunction. And they're not just for breakfast. Try an easy frittata recipe for dinner some night, for meatless magic.

FISH
Men's erections require a steady release of nitric oxide (and drugs like Viagra work on these pathways). This substance is manufactured in the lining of blood vessels, or endothelium, and the healthier his heart and vascular system are, the better he'll be in bed. The omega-3s found in fish are one of the most proven nutritional paths to heart health we've got. Worried about the high cost of seafood? Consider buying frozen in bulk. Costco and BJ's Wholesale Club often have amazing deals.

FLAXSEED
I don't use the word superfood lightly, but flaxseed is definitely one of them. A rich source of dietary lignans, these tiny seeds have been proven to be a powerful source of omega-3s as well,

TAKE IT FROM
Keri

LESS FIBER = MORE LOVIN'

By now, you've noticed that the Slim Calm Sexy Diet is very heavy on fiber. It's so good for you on many levels. It makes the foods you're eating seem more satisfying, keeps your systems functioning well, and has even been linked to longevity. But it can also lead to gas, and frankly, who wants to be thinking about that when you dim the lights? So for romantic dinners, stick to lower-fiber choices like proteins and healthy fat. Leave the beans for your night off!

and to be strongly linked to a healthier heart and vascular system. Flaxseed also has some very real connections to sexual health. Although there's plenty of conflicting data, it's considered to have some potential in helping men with prostate cancer, and it has a bigger impact on women's hormonal levels than soy. Flaxseeds are absorbed best when crushed, and you can buy them in oil form. Try it in the delicious Slim Calm Sexy Squares on page 228. Flaxseed oil is great on salads.

GINGER

Considered an old, reliable herbal remedy for nausea, ginger may also lower cholesterol and help prevent the blood from clotting, according to preliminary studies. Each of these effects may protect the blood vessels from blockage and, by extension, the damaging effects such as atherosclerosis, which can lead to a heart attack or stroke. Anything that benefits the circulation and the heart can make good sex even better. (Canadian researchers also say ginger is linked to increased sexual desire.) I keep some frozen and grate it right into recipes, but I also love the many varieties of ginger herbal teas out there.

GINSENG

In a study at the University of Hawaii, researchers found that women who consumed a supplement that contains ginseng saw a big increase in their libido in 4 weeks, and 68 percent said that their overall satisfaction with their sex life rose. Dabble in some of the yummy ginseng tea varieties at your natural food store.

MACA ROOT

The University of Guelph researchers found that this type of mustard plant, found in the Andes, increased desire in those who ate it. (Currently, there are studies under way to see how, specifically, it affects women with low libido.) But don't take the supplements—they make me nervous. As beneficial as products like this may be, they're not regulated, and it's hard for consumers to judge the potency and dosage. Stick to the maca teas and powders in your health food store. I add a teaspoon to my yogurt some days, when I feel like my libido needs a little lift.

NUTMEG

Researchers in India have shown that nutmeg makes male rats go nuts, increasing their sexual behavior whenever they get near a receptive female rat. (Maybe you want to be careful how much you give your guy!) We all grew up associating this heavenly smell with pumpkin pie, but it's also great with many vegetables. Winter squash and carrots are naturals, but you'll be amazed at how great it tastes on green vegetables. I like it sprinkled over spinach and almost any spring greens.

TAKE IT FROM Keri

USE YOUR BED WISELY

Here's another way going to bed slims you down: sleep! More and more researchers are finding that the connection between the hours you spend sleeping and the numbers on the scale are closer than we thought. New research from the Kaiser Permanente Center for Health Research in Portland, Oregon, looked at 500 overweight dieters enrolled in a comprehensive 6-month diet program. The ones who were most successful? Those who slept 6 to 8 hours a night.

Many people sleep more soundly postsex, so double your pleasure and let your z's do some of the weight-loss work.

OYSTERS These are rich in zinc, which is linked to sexual performance. Oysters are also a high-quality, low-calorie protein, tasty, and just plain sexy to eat. I like to order these at restaurants. It's a perfect way to feel like I'm splurging big-time, yet they're super low in calories.

PEACHES I love them for their creamy texture, beautiful color, and summery smell. But it turns out that their high vitamin C count makes them something of a fertility drug for your guy. Higher consumption results in better sperm counts and less sperm clumping (don't ask!). And here's a fun trick: Frozen slices, which I toss into smoothies, are actually a little higher in vitamin C than the fresh ones.

SAFFRON This gorgeous, bright yellow spice comes from the crocus flower. Its mild, delicate flavor is very popular in Spanish and other Mediterranean dishes. University of Guelph researchers report that saffron is among the very few substances that actually lives up to its legend and improves sexual performance. Treat it with respect: It's one of the most expensive spices there is. The best way to bring out its flavor is to soak the threads in hot (but not boiling) water or broth for 15 minutes and add the "tea" to your recipe. I love it in any grain dish, but also add it to my soups and stews.

SPINACH Women who eat spinach and other foods rich in B vitamins have a 25 percent lower risk of getting premenstrual syndrome, according to a new study in the *American Journal of Clinical Nutrition.* What could be sexier or more freeing than avoiding a few days of tension and bloating? For a surprisingly delicate flavor, toss some into a fruit smoothie. I think it works really well with pineapple and most berries.

STEAK Beef is a great source of zinc, plus plenty of endurance-fueling protein and B vitamins. And there's something so tantalizing about the sounds and smell of steak sizzling on the grill—like foreplay you can eat! It's good for sexual performance and has that special-occasion feel to it. Make it grass-fed, and it's extra healthy.

WATERMELON This juicy favorite has an unusually high level of an amino acid called citrulline, which the body uses to make arginine, an amino acid that's related to vascular health that can translate to healthier erections. It has also been linked to increased libido in women, according to research from the University of Hawaii. And there's something kind of slurpy-sexy about a big slab of melon on a hot day!

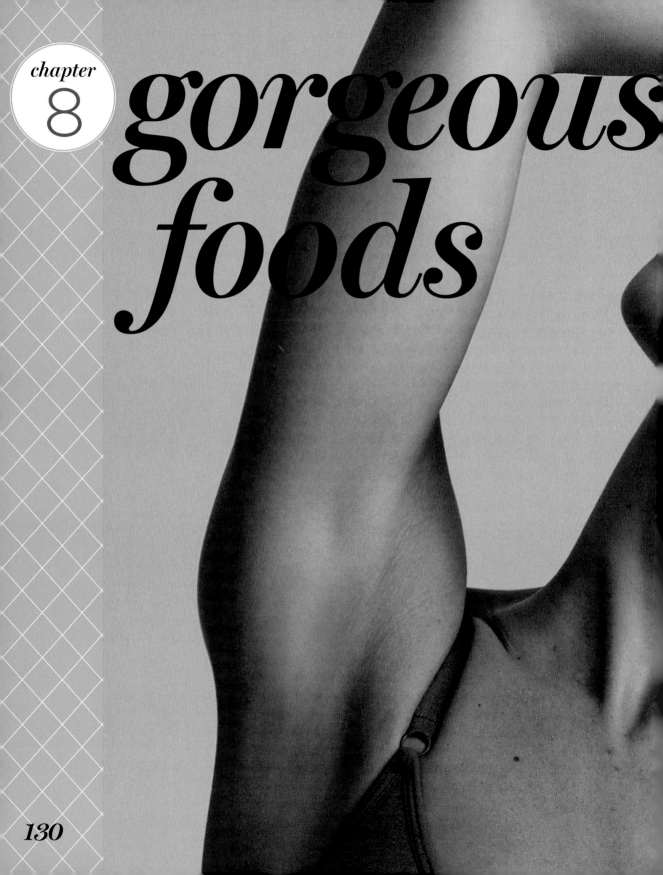

gorgeous foods

SLIM CALM

Eating

empowered delivers lots of perks besides weight loss. One of the most predictable fringe benefits? Within a week of starting the Slim Calm Sexy Diet, almost like clockwork, a new client will tell me "I'm not sure what's going on with my skin, but it looks really good. And I'm getting so many compliments on my eyes and hair, too. What's happening?"

These are the unexpected joys of the Slim Calm Sexy Diet. When you start on this journey to lose weight, the healthy foods you're eating are working all kinds of spa-worthy wonders. First, your skin: Expect blemishes to clear up, fine lines to soften, and skin tone to get brighter. Your hair will get shinier. Your eyes will get clearer. Your nails will look better. Even your teeth will get stronger.

This quick appearance upgrade is a combination of three different, equally important aspects of a slim, calm, and sexy life. First, the nutrients are from a wide array of foods. We're just scratching the surface of how smart Mother Nature is, but we know there are literally thousands of these substances, especially the antioxidants. The ones found in plants—phytonutrients—have been shown to be especially helpful in reversing the cellular effects of aging. Talk about a beauty boost! Many people notice an almost immediate improvement in their skin. It gets smoother, softer, and calmer.

Wondering what, exactly, I mean by calm skin? The opposite of calm—whether it's in your T-zone, your knees, or in the blood vessels in your heart—is inflammation. That means the body's white blood cells and chemicals are trying to protect us from infection and foreign substances such as bacteria and viruses. It's great our bodies can protect us, but it often means swelling, redness, and angry-looking spots on our skin.

Second, what we're not eating makes us look better, too. The absence of all those chemicals, artificial sweeteners, and manufactured fats make our eyes clearer. Just look at the whites of your eyes after 1 week. When was the last time they were that white? Besides the benefits of less chemical irritation, foods with plenty of antioxidants—especially vitamins C and E, as well as the healthy types of oils included on the plan—have been linked to clearer eyes.

Clear eyes are important. A new study from the University of Maryland reports that people read a lot into red eyes. When participants were shown pictures of people with very white, clear sclera (the white part of your eyes), they automatically assumed those people were more emotionally together. When shown images of people with the eyes tinted, even very subtly, to appear more red, they judged those people to be sadder, less healthy, and less attractive.

Finally, because of the first two, there's a super-beautiful shift in lifestyle: You're probably sleeping more soundly and finding the energy to exercise with more intensity. That's great for skin, because regular exercise is a proven acne fighter. It reduces stress and lowers the level of testosterone-related hormones that cause flare-ups, and sweating helps unclog pores. You're hopefully even having more—and better—sex. If that isn't a recipe for a healthy glow, I don't what is!

Keri's

3

FAVORITE
BEAUTY
FOODS

*Coconut,
mushrooms,
and
pistachios*

A Better Diet for Beautiful Skin

• • •   Of course, not all of your beauty problems can be addressed with a dietary intervention. But many of them can, and the connection between dermatology and nutrition seems to get stronger all the time. In recent years, there have been major changes in the way dermatologists look at food. For me, as a nutritionist, it's been really cool to observe this increasingly open-minded and respectful appreciation of the role diet can play. For almost half a century, dermatological researchers downplayed any connection between diet and acne. The notion that eating chocolate or french fries would cause an outbreak was just a teenage myth, they insisted. (I guess they didn't go to my high school!)

Not today. Dermatologists are now aware that while foods don't actually cause acne, they certainly have a big impact on acne-prone people. "Dermatologists can no longer dismiss the association between diet and acne," the *Journal of the American Academy of Dermatology* noted in a recent editorial. Foods with a high glycemic load—in other words, foods with lots of sugar that are absorbed very quickly into the bloodstream—make breakouts worse. And for many people, too much dairy may also aggravate skin, increasing the number and intensity of zits. Happily, there's compelling evidence that omega-3s, antioxidants, zinc, dietary fiber, and vitamins A, C, and E all contribute to make skin look and feel its best.

Skin docs have also broadened their field of inquiry beyond single foods and are now looking at the total nutritional picture. Another study in the *Journal of the American Academy of Dermatology* found that those whose diet was lower in saturated fat, higher in polyunsaturated fat, especially in omega-3s, and much higher in daily fiber had fewer breakouts. (They lost weight, too, and researchers can't be sure how much of an effect the weight loss, rather than the separate nutrients, had on skin.) If you're thinking, "This describes the Slim Calm Sexy Diet," you're right—it's a clear skin diet, too.

It's also an anti–skin cancer diet. Researchers have found that a Mediterranean-style diet—a meal plan quite similar to this one, which is loaded with dietary antioxidants, minerals, and phytochemicals, and plenty of healthy fats—has demonstrated "protective properties" against skin cancer. That's so important to me, especially since the Skin Cancer Foundation reports that the rate of all types of skin cancer is skyrocketing among women, even younger women. Skin cancer now accounts for more new cases of cancer than all other cancers combined.

Wearing sunscreen and a hat and swearing off tanning are all great, and vital. But isn't it a good feeling to know that the salads, snacks, and meals I'm asking you to eat offer another level of skin cancer protection?

Retinol and Vitamin A

• • •   Part of what has helped change the way dermatologists see skin is the rapid escalation of drugs containing retinol. Invented in the late 1960s, this drug took off in the 1980s and was used primarily to treat acne. But it was soon discovered to have powerful antiaging properties as well, smoothing fine lines, making pores look smaller, and even lightening dark spots. It's still the most proven antiaging drug out there and is now known to be effective for more than 100 different dermatological problems.

What does that have to do with nutrition? Retinol, also known as retinoic acid, is a nutrient. It's a form of vitamin A, a powerful anti-oxidant, and it's essential not just for healthy skin and teeth but also for bones, joints, mucous membranes, and eyes. (In fact, it's called retinol because it is also responsible for producing the pigments that appear in the eye.) While millions of women now put retinol on their face to control wrinkles, dermatologists sometimes prescribe oral forms of the medicine, too. Milk and eggs are terrific sources of vitamin A, by the way. Carotenoids, one of the most widespread groups of antioxidants and an important source of vitamin A, include many of the foods you'll eat on the plan—tomatoes, sweet potatoes, spinach, kale, and other greens.

My point is that there's now a tremendous crossover between vitamins in the foods we eat and in the products we put on our skin. I've come across skin creams so rich in food extracts I thought they might be edible. (Have you ever smelled a rosemary and mint shampoo? And there's a brown sugar body scrub I want to eat!) I spend a lot of time talking to clients about how some of my favorite foods are nourishing not just when you swallow them, but also when you put them on as a healing facial mask.

Medical professionals understand how healthy skin needs a well-rounded diet, consisting of plenty of real foods that are loaded with powerful phytonutrients—and they've made some breakthroughs about nutrition on the skin. Turns out retinoids aren't the only skin-friendly antioxidants. Your epidermis also loves to drink up vitamin C, vitamin E, and ferulic acid (found in wheat bran). All of these—as well as many other micronu-trients—keep your skin soft, smooth, and younger-looking. Vitamin K is helpful in reducing dark under-eye circles. Niacin, a B vitamin, also seems to fight the signs of aging, as well as to help manage breakouts.

Even the terminology that surrounds these products is fascinating, as the companies that sell them struggle to find the best way of explaining them to consumers. The word cosmeceuticals was coined to describe products that are both cosmetic and medicinal. Nutraceutical describes foods that are also medicinal, such as ginseng tea. Functional foods have nutrients added to them, such as orange juice with added calcium and

PROTECT YOUR SKIN WITH RAINBOW POWER

A big part of my empowered eating strategy is that I encourage clients to eat lots of different types of fruits and vegetables, to tap into the widest array of phytochemicals, both known and un-known. Researchers at the University of Wisconsin think that it is the broad range of antioxidants—such as tea poly-phenols, curcumin, genistein, resveratrol, lycopene, and pome-granate—that may prevent skin cancer, not just one or two "superfoods." So enjoy a rainbow of colorful fruits and veggies for maximum skin and health benefits.

eggs bred to have extra omega-3s. Now many companies even offer products described as nutricosmeceuticals, which are vitamin supplements engineered to make your skin look better.

But you don't have to buy any of those products if you don't want to. Just make sure you get plenty of vitamins A, B, C, and E, contained in a range of fruits and vegetables, which "help keep the skin elastic, protect it from age-related damage and help with the growth of new skin," according to an extensive report from the British Nutrition Foundation. "Not eating enough of them can cause problems such as dry, scaly skin."

Get-Gorgeous Foods

BRAZIL NUTS These are far and away one of the best sources around for selenium, a mineral that has attracted a lot of attention in cancer research. For one thing, experts have discovered that the incidence of nonmelanoma skin cancer is significantly higher in areas of the United States with low selenium content in the soil. And for another, selenium supplements significantly reduced the occurrence of death from total cancers. Brazil nuts are just a little more exotic than the usual almonds, walnuts, and peanuts. Eat 'em when you're bored. They're a little harder to crack open than other nuts.

CANTALOUPE This fruit helps anyone with a sweet tooth fend off cravings, and it's also a nutrient gold mine. A single serving provides more than your RDA of vitamin A. Most of us are aware that vitamin A products are good for the skin when applied topically. It's what gives products like Retin-A such an antiaging punch. But consuming enough dietary vitamin A is also essential for preventing a dry, flaky complexion. Melons also have plenty of vitamins B3, B6, and C. Besides promoting healthy cell turnover and aiding in the formation of collagen and elastin, vitamin C is key in countering the effects of sun damage. It's not just for breakfast: Serve thin slices with a mint garnish for a sophisticated dessert.

CARROTS Another food worth its weight in vitamin A, carrots also keep your peepers pretty, promote better night vision, and help provide protection against macular degeneration. For a new way to munch on them, try this: Soak some carrot sticks in hot water spiced with cayenne. Let the water cool, drain, and enjoy a little spice.

COCONUT

I love this tropical wonder in all forms, as well as in a good piña colada every now and again. Coconut improves the absorption of the minerals calcium and magnesium. Since these nutrients are crucial for a gorgeous grin, coconut is vital. And it doesn't hurt that coconut's medium-chain triglycerides help burn fat. Spread 2 teaspoons of coconut butter on a high-fiber cracker for a delicious snack.

FIGS

I am such a fan of these fruits that someday I want a fig tree. Researchers have found that just a handful of dried figs increased people's antioxidant plasma level for 4 hours (much longer than many foods)—enough to offset the oxidative damage done by a carbonated soft drink. Since biblical times, figs have been considered a topical beauty treatment. But the real reason I think of them as a beauty food is their heavenly smell. It makes me feel relaxed and serene. Halve or quarter them and add to a stir-fry for something different.

GREEN TEA

"All right, already," you may be thinking. "How many more times is this woman going to tell me to drink green tea?" But it definitely belongs on your beauty radar. Researchers have found that the polyphenols (a form of antioxidant) found in green tea prevent skin cancer. Even better, certain compounds in the tea have been shown to reverse the effects of damage from UV radiation. Turn it into a mocktail by serving it over ice, with mint sprigs.

HERBAL TEAS

I also love to drink herbal teas and have lots of flavors in the house. But eyebright, calendula, and chamomile are essential beauty foods. After steeping them in hot water, let them cool and use as compresses on your eyelids. These herbs are said to be super soothing for tired, puffy eyes. I think they make me look like I took a nap even when I didn't.

HONEY

I always call this nature's antibacterial agent. Used on your skin, this beauty food is good for treating acne and reducing redness, and it's been proven to help skin heal more quickly. It's also a natural humectant, which means that it keeps all that water you're drinking in the right places. A recent Welsh study of 665 people found that those who were enjoying honey regularly were healthier and had lower mortality rates over a 25-year period than those who weren't. For a sweet treat, drizzle a teaspoon over sliced figs and broil until it bubbles. Amazing!

TAKE IT FROM
Keri

BEST BEAUTY SECRET WEAPON

Dental floss! Neglecting your gums can lead to early stages of gum disease, called gingivitis. Warning signs include puffy gums that bleed easily, as well as bad breath. (Definitely not pretty.) Best way to fight it? Eat plenty of foods rich in vitamin C, and floss daily. Slimming bonus: Once you've thoroughly flossed and brushed, you're probably less likely to sneak back into the kitchen for a bedtime snack.

LEAN PROTEINS

Beef, chicken, and fish have proteins that contain coenzyme Q10, also called ubiquinone, which has antioxidant properties that are powerful in fighting aging and that help skin cells renew properly. This antioxidant, which your body can also manufacture on its own, is appearing in more and more skin products, too, because it's a small molecule that's easily absorbed. You'll be eating lots of these proteins on the Slim Calm Sexy Diet, so experiment with different cuts and varieties.

LOBSTER

As salmon prices have skyrocketed, lobster is much less of a splurge than many people think. Prices fluctuate by season, so keep your eyes open for bargains. Besides keeping you slim—it's an impressive source of protein, with only a gram of fat per serving—lobster is also a beauty bonanza, providing plenty of vitamin B12 and zinc, which help keep skin looking great. Too little zinc can cause hair loss and skin problems, while adequate amounts support faster wound healing and overall skin integrity. Like shrimp, they do have cholesterol, but don't worry: Studies have shown dietary cholesterol won't upset your levels. Just skip the drawn butter. Since the quality tends to decline as lobsters sit in the tanks, look for the lively guys. The tail should snap back when straightened. And if you're faint of heart, ask someone else to drop it in the boiling water.

MILK

Dairy products are wonderful skin smoothers when applied topically. That's why Cleopatra took milk baths. Eating these vitamin A–rich foods also makes for smoother skin, as well as stronger bones and healthier teeth. But for some people, it can cause flare-ups. Dermatologists have documented a connection between milk consumption and acne. The studies were done on acne-prone teens, and researchers speculate that the hormones naturally found in milk may be to blame. If you notice a few more spots, feel free to stay away from milk. Just make sure you're getting enough protein and calcium from other sources. There's a reason a warm glass of milk at bedtime is a nearly universal remedy for insomnia: It's soothing and nourishing. Try it after a tough day.

MUSHROOMS

While brightly colored vegetables get much more of the research attention, fungi are emerging as nutritional all-stars. They've got B6, folate, niacin, riboflavin, iron, potassium, and selenium. Once you start dabbling in 'shrooms, you'll be amazed at the variety—there are more than 35,000 kinds. (Careful: Many kinds are poisonous.) Branch out and try the deliciously woodsy maitake, also called hen of the woods; the melt-in-your-mouth oyster mushrooms; or the more strongly flavored shiitake. In ancient times, Chinese women ate them for a smooth complexion. They're a little pricier, but you can also buy presliced mushrooms in the produce aisle, to save you from washing, drying, and slicing them. You'll also find mushroom extracts in many high-end beauty products.

OLIVE OIL
It tastes great, and it's so good for you. Besides being among the healthiest types of fats, olive oil tends to be rich in polyphenols, which aren't just antioxidants—they're also antifungal and antibacterial agents. Eating olive oil is great, but you can put it right on your skin, too. I like to mix it with a little avocado, then apply it and leave it on for 10 minutes. It's so nourishing that you can almost feel your skin drinking it up.

If you're confused about which type of olive oil to buy, I can't blame you. America's appetite for olive oil has grown, and there are so many types, grades, and varieties that it's hard to know which to choose. But not all oils are equal, so whenever possible, I hope you'll buy "cold pressed," which means it's made simply by pressing the source of the oil. (The other option is that the oil is extracted chemically. Who needs that?) These are virgin olive oils, and are better for you because they contain lots of polyphenols and are proven to have greater cardiovascular benefits than processed olive oil. Extra-virgin olive oil is considered the finest grade available, because it contains less than 1 percent free oleic acid and has a superior taste, color, and aroma. It also contains more polyphenols, so it's the healthiest type of olive oil. Put a teaspoon of oil on a saucer next to a small amount of sea salt. Dip bits of whole wheat bread in both for a Mediterranean treat. (Just remember to keep track of it as a starch and fat serving.)

OYSTERS
These low-cal, high-protein sea creatures contain zinc, which has antioxidant properties, keeps your hair shining, and is especially important if you're prone to acne. If you're buying them in shells, they should be tightly closed or should snap shut when you tap them. If they're already shucked, look for ones that are plump, are even in size, and smell fresh.

PAPAYAS
These bright orange fruits contain vitamins A, C, and E and papain, a digestive enzyme that is a mild exfoliant. When you eat papayas, these chemical compounds help your skin look better and are good for your eyes, heart, and immune system. We've already explained how essential vitamin C is for skin, but vitamin E is also vital, and an important way the body wards off sun damage, such as age spots and wrinkles. They're wonderful fresh, but dried papayas are as sweet as candy and, in small amounts, naturally slimming.

TAKE IT FROM
Keri

"DO I NEED VITAMINS IN MY SKINCARE PRODUCTS?"

It's easy to get carried away when shopping for skincare products. But there is solid evidence that antioxidants, especially vitamins A, C, and E, make skincare treatments more effective. And vitamin K has been shown to help with dark under-eye circles. A study published in the Journal of the American Academy of Dermatology *found that a combination of vitamins E and C significantly increased the effectiveness of sunscreen products.*

PISTACHIOS These have all the advantages you might expect from a nut: great protein and heart-healthy fats. But to me, pistachios have a few added perks, especially in the beauty department. Because they are high in antioxidants—including beta-carotene, lutein, phylosterol, and gamma-tocopherol—they give your body a little extra firepower to fend off free radicals. Snack on them when you're feeling extra hungry. A single serving of pistachios is about 49 kernels, versus 18 cashews, so you can eat a more generous amount for the same 160 calories. If you're prone to snacking mindlessly before dinner, sit down with some pistachios. Because of the labor involved in getting them out of the shells, they are a wonderfully time-consuming snack.

PLUMS Like all foods rich in vitamin C, plums are a treat for your entire body, but are an especially good way to get anthocyanins, a type of antioxidant linked to prettier skin. That goes for their antioxidant cousins, too: blackberries, blueberries, and strawberries. They're so good that the famous poet William Carlos Williams even wrote a poem about stealing them from his sweetie's icebox:

> *Forgive me*
> *they were delicious*
> *so sweet*
> *and so cold*

While I tend to like most fruit at room temperature, I'm with the poet. A cool plum on a hot day is something special.

QUINOA This ancient grain has received a lot of attention lately, and I'm glad. It's so yummy and easy to cook, and it's an excellent source of the vitamin B complex, which keeps skin cells repairing themselves. If you don't get your Bs, you will have scaly, dry skin and sometimes even hair loss. It's usually served at dinner, but I like it for breakfast sometimes. It's quick, easy, and tastes great with pecans and cinnamon.

RED BELL PEPPERS I love the way these juicy, crunchy vegetables taste. I snack on them constantly. Fresh red bell peppers have a higher antioxidant capacity than other types of peppers and higher amounts of vitamins C (providing more than 450 percent of the RDA), A, B6, and E, plus fiber and other antioxidants. The unique combination of large amounts of vitamins A, C, and E makes red bell peppers a superfood for your skin. A study published in the *American Journal of Clinical Nutrition* looked at more than 4,000 women and found that those women who ate the most vitamin C on a regular basis had the best-looking skin. I slice red peppers into thin strips and bring them to my office. They are absolutely my favorite veggie snack.

ROSEMARY It smells terrific. But that isn't the only reason rosemary appears in so many hair and body products. Whether we eat it or use it topically, the fragrant oils stimulate circulation and act as an anti-irritant. I usually have a bottle of essential rosemary oil at work, and will sometimes put a few drops on a cotton ball and sniff it. It always brings me back to trips to places where rosemary grows in big flowering shrubs (ahh, Mexico!), and it's proven to help boost memory.

SALMON Besides its weight loss benefit, salmon reduces inflammation, calming the skin and making it glow. In fact, a recent study found that even a moderate intake of fish may reduce the likelihood of precancerous skin growths. Try cooking double servings at night, so you can eat the leftovers in a salad for lunch the next day.

STRAWBERRIES Smile! Natural-healing experts believe these berries remove surface discoloration from your teeth. I know some people who even make a paste and apply it. I like to slice them and arrange them in pretty patterns to serve with dinner. They're festive and a little unexpected.

SWISS CHARD I love eating this vegetable, as well as the way its red and yellow stalks look so pretty against the green leaves. Like all leafy greens, it rocks. But it's especially loaded with a B vitamin called biotin, which has been shown to strengthen brittle nails. If you're a chard virgin, be warned—the stalks can be a little sandy, so rinse them really well. Sauté them in a little broth and add them to your scrambled eggs.

TOMATOES Besides being a dynamite source of both flavor and vitamin C, they are rich in lycopene, a very efficient antioxidant. German researchers found that after a 12-week trial of consuming tomato products, people have more natural protection against photodamage from the sun. While I don't usually recommend juices—because fruit juices can pack many calories and not enough fiber—tomato juice is a major exception. Drink it up! Sip a tall Virgin Mary, complete with a little hot sauce and a celery swizzle stick, to make weekend mornings feel special.

WALNUTS Between the zinc and the omega-3s, this is one complexion-loving nut! A little sweeter than some other nuts, walnuts can elevate almost any dish to new levels. Try sprinkling them on a sweet potato.

WATERMELON Another lycopene-rich selection, this one provides 33 percent more protection against sunburn than other fruits. (You still have to wear sunscreen.) I like to take the seeds out first: Cut it in

Pamper yourself. If you don't treat yourself well, who else will?

half and then quarters, cut along the seed line with a paring knife, and use a fork to scrape out the seeds. Then slice it. For fun—and not just for kids—try cutting out shapes, like triangles, stars, and circles. You can even use cookie cutters.

Inside-Out Nutrition

• • •   When I talk about beauty foods, there's often a double meaning. Some foods make you beautiful when you eat them, and some foods make you beautiful when you wear them. Often it's the same foods. For example, the same yogurt that's such an important food to consume for healthier skin, because of its protein and abundant vitamin A, also makes a great base for masks and scrubs.

My clients sometimes dismiss my recipes for homemade masks as if they're just a silly, girlie thing to do. They couldn't be more wrong. These are effective skin treatments. Topical medications—whether it's birth control patches, pain relief, or even motion-sickness medication—are one of the most important trends to come along in the pharmaceutical industry in recent years.

Why not whip up a homemade beauty treatment in your own kitchen? They're great for days when you need a relaxing night in, when you've got leftover foods you don't want to waste, or when you just want to have a little fun. (My 5-year-old is certainly too little to be worried about zits or wrinkles, but she gets a huge kick out of watching me turn my face green!) An extra bonus: Because you make these potions yourself, they don't contain the preservatives that irritate so many people's skin.

Here's one of my favorites, a go-to cleanser for all skin types:

PINK DAIRY CLEANSER

Mix 2 teaspoons of milk with 2 teaspoons of pink grapefruit juice (with pulp) and 2 teaspoons of plain Greek yogurt or sour cream until blended. I love this recipe because the milk and yogurt (or sour cream) contain lactic acid, which gently exfoliates skin and stimulates collagen. The pink grapefruit pulp protects skin from sun damage. And the citrus fragrances are a mood booster and can even take years off your appearance. Fragrance researcher Alan Hirsch, of the Smell and Taste Treatment and Research Foundation in Chicago, has found that, to men, women who smell like grapefruit seem younger. Now that should give anyone an instant glow!

TAKE IT FROM

Keri

"WILL BER-RIES STAIN MY TEETH?"

I get so excited about the high antioxidant levels of blueberries, blackberries, and other darkly pigmented fruits that it's sometimes hard for me to acknowledge a downside. Besides the health benefits of the antioxidants, they're also packed with pectin, another way to slim smarter. So when I heard a dentist say, "But they do stain your teeth," I got bummed out. The good news is that it's not permanent. They do temporarily discolor teeth, since teeth are somewhat porous. Just be sure to brush after eating them, and you'll have nothing to worry about. Even rinsing with water will prevent any staining.

edible sunscreen!

While there's no getting around the need for sunscreen, researchers are learning more all the time about the foods that can naturally boost our skin's ability to defend itself against the sun's damaging UV rays. The sun is one of the leading causes of free radicals in the body, a major cause of skin cancer, and the source of those tiny lines that many women begin developing in their twenties.

EAT THESE . . .

Blueberries, black beans, cranberries, bananas, citrus fruits, broccoli, artichokes, walnuts, pistachios, cashews, dill, thyme

BECAUSE . . .
They all contain a type of antioxidant known as flavonol, which has been shown to improve the skin's appearance by decreasing sensitivity to light. Flavonols also increase bloodflow to the skin, improving its structure and texture.

Carrots, spinach, kale, apricots, butternut squash, sweet potato, cantaloupe, watermelon, tomatoes

BECAUSE . . .
Carotenoids, pigments found in orange and dark-green foods, are helpful in protecting the skin from sun damage by decreasing sensitivity to UV light. Specifically, lycopene and beta-carotene have been shown to reduce photosensitivity, contributing to a reduction in skin redness and overall damage caused by sunlight exposure.

Coffee, green tea, dark chocolate, cocoa

BECAUSE . . .
Alkaloids such as caffeine have been shown to eliminate UV-damaged skin cells and reduce skin roughness when applied topically after exposure to UV light. Several studies have shown that the caffeine in your daily coffee or tea prevents the formation of skin cancer.

Walnuts, flaxseeds, fatty fish, olive oil, soybeans, tofu, navy beans, kidney beans, winter squash, coconut oil

BECAUSE . . .
Using monounsaturated fats in place of saturated fats reduces the incidence of skin cancer. Omega-3 fatty acids are a type of protective polyunsaturated fat, which defends against damaging free radicals. This "good" fat reduces inflammation and gives cells stronger backup against oxidative damage.

Broccoli, brussels sprouts, cauliflower, cabbage, watercress

BECAUSE . . .
These vegetables contain sulforaphane, which has anticancer properties that protect skin from sun damage. This compound increases production of protective enzymes, which help the body fight skin damage from sun exposure.

the 10 worst foods

. . . What you don't eat helps shape your health destiny, too. Yet I know it can get frustrating trying to keep up with the latest headlines. (Red wine is good for you! No, wait, it's bad!) And believe me, sometimes the dueling-studies nature of what I do gets frustrating for me, too. I'd like to be able to give my clients definitive answers, instead of constantly hedging, saying, "Based on the balance of what we now know . . ."

Having said that, there are 10 types of foods I caution all my clients to steer clear of—at least for the next 6 weeks, when you're trying to build healthy new habits on the Slim Calm Sexy Diet. And I'm betting that at the end of this month, you will feel so much better that you won't want these foods back in your life anyway. I hear that a lot from my clients.

BAKED GOODS

For the next month, avoid all baked goods. Cakes, cookies, muffins, and other sweets are full of calories and often the worst kinds of fats. I'm not asking you to give up anything for life, but for the next 6 weeks, you need to get rid of empty calories, to make room for nutrient-dense choices.

COFFEE DRINKS

I'm all for a good cup of coffee, but America has gone insane for elaborate coffee drinks. Some of these are so loaded with fat and calories—as many as 1,000 calories—you're practically drinking a milkshake.

FAT-FREE FOODS

Thousands of products pretend to help people lose weight because they can claim to be "fat free." While I'm generally a believer in fat-free dairy products, there's a big difference between that and the many poor choices out there with "low fat" or "fat free" on the label. These foods offer little nutrition and they're rarely satisfying. People eat four servings of a "fat-free" dessert (like fat-free frozen yogurt, which often has so much added sugar that it can derail a day of perfect eating) and still feel deprived. Remember to always read labels carefully.

144

FATTY MEATS

Steer clear of high-fat meat choices, including sausage, bacon, poultry with skin, and ribs. If a cut of beef or lamb looks marbled, that means it's too high in fat. Researchers in Australia have found that diets high in meat and fat correlate with an increase in skin cancer, too.

FRIED FOODS

Whether it's french fries (including sweet potato fries), fried chicken, or even deep-fried pickles—yes, this is really served at some restaurants, as a side dish to buffalo wings—these foods all have way too much fat. And they often have way too many empty calories in the form of breading, plus more sodium than anyone needs.

NITRATES

Processed meats—hot dogs, salami, and bologna—aren't just high in fat. They're also made with nitrates, which have been linked to increased risks for colorectal cancer at double the odds from consuming other red meat. The ones I recommend are nitrate free, and I always advise reading labels carefully when buying cold cuts.

SOFT DRINKS

Soft drinks have been linked to obesity and adversely affect bone health. And there's no evidence that diet sodas are any better for you—there are even studies that suggest that people who drink them are more likely to be obese. (I've never found any research to support the claim that diet sodas actually cause cellulite, but I know many women who swear it's true.) For the next month, drink water and iced tea. If you are desperate for something fizzy, try a sparkling water.

SYNTHETIC SWEETENERS

Avoid all artificial sweeteners. I bet you'll feel so good without them that you'll avoid them for life! An important feature of the Slim Calm Sexy Diet is its ability to reawaken your tastebuds to the natural sweetness of things like cantaloupe, figs, and pears. Plus you'll avoid the frightening list of chemicals that make up artificial products. I know it seems hard to swallow, but these sweeteners have been shown to cause weight gain. Purdue University researchers found that rats fed artificially sweetened yogurt over a 2-week period consumed more calories and gained more weight than those that ate yogurt flavored with glucose, a natural, high-calorie sweetener.

STEALTH SUGARS

Besides avoiding certain foods you know are high in sugars, you need to dig a little deeper into ingredient labels. Most people are unaware of how much sugar is added to products that we don't even think of as all that sweet. Even if you are savvy at spotting safer sugars, like lactose (in milk products) and fructose (found in fruits), be on the lookout for high-fructose corn syrup. Watch how much added sugar you eat and the types of food that contain those sugars.

TRANS FATS

Read labels. If you see the words hydrogenated or partially hydrogenated, you'll know that food is a no-no. Avoid margarine, vegetable shortening, regular peanut butter, and packaged foods such as cookies, crackers, and chips. There's no known upside from trans fats, but there are plenty of risks. Although first developed to be healthier than other fats, we now know they increase women's risk of heart disease by 50 percent.

the slim calm sexy workout

I love

working out, but I know plenty of you just plain hate it. I have heard every excuse you can think of: "I hate to sweat." "They don't make sneakers with high heels." "I was traumatized by the rope-climb test in middle school." "Yoga gives me gas." "I hate those grunting noises some people make when they lift weights." "It hurts."

If you're someone who likes to exercise, I hope you'll keep reading. These workouts are challenging and designed to complement the Slim Calm Sexy Diet perfectly. If you're a sporadic exerciser, I know these will help you, too. But if you're among the 60 percent of Americans who basically don't have a consistent routine, I'm especially thrilled (and honored) that you are reading this, and here's why: I think I can change your mind about exercise.

First, I'm going to tell you the truth: Exercise alone won't help you lose weight.

As obesity researchers collect more and more data, there's less and less reason for me to sit here and tell you, "Exercise burns calories, and therefore, you will lose weight if you go the gym." There's too much evidence that exercise alone won't slim you down. It needs to be combined with dietary and behavioral changes, or it just won't work. So yes, you can lose weight on this plan—or any plan—and get slim without ever breaking a sweat.

However, you do need to exercise to be healthy. And you really need to exercise if you want to be calm and sexy. Knowing this, I believe, can transform your relationship with working out.

Once you break out of the mind-set that time on the treadmill is some sort of horrible penance for the last time you had pizza, you can be free to see fitness for what it really is. Life changing. Life prolonging. Relaxing. Freeing. Beautifying. Libido building. Cleavage boosting. Skin soothing. Mind clearing. Within weeks, you will be calmer and happier, look better naked, fit into clothes much better, sleep more soundly, and have better sex. Exercise is more powerful than many prescription drugs, including some antidepressants and blood pressure and diabetes medications. If we could bottle these benefits, we'd all be billionaires.

I'm not asking you to make me a lifelong promise, just a 42-day commitment. For the next 6 weeks, I want you to promise you will do at least one of these workouts, four times per week. If you've already got an exercise routine you like, that's great. Just toss these workouts into your mix, so you're upping the intensity and frequency. For example, if you're already active four times a week, pledge to make it six. If your favorite workout is a 3-mile walk with friends, add running intervals and some extra distance.

Again, I'm not asking you to do this forever. But if you want to get and stay healthy, you need to find a way to consistently be active in your life. Moving more while you're following the eating plan will maximize your weight loss results and put you in the healthiest frame of mind possible. And I have a sneaking suspicion that you'll start to look forward to lacing up your sneakers and pulling on your yoga pants.

Grab some workout clothes, and let's get moving!

The Slim Workout

THERE'S NO "FAT-BURN-ING ZONE"

Not long ago, gyms were buzzing with "fat-burning" workouts. The American Council on Exercise (ACE) reports that lower-intensity workouts, such as brisk walking, burn about 60 percent of the calories from fat, versus higher-intensity activities, such as running, which use 35 percent.

You're still better off doing higher-intensity interval training. ACE puts it this way: If you do 30 minutes of low-intensity aerobic exercise, you'll burn 200 calories—120 calories (or 60 percent) from stored fat. But if you exercise for the same amount of time at a high intensity, you'll smoke 400 calories, about 140 calories from stored fat.

• • •   This isn't just any cardio workout. Even though it's only 30 minutes long, it's supercharged with interval training to help you burn more calories both during and after your session. Intervals are short bursts of hard effort that alternate with easy recovery periods.

Why are intervals more effective than other forms of cardio? Whether you're always exercising at the same steady pace on the elliptical machine, taking a walk with friends, or even sweating it out in a Zumba class, your body quickly adapts and becomes efficient at that exercise. Unfortunately, the more efficient it becomes, the fewer calories it burns.

"Interval training breaks you out of that pattern, throwing your body constant surprises and torching calories along the way," says personal trainer Rachel Cosgrove, owner of Results Fitness in Santa Clarita, California, and author of *The Female Body Breakthrough*. "And you keep burning extra calories for up to 24 hours afterward."

To gauge whether you're working hard enough, rate your effort on a 1–10 scale. At levels 2 and 3, you should be able to talk and even sing along to your iPod. At levels 7 and 8, however, it should be difficult to carry on a conversation without getting short of breath.

WHAT YOU'LL NEED A cardio activity you enjoy. Intervals can be done on an elliptical trainer, a treadmill, a rower, a stairclimber—almost any machine at the gym. You can also take intervals outside and run, bike, or skate. In that case, a stopwatch will come in handy.

YOUR PLAN Do this workout at least once a week, or more if you want to see quicker results. You'll start off slowly, then each week you'll increase the amount of time you spend working at high intensity and decrease the time spent recovering. If you can't make it all the way through the high or very high intensity intervals, note how long you did last and build on it the next time.

DON'T FORGET Do the warmup and cooldown. They are not optional. Your muscles should feel loose, and you should be sweating lightly. In addition, drink lots of water—not just during your workout but also before. "Think of water as a fat-burning liquid," says Cosgrove. "If you head into your workout dehydrated, you won't get as much out of it." She recommends drinking half your weight in liquid ounces each day (so a 150-pound woman should drink 75 liquid ounces, or about 9 cups).

WEEK 1		
TIME	INTENSITY	EFFORT
4:00	Warmup	2
2:30	Easy	3
0:30	Hard	7
2:30	Easy	3
0:30	Hard	7
2:30	Easy	3
0:30	Hard	7
2:30	Easy	3
0:30	Hard	7
2:30	Easy	3
0:30	Hard	7
2:30	Easy	3
0:30	Hard	7
2:30	Easy	3
0:30	Hard	7
5:00	Cooldown	2

TOTAL: 30 MINUTES

WEEK 3		
TIME	INTENSITY	EFFORT
4:00	Warmup	2
2:00	Easy	3
1:00	Hard	7
2:00	Easy	3
1:00	Moderate	6
2:00	Easy	3
1:00	Very hard	8
2:00	Easy	3
1:00	Hard	7
2:00	Easy	3
1:00	Moderate	6
2:00	Easy	3
1:00	Very Hard	8
2:00	Easy	3
1:00	Hard	7
5:00	Cooldown	2

TOTAL: 30 MINUTES

WEEK 5		
TIME	INTENSITY	EFFORT
4:00	Warmup	2
1:30	Easy	3
1:30	Hard	7
1:30	Easy	3
1:30	Moderate	6
1:30	Easy	3
1:30	Very Hard	8
1:30	Easy	3
1:30	Hard	7
1:30	Easy	3
1:30	Moderate	6
1:30	Easy	3
1:30	Very Hard	8
1:30	Easy	3
1:30	Hard	7
5:00	Cooldown	2

TOTAL: 30 MINUTES

WEEK 2		
TIME	INTENSITY	EFFORT
4:00	Warmup	2
2:00	Easy	3
1:00	Hard	7
2:00	Easy	3
1:00	Hard	7
2:00	Easy	3
1:00	Hard	7
2:00	Easy	3
1:00	Hard	7
2:00	Easy	3
1:00	Hard	7
2:00	Easy	3
1:00	Hard	7
2:00	Easy	3
1:00	Hard	7
5:00	Cooldown	2

TOTAL: 30 MINUTES

WEEK 4		
TIME	INTENSITY	EFFORT
4:00	Warmup	2
1:30	Easy	3
1:30	Hard	7
1:30	Easy	3
1:30	Hard	7
1:30	Easy	3
1:30	Hard	7
1:30	Easy	3
1:30	Hard	7
1:30	Easy	3
1:30	Hard	7
1:30	Easy	3
1:30	Hard	7
1:30	Easy	3
1:30	Hard	7
5:00	Cooldown	2

TOTAL: 30 MINUTES

WEEK 6		
TIME	INTENSITY	EFFORT
5:00	Warmup	2
1:00	Easy	3
1:30	Hard	7
1:00	Easy	3
1:30	Moderate	6
1:00	Easy	3
1:30	Very Hard	8
1:00	Easy	3
1:30	Hard	7
1:00	Easy	3
1:30	Moderate	6
1:00	Easy	3
1:30	Very Hard	8
1:00	Easy	3
1:30	Hard	7
1:00	Easy	3
1:30	Hard	7
5:00	Cooldown	2

TOTAL: 30 MINUTES

EFFORT IS RANKED ON A 1-10 SCALE.

The Calm Workout

The key to success in yoga? Breathe. "Try to coordinate each move with your breath as instructed. It will help you get into the exercises and bridge the connection between your mind and your body," says Ingber.

• • • Serene and slow, yoga might not seem like an exercise that can help you lose weight. But this ancient art is an essential part of any diet plan. Yoga is not only a proven method to calm your mind, but it also lowers levels of the stress hormone cortisol, which can contribute to making you fat. Cortisol, which your body releases in response to physical stress, was designed to increase your appetite so you would replenish the energy you used to escape the stress (say, a lion chasing you). The trouble is, it also gets released when you're trying to escape an emotional stress (say, your boss yelling at you), and it makes you very hungry. The longer you stay stressed, the longer you stay hungry. But yoga helps short-circuit that stress response.

Yoga also helps further tone the muscles you're targeting in our strength-training Sexy Workout. The combination of stretching and toning makes you stronger and more flexible, while helping you lose weight. In addition to burning calories, yoga puts you more in touch with your body and helps you develop an appreciation of its natural strengths, says Mandy Ingber, the creator of this special workout and the trainer who regularly helps yoga devotee Jennifer Aniston get her "om" on. (She's also a contributor to *Women's Health*.) As a result, it makes you more mindful of your eating habits and can help change your entire relationship with food to a healthier one.

WHAT YOU'LL NEED A mat and a quiet place to practice.

YOUR PLAN Do this feel-good 30-minute workout at least once a week. If possible, perform it the day after you do your strength-training Sexy Workout to help stretch out the muscles you're building. On other days, even if you don't have time to do the whole routine, set aside a few minutes in the morning for several rounds of Sun Salutes. We promise you'll stand taller, and feel more engaged, calm, and energized as you move through the rest of your day.

DON'T FORGET TO Let go and enjoy yourself. Your goal is to have each movement flow into the next. Don't worry about doing each pose perfectly, especially if you're new to yoga. Instead, says Ingber, try to find what's perfect within each pose and enjoy that while you progress.

one

SUN SALUTE

A great way to warm up is with the Sun Salute (Surya Namaskar), 12 yoga poses performed in a single flowing sequence.

A **Mountain**
Exhale and slowly sweep your arms down to your sides, and bring your hands into the prayer position.

B **Upward Reach**
On an inhale, slowly sweep your arms overhead, gently arching your back as far as it feels comfortable.

SLIM CALM SEXY DIET

Standing Forward Bend

As you exhale, bend forward until your hands rest by your feet (it's okay to bend your knees if you need to).

D Lunge

Inhale, bend your left knee, and push your right leg back into a lunge.

E Plank

Exhale and set your left leg back so you are in the plank position. Inhale and, pushing forward from your crown and back from your heels, try to make a straight line with your body. Keep your shoulders directly over your wrists and your arms straight without locking your elbows.

F Low Pushup

Exhale and lower your body as though coming down from a pushup, but remain hovering a few inches above the floor. Try to maintain a straight line with your body. Keep your arms at a 90-degree angle and do not allow your shoulders to sink below your elbows.

G Upward Dog

As you inhale, uncurl your toes, press the tops of your feet into the floor, and reach your chest up and forward, straightening your arms. Try to keep your thighs and knees off the mat. Make it easier by bending at your elbows and placing your forearms on the mat.

H Downward Dog

Exhale and, lifting from your hips, press back and up into an inverted V shape, keeping your arms and legs straight and reaching your heels toward the mat.

I Lunge

Inhale, bend your left knee, and push your right leg back into a lunge.

J Standing Forward Bend

Exhale, bring your right foot forward to meet your left, bend at the waist, and bring your head as close as possible to your knees, placing your hands by your feet (it's okay to bend your knees if you have to).

K Upward Reach

Inhale and slowly sweep your arms overhead, gently arching your back as far as it feels comfortable.

L Mountain

Exhale, slowly sweep your arms down to your sides, and bring your hands into the prayer position.

Repeat the entire sequence, this time pushing back with your left leg. If you have time, repeat the sequence three to five times on each side.

TAKE IT FROM
Keri

FITNESS ON THE GO

I travel fairly often for work, and I know how air travel and rescheduled meetings can derail an exercise plan. Here's what helps: Pack a jump rope and a resistance band. They can fit into even the most overstuffed suitcase. If your hotel doesn't have a gym, you can get in a reasonable workout right in your room. And travel in comfortable shoes. Airports offer plenty of opportunities for walking, and a few brisk laps around the terminal can be an effective workout—not to mention one that can help you relax (or sleep) during your flight.

two

CHAIR POSE

Stand with your feet together. Inhale, bend your knees, and reach your hands overhead. Tuck your tailbone toward your heels and scoop in your abs. Turn your palms to face each other and release your shoulders by sliding your shoulder blades down your back. Hold for 10 slow breaths.

TREE

Step your feet together and place your hands on your hips. Transfer your weight to your left foot as you bend your right knee and place your foot on your left ankle (or at your knee or even thigh, if you're advanced). Bring your palms together in a prayer position and hold for 10 breaths. Switch sides and repeat. Make maintaining your balance easier by gazing at something that doesn't move and focusing on your breath. Press your lifted leg to your standing leg and your palms together. If you can't make it all the way to 10 breaths at first, work your way up.

**WARRIOR
SEQUENCE**

A Warrior 2

To get into Warrior 2, step your right leg behind you and turn to the right. Lift your arms
up to shoulder height with your palms facing down. Then turn your right (back) foot
out, lining up the heel with the arch of your left (front) foot. Inhale, and as you exhale,
bend your front knee into a right angle. Make sure to keep your knee directly above your
ankle and your thigh parallel to the floor to protect your knee from injury. Turn your head
to look out over your front hand. Hold for five slow breaths. Straighten your front leg
slightly, then bend and straighten a few times along with your breath.

Repeat the Warrior 2 and Reverse Warrior sequence, this time stepping your left foot behind you and bending your right knee.

B Reverse Warrior

From the bent position, move into Reverse Warrior. Slide your right (back) hand down your right (back) leg toward your ankle. Arc your front palm up and over your head and reach behind you without moving your legs. Look up at your hand and hold for five breaths.

five

TRIANGLE

From Reverse Warrior, straighten your leg and rise up into Triangle. Standing again with your feet spread wide, turn your right toes out and line up your right heel with the arch of your left foot. Lift your arms to your shoulders, palms down. Exhale. Extend your right arm and, keeping the right side of your torso long, reach down toward the floor to touch the outside of your calf or ankle. Inhale and lift your left arm so it's in line with the right, and look up at your left thumb. Try to lengthen your spine and rotate your chest toward the ceiling. Then, keeping your arms extended, exhale, tighten your abs, and lift your torso upright. Switch sides and repeat.

164

six

BOAT

Sit down on the mat with your legs together and straight in front of you. Balancing on your sit bones, gaze up, lift your arms to shoulder level, and extend your chest upward. At the same time, extend your legs so that your toes are at eye level. Hold for five breaths, then lower your arms and legs with control. Repeat three times.

"Excellence is not a singular act but a habit. You are what you do repeatedly."

—SHAQUILLE O'NEAL

seven

BRIDGE

Lying on your back, place
your arms at your sides,
palms down. Place your
feet on the floor, hip-
width apart, as close to
your butt as possible.
Press into your feet as you
raise your hips, making
a straight line from your
shoulders to your knees.
Hold for five breaths, then
lower your hips with con-
trol. Repeat three times.

eight

PIGEON

To get from Bridge to Pigeon, hug your knees to your chest,
rock up into a sitting position, and extend your legs in front of
you. Swing your right leg long behind you and bend your left
knee so that your knee is aligned with your left hip and your
shin is parallel to the front of your mat. Walk your hands as far
forward as you can and try to rest your forehead on the floor.
Hold for 20 breaths. Switch sides and repeat.

SEATED
TWIST

Sit up and cross your legs in front of you. Gently twist to the left side, placing your hand on the mat behind you. Hold for 10 breaths and try to deepen the stretch with each exhale. Switch sides and repeat.

ten

SAVASANA

Lie on your back with your arms relaxed at your sides, palms up, and your feet slightly wider than your hips. Close your eyes, breathe, and empty your mind for at least 5 minutes (about 50 slow breaths). Yep—that's really all you have to do. But don't blow off this pose. It's actually a key part of the whole routine.

THE PERFECT PRE-RACE MEAL

Sometimes clients ask if there is a "perfect" meal to complement their exercise goals, and in all honesty, I think there are probably thousands of them. But there's some compelling new research that loading up on protein in the days prior to an endurance event—a really long run or an intense day of biking, for example— not only improves performance but also alleviates the stress that comes along with a hard workout. Scottish researchers think the explanation may be in tyrosine, an amino acid found in protein that's known to boost mood.

The Sexy Workout

• • •   Do you want to turn your body into a calorie-burning machine? Grab some dumbbells. Strength training is the fastest way to build sexy, lean muscles that torch way more calories than fat does. And don't worry about bulking up. The light weights used in this speedy workout will firm you up without giving you man muscles. The result: a slim, toned, totally feminine figure.

Do this circuit workout at least once a week—or on up to three nonconsecutive days, to muscle your muscles into sexy shape even faster, says Jennifer Nyp, owner of ZenGirlFitness in New York City's Soho (and the creator of this workout). At first, you'll do the entire circuit just once, and you should be done in 15 minutes or less. Over time, you'll work your way up to completing it three times, which should still take only about 30 minutes.

WHAT YOU'LL NEED

TWO SETS OF DUMBBELLS: Use 3- and 5-pounders if you're a beginner, or 5- and 8-pounders if you're used to strength training. "When it comes to dumbbells, it's always smart to try before you buy," says Nyp, who also teaches Pilates, yoga, and TRX. She recommends small dumbbells covered with gripping material. Your best bet is to shop in a real store rather than online. Do a few bicep curls in the store to make sure the weights aren't too light or heavy. If you prefer, you can do the workout with resistance bands with handles instead (choose medium resistance).
A STABILITY BALL: Check on the package to make sure you're buying the right size for your height, as well as whether you need a separate air pump to inflate it.

YOUR PLAN

Perform 10 reps of each exercise. If the 10th rep still feels easy, increase your weights a little. If it feels too hard, decrease them.

WEEKS 1–2: Do the circuit only once in each workout, using your lighter weights.

WEEKS 3–4: Do the circuit twice through in each workout, and advance to your heavier weights if possible.

WEEKS 5–6: Challenge yourself to do 3 circuits total in each workout with your heavier weights.

SQUAT WITH OVERHEAD PRESS

TARGETS:

glutes, hamstrings, quads, shoulders, triceps, upper back

A. Grab a pair of dumbbells and bring them to shoulder height, palms facing out. Place your feet hip-width apart and parallel. (If using a resistance band, stand on it and start with your body in the same position. Then follow the rest of these instructions.) Inhale and lower your butt into a squat. Keep your head up and facing forward. Inside your sneakers, lift your toes slightly and shift your weight to your heels. Lower until your thighs are parallel to the ground. Pause.

B. Exhale as you stand, raising the dumbbells over your head until your elbows are fully extended but not locked. Slowly lower the dumbbells to starting position.

STANDING ROWS WITH TRICEP KICKBACKS

TARGETS:
back, shoulders, biceps, triceps

A. With your feet hip-width apart and knees slightly bent, bend over so that your back is almost parallel to the ground. Stick your butt out and your stomach in. Grab a dumbbell in each hand with palms facing in, and let your arms hang. (If using a resistance band, stand on it and follow the same instructions.)

B. Pull the dumbbells toward you until they touch the outside of your chest. Pause.
C. Keeping your elbows up against your sides and arms bent at a 90-degree angle, extend your arms back so that they're parallel to the floor. Pause and squeeze your triceps, then return your arms to a 90-degree angle.

ALTERNATING LUNGES WITH BICEP CURLS

TARGETS:
glutes, hamstrings, quads, calves, biceps

A. Hold the dumbbells at your sides and stand with your feet hip-width apart.

B. Step back with your right foot, and bend both knees to lower your body until they are at a 90-degree angle. (If using a band, place it under your right foot.) At the same time, curl the dumbbells to your chest. Then lower and return to a standing position. Repeat with the other leg to complete 1 rep. To make this exercise more challenging, step forward for a front lunge instead of a back lunge.

A GREAT POST-WORKOUT SNACK

University of Texas researchers found that a bowl of whole grain cereal and fat-free milk was ideal. Not only is this satisfying protein-carb combo cheaper than a sports recovery drink, but researchers say it may promote protein synthesis, helping to build muscles.

④ KNEE STRETCHES ON THE BALL

TARGETS:

abs, arms, back, chest, triceps—everything

A. Lie facedown with the stability ball under your midsection and your palms on the ground. Walk your hands forward until just your shins are on the ball.
B. Slowly pull your knees toward your chest, rolling the ball forward and taking care to keep your legs hip-width apart and knees pointed straight ahead.
C. Slowly straighten your legs. Keep your upper body still and your butt as low as possible. Bend and straighten your legs for each rep. Make this exercise more challenging by starting with the ball at your ankles and straightening and bending more slowly.

5 ▸ SIDE PLANK WITH HIP LIFT

TARGETS:
core (especially obliques), shoulders

A. Lie on your side with your legs straight and stacked directly on top of each other. Tuck your tailbone under. Place your bottom arm at a right angle to your body with your elbow directly below your shoulder. Place your top hand on your hip (make it more challenging by lifting your top arm straight to the ceiling). Push straight up until your weight is resting evenly along your forearm and the outside edge of your bottom foot. Your body should form a straight line from your head to your feet. Hold for 30 seconds.

B. Lift your hips up as high as you can for three counts. Then lower for three counts, tap down on the floor, and raise yourself up again. Each raise and lower counts as 1 rep. If you can't complete 10, work your way up to it. Switch sides and repeat.

6 KNEE PUSHUPS

TARGETS:
abs, chest, shoulders, triceps

A. Get down on all fours with your legs together. Place your palms on the floor slightly wider than your shoulders. Your wrists should be directly below your shoulders. Cross your ankles behind you.
B. Keep your body from your knees to your shoulders in a straight line throughout the entire pushup (don't stick out your butt) and lower your chest until it nearly touches the floor. Pause, then push yourself back up until your arms are straight, but do not lock your elbows. Keep your abs tight and do not let your hips sag. Repeat. Make the move more challenging by straightening your legs and keeping your weight on your toes.

IS SEX A GOOD CALORIE BURN?

There's so much debate on this topic, and honestly, it all depends. Haven't we all had that exhausted, low-energy kind of sex where we barely move a muscle? Obviously, that's different from the running-around-the-house-why-not-use-the-kitchen-table sex, right? In their book, The Pritikin Edge, *Robert A. Vogel and Paul Tager Lehr say that 100 to 200 calories per romp is a healthy estimate. Still, even just a few minutes of active sex is a great addition to your weekly workouts.*

7 HALF TURKISH AB GET-UP

TARGETS:
core, abs, shoulders, back

A. Lie on your back with both legs bent and your feet flat on the floor. Grab a dumbbell in your left hand and lift it straight up from your shoulder, palm facing in. Extend your right arm straight out to the side, palm facing down.
B. Tighten your abs and curl up to a sitting position. Pause, and slowly lower your back to the floor, one vertebra at a time. Repeat.

SIDE LEG LIFTS AND CIRCLES

TARGETS:
core, inner and outer thighs

A. Lie on your right side with your right upper arm on the floor and your head resting on your right hand. Without moving the rest of your body, raise your top leg 6 inches. Pause and lower. Repeat 10 times.

B. Keeping your legs straight, bend forward at your hips to form a slight angle. Raise your top leg 6 inches and make 10 small forward circles. Move from the hip and try to raise your leg higher with each circle. From the highest point, make 10 more small circles in the other direction, and lower your leg. Make this exercise more challenging by tying a resistance band around your thighs right above your knees.

SPECIAL BONUS SECTION

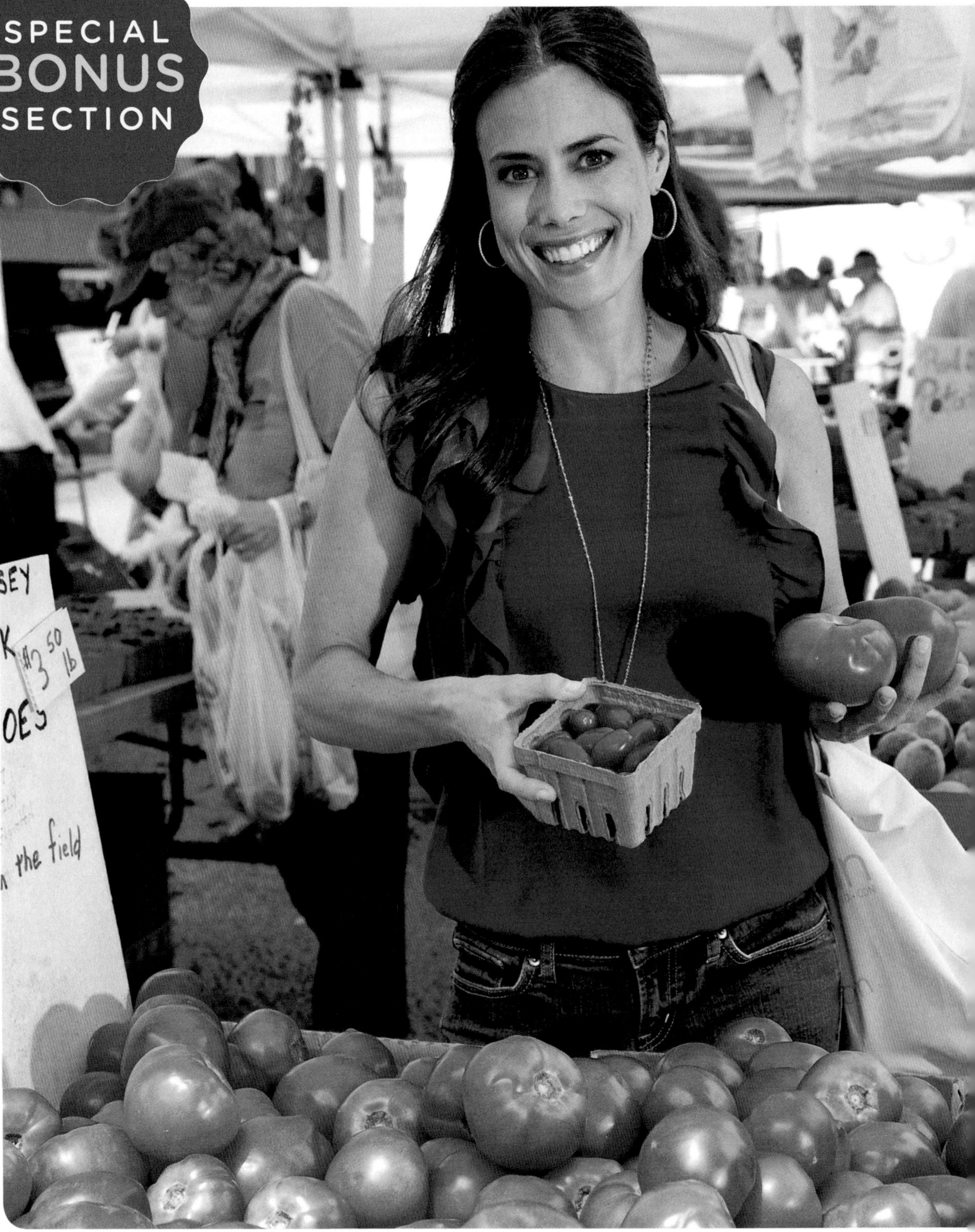

a slim calm sexy life

a day with Keri

Some

decisions—whether to take a new job, paint your living room, get a puppy, or wear high-heeled boots to work—have a kind of finality to them. You think them over, make the call, and boom, you've done it. There you are, with a dog and a jade-green living room.

Living a slim, calm, sexy life is a little different. That's because living each day well is based on thousands of small decisions that we make all day, every day. I don't just mean deciding what to have for breakfast (although that's one of my favorite decisions each day). It's about deciding whether you'll eat that meal mindfully, happily, and appreciating what's good about it, or chew it without thinking while you check Facebook.

We all know there are many ways to send a perfectly good morning in a bad direction. Who hasn't let a traffic jam, a nastygram from a boss, or a guy's failure to text put us in a funk that lasts all day? But the reverse is equally true. I'll show you how many chances there are in your day to make conscious choices that will make you feel better, stronger, happier, and more complete. Lots of them are about what to eat. But some are much bigger than that.

Today, you'll be presented with thousands of opportunities to live a slimmer, calmer, sexier life. That's why I wanted to write this chapter about a typical day in my life. And please, do NOT think I'm saying, "Oh, I'm so great. I live slim, calm, and sexy every day." That's not my point at all. And let me be clear that anyone who knows me can tell you I have gone through many days being far from slim, calm, and sexy. I'm not Wonder Woman, but I want you to understand that the more you do these things, the more they will become habits.

05:30 Welcome to "me" time I'm awake—without an

alarm. You may think I'm annoying for being that perky morning person, but I can't help it. (It's nice to know I'm not alone: About 55 percent of Americans describe themselves as early birds. We usually smile at each other when we pass on the street.)

These early-morning hours have taken on a lot more meaning to me since I had kids. Now that my little nuggets sleep in, this is a chance for me to have the best quality "me" time. I always say I get more done from 5:30 to 6:30 than in 3 hours at any other part of the day.

First thing? Coffee. I love it, and I have one of those coffeemakers I can program ahead, so it's already made, sitting on the counter waiting for me. I sit down and drink that cup quietly and peacefully. It's heaven. I may check my e-mail or read a little news, but not for long. My main objective is to get straight to the gym or head outside for a run. There is nothing like running down the quiet city streets and actually being able to hear the birds chirp in New York City. Watching the sun rise over the reservoir in Central Park is a gift I never take for granted.

If I go to the gym, I try to mix it up. Each morning, I do some form of weight lifting, some stretching, and some cardio. My current favorite is a stairclimber, but I will sometimes use the bike and the rowing machines to keep it fresh. Really, the idea of doing the same thing day after day strikes me as monotonous. I don't like to be in that much of a routine.

I also change how I exercise. Some mornings, I might read, maybe something work-related or something inspirational, even a novel now and then. I often listen to music—really up-tempo stuff when I feel energetic (or just need an energy boost) or mellower tunes when I feel like letting my body adjust more slowly to the a.m. workout. To get really inspired, I use visualization tricks: I'll imagine myself hiking up a favorite mountain trail.

07:00 **Beautiful breakfasts** I'm back home for breakfast. You already know I'm a big believer in changing things up, so there isn't one typical breakfast for me. One day, it might be a slice of really good whole grain bread, maybe with almond butter, a little cinnamon, and then a hard-cooked egg. Or it might be Greek yogurt with some matcha powder, pomegranate seeds, and a handful of pistachios.

By now, my kids are waking up, so in between giving them breakfast, I'm also making their lunches as well as my own. While I don't expect you to eat like little kids do, I often pack myself some version of what my kids love: a sandwich made with whole wheat bread and usually cheese, turkey, hummus, or peanut butter. I'll add a fruit, like sliced strawberries or apples. There is always a vegetable, too—maybe slices of red pepper, carrots, or sugar snap peas. Some days, I might include a little extra, like a piece of cheese, yogurt, or edamame. All of these foods are on the Slim Calm Sexy Diet, and it's nice to know I can nourish my entire family with healthy, feel-good foods.

Next, while the kids are getting themselves dressed, it's time for me to shower (if you're a mom, you already know about multitasking). I'm super quick, but I always use natural cleanser and an exfoliating scrub. And even though it's a weekday and I'm on a tight schedule, I always moisturize afterward, from head to toe. I even inject a healthy food into it, mixing a little Nutiva Coconut Manna—yep, the same food I spread on crackers sometimes—in with my moisturizer. I love everything about it: the smell, the texture, and the way it softens my skin. The point is, there are little things any of us can do to start the day feeling calm and a tiny bit pampered, even on our busiest days, and mine is moisturizing. What is it for you?

On the flip side, there's never enough time for every beauty ritual. So what to skimp on? For me, it's washing my hair. It has to be a very calm day for me to squeeze that in. You can count on me having "dirty" hair most other days. But it's not really a sacrifice. The secret to shiny, healthy hair is actually to let its natural oils do their job. Too much

TAKE IT FROM Keri

IS SLEEPING NAKED REALLY BETTER FOR YOU?

My guess is that whoever told you that was just trying to get you to take your clothes off. I've never been able to find any solid research to prove this, but it's something I've often heard from my outdoorsy friends, who argue that sleeping in the buff keeps you warmer in a sleeping bag. I can tell you this: We know that having lots of sex is healthy, right? If going to bed without clothes leads to more sex, then yes, sleeping naked is a good move!

Researchers found that being outdoors was associated with greater feelings of revitalization and increased energy.

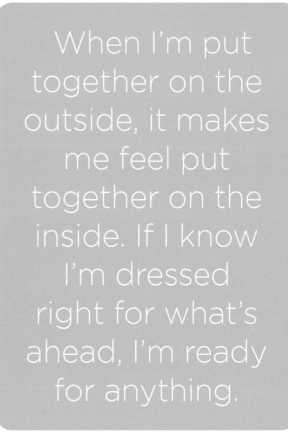

When I'm put together on the outside, it makes me feel put together on the inside. If I know I'm dressed right for what's ahead, I'm ready for anything.

shampooing and blow-drying dries out your mane and creates extra frizziness. My secret is to use a little dry shampoo if I have a few minutes, or I pull my hair back in a ponytail with a headband. Unwashed hair is actually the best for updos. It has a messier texture that holds styles really well.

Next, what to wear? This is a decision that's essential to having a calm day. I'm not a crazy fashionista, but when I like what I'm wearing, I have more confidence all day. And that makes me feel calm—or sexy, depending on the occasion. When I'm put together on the outside, it makes me feel put together on the inside. If I know I'm dressed right for what's ahead, I'm ready for anything.

On days with clients, business meetings, or TV appearances, I often wear dresses. It's only one piece of clothing I have to put on! There are other days at Nutritious Life when the schedule is way more relaxed. Maybe I'm just catching up with the other registered dietitians or doing paperwork. I like to dress casually and comfortably on those days, and leggings and boots are a standard. (And yes, I'm as addicted to black basics as every other working girl in Manhattan. I love bright jewel tones because I feel like that a splash of color makes me happier, all day long.)

My makeup mirrors my clothing decision. I'm already a little bit of a minimalist, and if I don't have to appear on TV, I wear very little. I've gotten spoiled lately, because I've been doing more TV appearances. Those days are easy—you just show up at the studio and let the wonderful professionals do their thing. It's way better than what I pull off on my own.

08:30 **A calmer commute** After I take the kids to school, I get on the bus or take a taxi, depending on where my first meeting is. En route, I catch up on e-mail using my BlackBerry. E-mail is such a great way to communicate, but if you're not careful, it can also be an enemy of your mental health. E-mail usage is growing at the rate of 66 percent a year, according to technology workers, and the average person working at a desk checks e-mail 50 times—and instant messages 77 times—every day. No wonder so many of us feel we can't get anything done. These interruptions steal about 2.1 hours of productivity out of every day. That's why we're all running around like our hair is on fire.

It's taken me a while, but I'm finally figuring out how to use technology to make my day more efficient, not more frazzled. My BlackBerry is usually buzzing with e-mails from all the different parts of my life—making dinner plans, finalizing playdates for the kids, responding to a client, or touching base with an editor. By handling all those e-mails

TAKE IT FROM Keri

SLEEP BECOMES ME

I've certainly been guilty of cheating myself on sleep. But I know how critical it is to maintaining a healthy weight. A recent study from Columbia University found that women who are sleep-deprived eat 329 more calories per day on average than when they are well rested. So even though I can push myself to stay up later—and I love a great party as much as the next girl—on weeknights, I try to admit that I'm zonked by 10 p.m. I've learned that "sleep hygiene" is almost as powerful a tool in staying slim, calm, and sexy as nutrition is.

CALM AND SEXY—IT'S IN THE BAG

I've learned that life is much easier when all the makeup I own is in one little bag, and it's with me all the time. For me, it's as easy as these six pieces: Bobbi Brown tinted moisturizer, a concealer, a few MAC eye shadows, mascara, blush, and lip gloss.

before I get to work, I can settle down at my desk and concentrate on the day ahead. For most people, the hours between 9 and 11 a.m. are the most productive, and I like to put them to the best possible use for my clients. Clearing out my inbox first thing helps me focus.

10:45 Time out for tea

In my job, I talk to a lot of people—clients, co-workers, and business partners. I swear, sometimes my mouth hurts! (Okay, I never really get tired of talking, but it can still be exhausting.) So midmorning, I take a quiet 5 minutes just for me. (At least I try to do this daily!) I step out from behind my desk, shut the door to my office, and settle into the couch. (I even keep a cozy throw there, for chilly days.) I make a cup of green tea, grab a handful of nuts, and just sit still and nibble. Even though it's not easy for me to be quiet, I try to quiet my thoughts and breathe deeply using the yoga techniques I've learned. This simple, 5-minute exercise makes a huge difference in how the rest of my day goes, and it's usually better because of it.

My couch also faces one of my favorite possessions in the world: a great big photo by Monica Hoover that's a funky, hippie image with lots of grass and the word "health" painted on the side of a funny old camper. I call it a photo, but a psychologist would call it "a visual cue." The idea is that all of us—even though we think we're such verbal creatures—really respond to images. The old saying that a picture is worth a thousand words turns out to be true, and focusing on this picture I love—with the single word that sums up everything about what I'm trying to accomplish in my profession—helps me remember why I get up and show up every day.

My heart rate slows down. My thoughts settle. I can shake off the conversations that didn't go so well and refocus on what I need to get done for the day. It always surprises me how often, in these little breaks when I don't seem to be thinking about much of anything, I'll get a really good idea. I think forcing myself to take a little downtime every morning boosts my creativity. When I sit back down at my desk, it's often the most productive time of day for me.

12:30 Long-lasting lunches

Lots of people eat tiny lunches when they're trying to lose weight—a little container of yogurt, maybe, or a very skimpy salad. Not me. I need a major refueling midday and have learned that a carefully thought-out lunch translates into a much more effective afternoon.

Some days, it's a lunch I've brought from home. Maybe it's a version of what I made for the kids, or maybe it's fish left over from dinner the night before. Other days, I'll meet at a restaurant for a business lunch.

Having the kids around as I chop vegetables is fun, and I like when they get involved. It makes me feel like more of a hands-on mom and less like a short-order cook.

I'll usually order one of my favorite protein foods—scallops or salmon— and a lot of greens. (For busy women, having someone else do all the dicing and slicing is like a splurge.)

01:30 Time to refocus

Back at the office, I check my Post-it notes (more visual cues to help me remember) to make sure I'm tracking on the day's most important tasks, and dive back in for a few hours.

I don't do it every day, but most afternoons I try to take a break from my regular work to call a friend. I love my friends. I'm still in touch with people from grade school, middle school, high school, college, and just about every job I've ever had. I try to stay in touch with everybody.

And like most women I know, I feel guilty sometimes that I don't do a better job of it. My lists always include things like "Call Deirdre" and "Stephanie's birthday." I try to make sure that I always have something fun with my girlfriends to look forward to. "Dinner with Tufts girls" or "Spin with Tara" is a special treat.

More than a decade ago, psychology researchers explained why this is so important to me and so many other women. Friendships like these ("social support" is the colder, clinical term) produce physical, stress-fighting changes in our body. The idea of the "fight or flight" response to stress, these researchers found, came from studying men. Women are more likely to "tend and befriend," a response that releases soothing oxytocin. And researchers from Harvard University have found that the more friends women have, the fewer health problems they suffer from. A recent Australian study even quantified it: People with a large circle of friends were 22 percent less likely to have died during the course of the study. So take a few minutes from your day, and dial (or e-mail) that girlfriend. She really is a lifesaver.

04:00 Fending off the slim slump

This is a critically important part of my workday. By now, reality has sunk in. My 24-item to-do list has grown to 33, and not enough tasks are crossed off. I repeat my favorite word again—"focus"—and look at my Post-its. Fighting the urge to feel frustrated or tired or overwhelmed, I take my second tea break of the day: this time, green tea with steamed milk. I love that little bit of caffeine and antioxidant blast I get from the tea, and that comforting smell of the steam. I have another snack, too. This is when I'll have a piece of Dagoba Organic Chocolate (my fave) or yogurt and nuts.

Often, I fight myself when I take this break. A voice in my head will always say something like, "Aack! There's no time to slow down. You have to finish _____. You have to call _____." But I try to do it anyway, especially because I'm inclined to fight things that help me relax. (Trust

TAKE IT FROM Keri

MY ULTIMATE WEEKEND TREAT? A NAP!

I don't get to nap very much, but when I can, I do. New research from Allegheny College finds that people who sleep just 60 extra minutes in the daytime have lower blood pressure after a stressful event. In other words, sleep helps our body bounce back from stress more quickly. Whether it's on the couch in my office, on an airplane, or in my own bed, I can fall asleep anytime, anywhere.

me, anything approaching a Zen-like calm is really not me at all.) But I want to have access to that level of calmness. When I'm high energy, I want it to be because I'm choosing it, not because I don't know how to control it. So I force myself to take this quiet time, to build this habit of calmness. And it really works. If I can learn to do it, anyone can.

Relaxed and refocused, I sit back down at my desk and take a close look at the A-list Post-it. Once the high-priority things are done, I shift gears a little and set myself up for success the next day by writing tomorrow's list. It helps me in two ways: First, I get to give myself a little pat on the back for what I did get done. (Tearing up that little A-list Post-it note and tossing it into the trash feels great.) Second, it lets me organize my desk for a productive day tomorrow. That means I will be able to come into work feeling energized and ready to tackle my day, not dreading a mountain of chaos on my desk.

As a nutritionist, I know how important this is. It's no accident that for many people with demanding jobs, this is the part of the day when they feel most overwhelmed, tired, and frustrated that they didn't accomplish what they needed to. Is it any wonder that the minute they get home, they start to eat in a reckless way? The calmer I feel leaving work, the more peaceful I feel when I step into the kitchen—and the more likely I am to prepare a meal that represents the way I want to eat. I want to sit down to a plate full of nutrition, not frustration.

05:30 Easing into evening

When I walk in the front door, my kids literally bowl me over. I love the way they pounce on me and even to fight over me. This is such a delicious age, and I try to make sure I drink up every one of those hugs. I know they won't last forever. I like to hear about their day, and then I head straight into my room to change clothes. It's such a small thing, but I've learned that slipping out of my work clothes and putting on my domestic goddess attire—sweat pants—makes a world of difference in my mental health. I even know why: Researchers have figured out that the more roles a woman plays in her life, the more buffers she has against stress. To me, clothes are part of that. There are many days when I have to change four times. I'm an athlete, a mom, a nutritionist, and a friend, right? That means workout clothes, jeans, and a tank to drop off the kids, work clothes, and then something more fun if I'm going out to dinner. (Don't get me wrong— I know these multiple roles can sometimes add stress, too. Researchers have found that these many roles both wear us out and energize us in different ways.)

Though I do go out to dinner with friends and colleagues quite a bit, if it's a night when I'm staying home, I head back to the kitchen, ready to start dinner. I'm a pretty good cook (at least my kids think so), and

On days when I feel like my life is just a little too full, I remind myself of my all-time favorite Julia Child quote: "Life itself is the proper binge."

I try not to get into ruts. But on weeknights, there is a certain familiarity. For me, it's a togetherness thing, too. Having the kids around as I chop vegetables is fun, and I like when they get involved. It makes me feel more like a hands-on mom and less like a short-order cook. These days, my daughter, Maizy, likes to put on her own cooking show, preparing imaginary meals while I'm working on the real thing.

Proteins are usually the star of this meal: grilled salmon, broiled chicken, or grass-fed beef. But I always try to have at least two vegetables—a salad, for example, and steamed broccoli with cashews, or a soup that's loaded with different tastes and textures of vegetables. The more different kinds of food on my plate, the more luxurious it feels. There's too much good food in the world to skimp.

After doing the dishes, it's time for me to focus on my family: homework, games, baths, bedtime. It's precious time, but can be just as hectic and involved as my workday. Once the kids conk out, I can really unwind.

This is when I try to catch up on personal e-mail, surf the Internet, and check in with friends and family. (Is there anything as nice as settling into a comfy spot on your couch, whether you're reading a magazine or just zoning out in front of your favorite TV show?) Through it all, I am taking deliberate steps to calm myself down. I'll usually sip herbal tea (or sometimes a glass of wine). Some nights, I put on one of those wonderful Naturopatches. I usually put them on my upper arms. I like the soothing Bergamot.

10:00 Sensual sleep

By 10, I'm toast. I make myself a last mug of herbal tea and head into the bathroom to get ready for bed. My routine is simple but luxurious, as pampering as can be for a weeknight. I take my makeup off and dig out the potions I'm in the mood for. I know many women have a handful of reliable products they always use, and that's great, but it's not me. I change things often. Whatever types of cleansers, toners, and moisturizers I use are usually natural, and—the most important rule in my book—they smell great. Vanilla and lavender are associated with calming down and going to sleep; citrus smells cheer me up; and certain florals make me feel very sexy. It may seem like a tiny thing, but I love the idea of pampering myself just before I slip off to dreamland.

To help shake off an especially exhausting workday, I try to do things that are sexy and sensuous. I'll take a bath with lavender salt sometimes, or even just a quick shower, and use spray-on oils for more moisturizing. And I pay attention to what I wear to bed. To me, soft, silky boy shorts and tank tops are the sexiest, most incredible sleepwear imaginable. Ahhh, sweet dreams.

Who doesn't love weekends? It's such a nice change of pace.

How I Make Weekends More Wonderful

• • • Who doesn't love weekends? It's not that my weekday life is a bore—far from it!—but it's such a nice change of pace to not be so fiercely scheduled and to not feel like I have to use every moment as efficiently as possible.

For me, and for most of my clients, time is the biggest luxury of all. Here's what I like to do with my downtime on weekends, to truly feel like I'm a living a full life:

COOK UP A STORM I know plenty of people have a hard time staying on track during the weekends and will eat all kinds of things on a Saturday that they wouldn't go near on a Tuesday. But for me, the reverse is true. Since weekends are when I do have time to go the extra mile, I will. Saturdays and Sundays are the days I'm more apt to experiment with new foods and recipes. Sure, sometimes I try to focus on efficiency, and in my shopping, I'll think ahead for a week's worth of healthy choices. But I like to go a little wild, too. Maybe I'll buy a pepper I've never seen before and fool around with a new salsa recipe, or take time to soak split peas I buy from an Indian specialty shop nearby, or look for that perfect cut of steak. The point is, it's my time to play with food, not just eat it and rush off to work.

EXERCISE THE WAY I LOVE TO For someone who loves working out, and working out hard, weekday workouts are adequate but a little unfulfilling. On weekends, I'm much more likely to let myself have a good long run in the park, or spend time at the playground with the kids. Getting outdoors means the world to me. It doesn't surprise me that new research from the Peninsula College of Medicine and Dentistry confirms that exercising outdoors is better for your mental health than staying in the gym. Specifically, the research-ers found that being outdoors was associated with greater feelings of revitalization and increased energy, and while all exercise lowers tension, confusion, anger, and depression, outdoor workouts are even better at it. So get out there and soak up some sun while you sweat.

PURSUE ALL MY PASSIONS Weekends are the time when I try to nuture my soul with my favorite hobbies, things like hiking, art, or photography. Even though I don't have much time to spend on them, they mean a lot to me. They're little reminders that I'm multifaceted and that my life is full of all kinds of possibilities.

I'll think ahead for a week's worth of healthy choices. But I like to go a little wild, too. It's my time to play with food, not just eat and rush off to work.

PLAN A TRIP I love to travel, whether it's hiking in the mountains in Colorado (my all-time favorite happy place), soaking up the sun in Mexico, or traveling to Florida to see family. I'm lucky that my job has me on the road just enough to make it exciting but not so much that it's a chore. I do some of my best thinking and writing on airplanes. But I ran across some fascinating research recently. It's actually planning the trip that makes us happiest, not the trip itself. In fact, trip planning elevates happiness levels for a full 8 weeks. That makes sense to me. Sometimes just surfing travel Web sites is enough to send me on a blissed-out mental trip. Paris? Tahiti? Prague? Maybe Costa Rica? It doesn't cost anything to daydream, and it boosts happiness.

Rewrite Your Bucket List

• • •   If you're like me, you have a whole lot of ambitions—all kinds of things you want to do before you're too old to enjoy them. I've already crossed a few off my list. Finishing my first marathon brought an incredible sense of achievement.

You don't have to be old or have a fatal diagnosis to focus on this stuff. Living like every day could be our last really does make us happier. You may think this has nothing to do with successful weight loss, but you'd be wrong. Feeling in control of your life (like whether you will or won't jump out of an airplane this year) adds to what psychologists call our sense of mastery and control—and you better believe both of those are important for long-term weight loss success.

SO HERE'S MY LIST:

This year, I will _go skiing with my kids_

Within 5 years, I will _run an Ironman Triathlon (I hope!)_

Before I die, I will _climb Mount Kilimanjaro; see the pyramids_

YOUR TURN:

This year, I will _____

Within 5 years, I will _____

Before I die, I will _____

My Thoughts on Supplements

• • •   The Centers for Disease Control and Prevention says 53 percent of adults now take some form of supplement, up from 43 percent back in 1994. And women are far more likely to do so than men—about 59 percent compared with 49 percent. Calcium is the most common, taken by 69 percent of all women, and both vitamin D and fish oil supplementation are up, as well.

In recent years, many studies—including one that looked at more than 160,000 women—have shown that there's no benefit at all to taking a multivitamin. Other research, also very substantial, has found health risks in taking supplements, even calcium. Add to that the growing concern in the United States about contaminants in the food chain and the fact that most supplement sales are only very loosely regulated, and it would be easy to say no to all supplements. It's true that the standard line from nutritionists is usually that supplements are an unnecessary expense because you should be getting all the nutrition you need from a healthy diet.

But I'm not just a nutritionist—I'm also a realist. Very few people (even me) eat a perfectly well-rounded diet all the time. And often when people are dieting, they may be at risk for a nutrient deficiency. (I promise, if you follow the Slim Calm Sexy Diet, you're getting everything you need.) But because I feel there is usually a place even in a healthy diet for additional nutrition, I take an omega-3 every day. And I usually take a multivitamin, an extra antioxidant, and a calcium supplement.

If you want to take supplements, all I ask is that you still consciously track what you're eating, with the goal of getting everything you need from your food. And please check out the brand of supplements you're consuming. Consumerlab.com is a good start

The Slim Calm Sexy Staples

Over the years of helping people get and stay slim, I've learned that the best defense against eating the wrong foods is making sure plenty of the right ones are always available. Here are 10 things I can't live without. If I run out of these, you know I'm making a 10 p.m. dash to the market:

Peanut butter	Eggs
Greek yogurt	Tea (green and herbal)
Avocados	Apples
Whole grain bread	Fresh mozzarella
Artichokes	Hummus

101 ways to stay

slim calm sexy—for life

SLIM CALM SEXY DIET

Seeing

clients reach their weight loss goals is just about the most thrilling part of my job, and you can bet when that happens, there is plenty of celebrating and high-fiving around the Nutritious Life office. (I've yet to buy a confetti cannon, but I've come close!) If you stepped on the scale this morning and saw that magic number, I hope you'll give yourself a huge standing ovation. What you've accomplished isn't easy, and in my book, you're a rock star.

But chances are you're a little nervous, too. You may be thinking, "I've done this before and regained the weight. How can I protect this brand-new weight and make it mine forever?"

Here's where I step in with a reality check. It won't be your weight forever. Those numbers will continue to fluctuate a little—by as much as 3 to 5 pounds—as you transition from a fairly restricted pattern of eating to a whole new path. I'll be honest with you: This new road will entail a lot of trial and error. It has to be that way. Only you can figure out what works for your body as you make this shift from losing to maintaining. And it's only by paying close attention to what you eat each day and to the numbers on the scale that you will learn what your healthy-for-life eating style should be.

I'd love to tell you that now you don't have to think about what you eat anymore, but that's just not true. In fact, the minute you start thinking you can go "back to normal" with your eating, the less likely you are to keep the weight off. "Maintenance" doesn't mean blindly resuming your old habits. I like to compare it to driving. You have to stay on the road, right? That's done by constantly making tiny corrections and paying attention to what's in front of you. Some people are great drivers from day one, and others drive right into the ditch a few times until they get the hang of it. Learning how to self-correct may take some time, but the end result is worth it: a slimmer, calmer, sexier, and more confident you for the rest of your life.

I hope you're not thinking, "What? Do I have to be on a diet the rest of my life?" Absolutely not! In fact, as you settle into your new identity as an empowered eater, you'll find—as I have—that the conversations in your head about what to eat or not eat will become incredibly brief. "Hmm, what am I in the mood for? And how does that stack up with everything else I've eaten today?" are about as dramatic as it'll get.

You may even gain a few pounds, then pull back and say, "Okay, what do I need to adjust?" Don't beat yourself up over it. Just get right back on track. Maintaining your new weight means not only doing the right things; it means doing them over and over. Soon it will become second nature.

Do I expect you to be perfect at each meal? No way! In fact, I hope you'll strive for 18 "on-track meals" per week. Of course, you can't go crazy for those 3 other meals. Use what you've learned on the plan so far to guide you, but you can be a little more relaxed. Add foods into your daily meal plan gradually, starting with a protein and a carb. See how you feel for a week—is your weight staying about the same? If you're still losing, add another fat each day.

How to Keep the Fire Burning

• • •   Losing weight means changing many habits, and that takes constant attention and plenty of new ideas—not just new foods, but also a new way of seeing your relationship with food. And even once a client achieves that goal weight, "same old, same old" doesn't keep her there. She needs a constant stream of new ideas to stay fresh and motivated.

Let's say you've achieved your goal weight, and you're 25. That means you're going to eat roughly 1,095 maintenance meals in the next year, or 65,700 meals before you move on to the Great Big Blueberry Patch in the Sky. (You might notice I tacked an extra 5 years onto the average life expectancy of 80.1. I'm that confident that all your hard work building healthy habits will pay off.) It's my job to help you stay inspired.

So where do I find all my ideas? Everywhere I go, I am constantly looking for ideas and inspiration for myself, my clients, and my family. I find them from the weight loss, nutrition, and exercise worlds, as well as from entirely different areas. There's great, motivating information from fields like psychology, behavioral change, even history. (People in my line of work are prone to collecting odd facts about food. For example, Alexander the Great supposedly banned soldiers from chewing on mint because he worried that they would become too sexually aroused to fight well.)

If I can adapt an idea as a way to help my clients stay slim, calm, and sexy, I do. We live in a world with lots of pressure to eat too many foods that are so unhealthy, so why not constantly prowl around for ways to eat better? While the Slim Calm Sexy Diet is a great start, a Slim Calm Sexy life requires that you be flexible and inventive, too. I don't believe in letting anything get stale—not food, not workouts, or even my sex life!

Here are 101 inspirations.

Use them to constantly reinvent and revitalize your commitment to staying slim, calm, and sexy.

1 | Start an indoor herb garden

Having a few pots of herbs on your windowsill not only boosts the nutrient density of your diet and wows your tastebuds, but it's also a great lesson in patience. Growing herbs in pots typically takes about 6 weeks, just like the Slim Calm Sexy Diet. You can measure your progress along with your basil.

2 | Add to your list of nonfood rewards

Treating yourself to something special as you lose weight is a great idea, but some of us run out of ideas right after mani-pedi. Think bigger: How about a weekend nap? A whole day of antiquing? A nice sauna at the gym? (They build them for a reason, you know.) All of us need more ways to give ourselves an "Attagirl."

3 | Outsmart a buffet

Limit yourself to only one trip through the line—for salads, an entrée, and even dessert. People who make one trip through the buffet typically eat about 14 percent less than those who go back for seconds or thirds, according to research from the Cornell University Food and Brand Lab.

5 | Beef up your pit crew

Weight loss experts have known for a long time that social support really helps people in their efforts to lose weight. It's what has made groups like Weight Watchers so popular and so effective. But it doesn't need to be formal. Just getting into a buddy system for diet and exercise is beneficial. One study found that 66 percent of people who dieted with friends managed to keep the weight off. That's really impressive.

6 | Add a 1-minute challenge move

Twice this week, I want you to try something very hard for you, and do it—but only for 1 minute. Some ideas: jumping rope, jumping up on a step, bursting into a run from your walk, or holding a plank pose. Exercise pros say that, even though it's only for 60 seconds, this extreme exertion will both energize and inspire you. Each time, it will be a little easier and a concrete measure of your progress.

---

number

Chill out

Adding ice cubes to your water can help you burn more calories without doing any extra work. A German study found that drinking 17 ounces of cold water boosted metabolic rates by 30 percent within 10 minutes. Nutritionists speculate that the energy it takes to bring cold water—let's say, 40°F—up to your body's temperature of 98.6°F will burn even more.

7 | Start studying Sophia Loren

Several years back, Dove—as part of a massive research effort into women's attitudes about beauty and self-esteem—asked women all around the world, ages 16 to 54, how they felt about themselves. Of all the nationalities studied, Japanese women had the highest desire for physical change, closely followed by British women. Italian women, on the other hand, had the least desire to change the way they looked. Loving the way you look right now—that's what I call la dolce vita!

8 | *Nutritious Life-ism:*

Tell me what you eat, I'll tell you who you are. —ANTHELME BRILLAT-SAVARIN

10 | Take a one-night education excursion

Even though I love nutrition so much I got a degree in it, I don't expect you to. But a wonderful thing about the healthy-eating trend is that there are now all kinds of ways to learn a lot—in a flash. Many stores now offer lectures that are really informative, fun, and helpful. Why not sign up and spend an hour to become an expert in local cheese, learn to make your own sushi, or become knowledgeable about organic wine?

11 | Use sex to de-stress your cycle

Turns out that the more often we have sex, the more likely we are to develop regular menstrual cycles, according to studies done at Columbia and Stanford Universities. Predictable periods give you a little less to worry about.

12 | Know that every minute matters

Here's another reason to salute your decision to lose weight now. While many people spend years—sadly, even a lifetime—trapped inside a body that weighs too much, a new study from Monash University in Australia found that there's a direct link between the length of time people are obese and their mortality rate. In other words, the sooner you shed the excess weight, the better your health profile. The study, based on the Framingham Heart Study, found that for those who had lived with obesity between 5 and 14.9 years, the mortality rate doubled. And those who had been obese for 15 or more years? It tripled.

---

number

9

Drizzle on real salad dressing

You know how I've been saying that real foods are better than fake? Researchers at Iowa State University found that when people ate a green salad with fat-free dressing, they absorbed almost no nutrients. Those who ate the salad with regular dressing got plenty of the good stuff. Bring on the olive oil!

14 | Broaden your definition of a food journal

Keeping a food journal can double a person's weight loss, according to a study from Kaiser Permanente's Center for Health Research. (This data comes from one of the largest, longest-running weight loss studies I know of.) But what intrigues me is that there doesn't seem to be any need for a formal food journal (although many women feel more organized that way). Even leaving Post-it notes, texting, or e-mailing themselves about what they had eaten that day was enough to keep them on track.

15 | Cultivate your compassionate side

You know how the Dalai Lama says that compassion for others leads to happiness? It does—and it also leads to lower stress levels. Researchers measured compassion in a group of 59 women, as well as their receptiveness to getting social support. Those who were the most compassionate and receptive handled stressful situations better and had a higher level of overall well-being.

16 | Dim all the lights, sweet darling

The darker your bedroom, the better you'll sleep, which will make it easier for you to lose weight. What's more, one study recently found that women who sleep in rooms that are completely dark (versus those who sleep with some lights on or have lights shining in their window from outside) are 40 percent less likely to get breast cancer.

17 | Stress less about the pill

Many women worry that their birth control pills cause them to gain weight. But a new study from Oregon Health and Science University has shown that the commonly held belief that the pill causes weight gain is more fiction than fact. Researchers found that heavier individuals who keep their diet stable may actually see a weight loss. Why the misperception? The researchers think that the weight gain that seems to occur with age is being attributed to the pill. All the more reason to enjoy safe sex.

18 | Work out for another good reason

It turns out that besides burning calories, exercising restores the sensitivity of neurons involved in the control of satiety, that nice feeling of fullness we get after eating well. That, in turn, contributes to reduced food intake and then weight loss, according to new research from the State University of Campinas in Brazil. Using rodents and measuring hormones such as insulin and leptin, researchers proved that physical activity not only increased calorie burn, but it also regulated that feeling of fullness.

number

13

Don't skip a meal as penance

Go a little nuts last night, eating something you regret? Don't do some weird kind of penance when you make a mistake. Instead, make your next meal deliciously pampering. Choose your absolute favorite healthy foods, even if it means making a special trip to the store. Then sit back and enjoy. You're trying hard, so celebrate yourself.

19 | Think like a German

One reason Germans may be doing so much better than Americans in the weight control department? They believe in breakfast. About 75 percent of Germans eat breakfast each day, compared with only 44 percent of Americans. Go on—pour yourself a bowl of muesli.

20 | *Nutritious Life-ism*

We like to remind clients that there's no such thing as failure—it's all feedback. Every time you have a setback, just ask, "What did I learn?"

21 | Become a corn connoisseur

Maybe it's because it has such a short season, or maybe it's because it is naturally as sweet as candy, but there is nothing like freshly picked sweet corn. (In fact, author and entertainer Garrison Keillor insists it's better than sex.) When you can get your hands on the good stuff, invite your friends over and make a meal of it. It's loaded with vitamins A and C.

22 | Know your numbers

While most young women tend to obsess about weight and BMI—which I agree are very important—they often ignore another key number: blood sugar. Your doc will likely check this every 3 years or so, and ideally your fasting blood sugar should be 99 mg/dL or less. But if it has been higher in the past—between 100 and 125—you have what is known as prediabetes, a precursor to type 2 diabetes. In that case, your doctor may well want to test your level annually. And the more you control the weight, the less likely you are to develop full-blown diabetes.

23 | Take tea, Japanese style

By now, you're probably drinking a lot more tea than you used to. I know I've talked to you about mindful eating and drinking, but if you want to take it to a whole new level, search YouTube for a few Japanese tea ceremony videos. Every aspect of the ceremony is thoughtful and symbolic. Once you see how many steps people take to get every detail of the preparation just so, it will make you really aware of how we rush through things. Slow is better.

number

25

Spend more time in the park and less on housework

One of my favorite bumper stickers? "Dull women have immaculate homes." On weekends, get outside and live it up, doing all the things you need to recharge and refresh yourself first. The dust bunnies can wait.

24 | Slim down your potluck contributions

While it might not be quite accurate to say that religion is fattening, an intriguing study from Northwestern University Feinberg School of Medicine found that normal-weight young adults are 50 percent more likely to be obese by the time they reach middle age if they are actively involved in religious activities, compared with people who aren't observant. Researchers aren't sure why, but they think it may have to do with the types of food brought to church-related events. So when it's your turn to go to a potluck, bring a nice big salad.

27 | Give the office candy jar a makeover

With office candy, out of sight really is out of mind. One study found that people ate an average of 2.5 more pieces of candy when it was left out in a clear dish than when it was in a covered, opaque bowl. Over a month, that translated to 1,920 calories, and in a year, 24,960—or 7.13 pounds. Find a pretty dish with a lid to keep candy covered.

28 | Check your conscience: Are you a fattist?

Obesity is complex. It's not that heavy people are lazy or lack willpower. Because of my work, I've become really attuned to just how much our society likes to blame obese people and make them them feel bad. Really bad. What seems to be happening is that in the public-health zeal to end with the obesity epidemic—a campaign that I am admittedly a part of and a huge proponent of—we are getting meaner all the time. A new study from the University of Manchester in England reports that anti-overweight sentiment is up sharply, both in the general population and among health professionals. A separate study, from Purdue University, found that discrimination against obese people is so profound that it may actually harm their physical health.

   The British scientists learned that simple educational interventions, such as explaining some of the difficulties involved, helped prejudice decline by as much as 27 percent. You don't need me to give you a speech to remind you to be nice. At least once today, make eye contact with an obese person instead of looking away, and give him or her your friendliest smile. The more compassionate you are to others about weight struggles, I believe, the more compassionate you'll be with yourself.

29 | Try some meditation

I've already said how I believe that stress is closely linked to overeating, so it doesn't surprise me that stress management efforts help people lose weight. But sometimes it impresses me just how strong the connection is. A new study from Oregon Research Institute introduced

number

26

Go home and get frisky

Sex is a stress buster. I know it's easy to avoid sex when you're all tied up in stress knots, but it really does help. Scottish researchers have found that it lowers blood pressure and reduces overall stress measures. Hugs from your partner and hand holding lower stress, too. Get closer, and you'll relax in no time.

a group of obese adults to a 6-week mindfulness training program, which involved very basic meditation. Participants not only lost a significant amount of weight, but they also showed decreases in binge eating, depression, perceived stress, and physical symptoms, including levels of C-reactive protein, a marker of inflammation in the body.

30 | Pick a boredom buster

Seasoned exercisers are a little more vulnerable to falling into mental ruts. No matter how devoted you are to your routine, pick one new thing to try each week—maybe on the weekend, when you have a little more time. Try a new class at the gym, rent a workout DVD on Netflix, or borrow the neighbor kid's scooter. The point is to spend at least a little time each week finding something new to love about exercise.

31 | *Nutritious Life-ism:*

"Laughter is brightest where the food is."

—IRISH PROVERB

32 | Become a superfruit smarty-pants

Sometimes, keeping up with the next big thing in nutrition is a full-time job. But by simply fine-tuning your radar, you can be the first in your crowd to know, for example, that African baobab is going to be the next big thing. (Fans say it tastes like a wonderful cross between citrus, pear, vanilla, grapefruit, and caramel.) An easy way to stay in the loop is to visit Frieda's (www.friedas.com), a specialty produce company that does a brilliant job of keeping foodies up on the latest trends. Frieda's explains fruits such as oroblanco (a sweet grapefruit-pomelo cross) and Angelcot (a white-fleshed apricot), and vegetables like black radishes and Asparation (a broccoli crossed with kale).

34 | Shape the future: Mentor a girl

Volunteering is good for us, is linked to longer life, and lowers rates of both heart disease and depression. But it's also good for others. Big Brothers Big Sisters says that its "Littles" get along better with their families, are 52 percent less likely to skip school, and are more confident. Think about volunteering for a local school or sports team. From preschool soccer to high school basketball, girls need strong, supportive direction.

number

33

Get chummier at work

Having good friends at the office isn't just a good all-around stress reliever. It turns out that it can actually help you live longer. Women who say they work with people who help them solve problems and provide peer support live longer than those who don't, according to researchers at Tel Aviv University.

35 | Don't flirt with that croissant

Some women are simply able to think about food less. It's almost like they have a remote control and can click away from the Food Network anytime they want. But others have a much tougher time. A recent study from the Netherlands found that the more often women who were struggling to lose weight were shown images of high-calorie snacks, the more they craved them and the more likely they were to overeat. You know what that means, right? Window shopping in the bakery aisle is not a good idea for you, especially if you're feeling at all vulnerable.

37 | Rethink your standards

Okay, we've all heard a million times that the media portrays women as scary-skinny. But the next time you get the blues because a certain style or cut of clothing seems utterly wrong for you, think of this: Only 8 percent of women in the United States naturally possess the body shape defined by the fashion industry as "ideal." That means 92 percent of us don't. Repeat after me: It's not your fault—it's the clothes. Focus on finding styles that fit and flatter your natural shape, and you'll feel like a supermodel.

38 | Turn off the tube

Members of the National Weight Control Registry are superstars in my book—not just because they've lost a great deal of weight, but because they've been so successful at keeping it off. One of their secrets? Sixty-two percent say they watch 10 hours or less of TV per week.

39 | Make your home-cooked meals happier

While experts have long known that people tend to eat healthier meals at home than they do in restaurants, they weren't sure why. A new Canadian study finds it's because we're often happier there. The study looked at 160 women, and found that positive emotions have a major impact on what we cook and eat: People who are in a good mood at home tend to prepare healthier meals, and then feel more emotionally rewarded after eating them. That cycle of positive reinforcement was more pronounced at home than elsewhere. So anything you can do to increase your home's ability to make you happier, whether it's soft lighting, music, home design, or new kitchen equipment, is likely to increase that effect.

40 | Give your calorie burns a reality test

I always say calories are sort of beside the point, and when you follow the Slim Calm Sexy Diet, you don't have to track them—I've already done the work for you. But it is important to be aware of roughly how many calories you burn in your typical workout. Otherwise, it's too easy to think you "earned" more food than you really did. Forty-five minutes

---

number

36

Pay attention to how your fat fights back

One reason losing weight is difficult is that as you lose fat, your body has a little panic mechanism: Even though being overweight isn't healthy, your body thinks it is. One study, published in the journal *Appetite,* found that for every pound of fat lost, the desire to eat increases by about 2 percent. (Imagine how hard that makes it for someone who has lost 50 pounds.)

of yoga, for example, is a wonderful de-stressing workout but likely only blasts 128 calories—roughly what you'll take in with 5 ounces of your favorite red wine. A 45-minute walk, at 3 mpg, will burn 168 calories. A nice slow jog at, say, 5 mph? You'll free yourself of 408 calories.

41 | Embrace your rural roots

Want another reason to eat a diet that includes more plants and less processed food? As Americans, we often believe, and are told, that we have some of the best medical treatment and health care options in the world. And often, that's true. But our Western diet has given us big problems, as Gary Taubes points out in *Why We Get Fat:* "Colon cancer is 10 times more common in rural Connecticut than in Nigeria. Alzheimer's disease is far more common among Japanese-Americans than among Japanese living in Japan; it's twice as common among African-Americans as among rural Africans." We all know the answer: More plant-based foods, simply prepared.

42 | *Nutritious Life-ism:*

"A crust eaten in peace is better than a banquet partaken in anxiety." —AESOP

44 | Have more orgasms

Okay, I'm sort of fibbing. I've yet to find research that confirms my heart-felt theory that women who have more orgasms lose more weight than those who have fewer. (If you find it, please send it my way.) But some fascinating data from the Longevity Project confirms that women who have more orgasms do live longer—so the more orgasmic we are, the more chances we have to enjoy a healthy, nutritious life.

45 | Thank a woman for that salad

The more I learn about how the world's food is produced, the more it boggles my mind. Women put in two-thirds of the world's working hours and produce half of the world's food, yet they earn only 10 percent of the world's income and own less than 1 percent of the world's property. When possible, buy products that are labeled "Fair Trade," which means the workers are likely to be paid a decent wage.

46 | Carve out a weekly "You-day"

Try to make one day of the week especially about taking care of you. For me, it's usually a few hours on Friday. That's the day I allow myself to take a

number

43

Think small when eating out

You're more apt to get a right-size amount of food ordering an appetizer or splitting an entrée with a friend, than by ordering a "normal" entrée. In case you feel self-conscious about it, repeat after me: "In America, 'normal' means overweight. Is that what I want for myself?"

208

long run, a leisurely cooldown, and as much time as I want to stretch. Your body benefits from having one day of training that is more demanding; your spirit benefits from knowing you're devoting extra time to your health.

47 | Give your sweet tooth a date

I love dates because they've got tons of nutrition and they're as sweet as candy. I bet one or two will truly satisfy any sugar craving that comes your way.

48 | Go with the vinaigrette, please

Eating vinegar before a high-carb meal will help control your blood sugar levels, according to a study from Arizona State University. Researchers think the acetic acid in vinegar may inactivate certain starch-digesting enzymes, slowing carbohydrate digestion.

50 | Pick a theme song

Your iPod may be loaded with great tunes, but make sure there's one that is "your" song. Researchers at John Carroll University in Ohio have found that the act of choosing a personal theme song helps increase self-awareness.

51 | Pick up the pace

Walking can be a great way to work out, but you have to make it count. A study from Harvard University tracked women for 16 years, and found that those who more or less strolled when they walked weighed about the same as women who never exercised at all. But those who walked at least 4 mph had healthier BMIs.

52 | Try a little Mozart with dinner

The *Journal of Culinary Science and Technology* tested types and volume of music on people eating in a swanky restaurant. It turns out that classical music, played at a soft volume, made the meal most appealing.

53 | *Nutritious Life-ism:*

"Worries go down better with soup."
—JEWISH PROVERB

54 | Get sneaky about vegetables

Eating more vegetables is a proven weight loss winner—even if you have to fool yourself to do it. Researchers from Penn State added vegetable purees to meals to bulk them up and found that dieters didn't just up their produce

number

49

Enjoy a sharper memory

Another reason to celebrate losing weight? Your memory is probably getting better. A study at Kent State University found that measures of both memory and cognition increase after weight loss. Researchers think it's because many of the problems that come with obesity and may damage the brain—high blood pressure, type 2 diabetes, and sleep apnea—may be reversible.

consumption, but that they ate less overall—about 200 calories less. (One recipe, for example, used 1 cup each of pureed cauliflower and summer squash in a macaroni and cheese dish made with fat-free milk and reduced-fat cheese.) Puree vegetables yourself, or make it easy by keeping cans of pureed pumpkin in the house, which I like to add to soups and stews.

55 | Redefine "plateau"

I can't tell you how often I get "Keri, help! I'm stuck!" messages from clients. And weight loss plateaus are very real. In fact, one study found that no matter what weight loss program people followed, most of them stalled at around 6 months. But if your weight loss slows or even remains the same for a few weeks, that's normal, and I wouldn't say you're stuck. If it goes beyond that, however, it's time to make a change—either by reducing the amount of food you're consuming (or sometimes increasing!), and the same goes for exercise.

56 | Track your favorite fish

We all want to eat more fish, and I love the idea of rebuilding the seafood industry in the Gulf of Mexico. But it's hard for an average shopper to tell where fish is from. A fishermen's alliance recently launched a program called My Gulf Wild (www.mygulfwild.com), which lets consumers enter a tracking number that's attached to the gill of each fish after it's caught to see exactly where their fish is from. You can even see a picture of the boat captain!

58 | Have that pity party, but set a timer

You probably have a few friends you can call and whine to whenever things get bad. But watch the clock when you do so. Experts are finding that while a certain amount of venting is useful—since we all need to feel understood—too much is a bad thing. Research from the University of Arkansas found that too much venting actually increases aggression. So what works better? Deep breathing, or simply giving yourself a time-out.

59 | Work out in intervals

"I've always liked working out," says test panelist Kim Hartung, 33, of Clinton, Iowa, "but adding the intervals in the Slim workout to my usual running routine has been fun. I'm actually using the sprinting intervals. I'm starting to do some local road races, and this plan really helped me step it up." Viva la intervals!

60 | Broaden your global view

It's easy to think Americans are the fattest of all, and certainly, when it comes to overweight and obesity, we're well ahead of the curve. A recent study of some 9.1 million people around the globe showed that

number

57

Splurge away from home

There are times when a girl's gotta have ice cream. But when you do have a conscious indulgence, please do it somewhere else—at a friend's, a restaurant, or the ice-cream shop. That way, it's a one-time, special occasion. Bringing a half gallon of rocky road into the house? Now that isn't okay!

American women do have the highest BMI and that BMI levels increased the most among high-income countries in the past several decades.

But we've got plenty of company. Women in Australia and New Zealand came in second in weight gain among high-income nations. And overall, the biggest jump in female BMI occurred in Oceania and southern and central Latin America. That's certainly not good news, experts say, but it will help if we can all begin to think of obesity as a global problem and find global solutions.

Where are women doing the best in terms of maintaining weight? Central and Eastern Europe, central Asia, Brazil, Japan, and Taiwan.

61 | *Nutritious Life-ism:*

"The belly rules the mind." —SPANISH PROVERB

63 | Get down on the farm

In a trend that I'm sure would tickle our peasant forefathers, more of us are trying to get back to the farm, by buying local and organic produce. It's so much healthier for us and better for the planet. Farmers' markets are getting more and more popular. The USDA estimated that in 2011 there were 6,132 of them around the country, a 16 percent increase from the year before. Get the most out of every visit by challenging yourself to do two things. First, taste something brand new, even if it's just a different type of tomato or green bean. Second, chat with a farmer about what he or she is selling. Farmers can usually give you recipes and nutrition information for what they grow.

64 | Think addition, not subtraction

Empowered eating means thinking about food in terms of abundance, not deprivation. It may seem like semantics, but it's a big difference. If you allow yourself to drift into "can't have this, can't have that" thinking, you'll set yourself up for a binge. Next time you shop, make an effort to find at least three new items you can point to and say, "Yep—I'll have some of those, some of those, and some of those."

65 | Lie down and belly breathe

Yogis love this one, and so do I. Just lie on the floor with your hands on your belly, letting them rise and fall as you breathe. Breathe deep into your belly, letting the air fill your rib cage, and then your chest, right up into your throat. Then exhale, emptying your throat, chest, rib cage, then belly last. Just 5 minutes of breathing will make you feel calmer and more relaxed.

number

62

Declutter your kitchen

Easier is always better, at least in my book. So once a week or so, look around your kitchen and ask, "What's in my way? What's missing?" If you hardly ever use your toaster, put it away. Is your blender easy to reach? In your pantry, cabinets, and fridge, make sure the foods you use most are at eye level.

67 | Become a pickle person

Evidence is growing that acetic acid, the main component of vinegar, reduces blood pressure, blood sugar levels, and the formation of fat. So slow down the next time you go through the condiment aisle. Try a new type or two of cucumber pickles, and also dabble in pickled peppers, cabbage, or even tomatoes.

68 | Bite the spice bullet

I've already talked about the weight loss powers of hot red peppers, but here's something spice avoiders should know. A recent study from Purdue University measured the effects of cayenne pepper in tomato soup on people who liked spicy foods and people who didn't, and found that those who disliked spicy foods actually got more of a calorie burn from the meal than those who liked them. While researchers think that people will likely become desensitized to the effect as they become more accustomed to spicier foods (and eat more of them), if you can learn to put up with a little heat, you can get a caloric advantage.

69 | Expand your metrics

I know you're closely watching the scale and probably the waistband of your best jeans. But as you continue in your weight loss efforts, that gets boring, and both are a pretty one-dimensional measure of your progress. Research has shown that the more accurately you track your progress, the more inspired you'll be to stay on track. So measure something new. Maybe your thighs? How many pushups you can do? How long can you hold a plank position?

70 | Get paid to work out

More and more companies are adopting wellness programs to encourage employees to get fit—and some even include perks such as paying part of your gym membership. Some plans will also help you find a lunch buddy. Having someone to take a brisk 15-minute walk with will make a big difference in your activity level and also make it easier to stick with your goals. The American Heart Association makes starting a work program easy: Go to www.startwalkingnow.org.

71 | Focus on short-term gains

It's easy for people like me to talk about the health benefits of slimming down for the long haul—you can prevent problems such as diabetes and heart disease. But experts at the University of Cincinnati have found that short-term benefits, such as reduced knee pain, are much more motivating. They also discovered that losing as little as 10 pounds reduced pain by 20 to 30 percent.

number

66

Meatless Mondays

I love steak as much as the next girl and it has its place in this diet, but the less red meat we eat, the healthier we'll be. A large study found that women who had red meat at least five times a week had a 29 percent higher risk of type 2 diabetes than those who ate it less than once a week. And those who ate processed meats, including bacon and hot dogs, at least five times a week had a 43 percent higher risk.

212

72 | Develop your own specialty of the house

Test panel secrets: "I fell in love with the hummus sandwich and made it even better. I use thin bread, a cilantro-laced hummus I discovered, thin slices of red onions, and chopped red peppers," says test panelist Teresa Klein, of Shipshewana, Indiana. "It's my favorite lunch—and just incredible."

74 | *Nutritious Life-ism:*

"I was 32 when I started cooking; up until then, I just ate." —JULIA CHILD

75 | Become an honorary Brazilian

A study in the journal *Obesity Research* found that Brazilian women who eat plenty of that country's traditional rice-and-beans dish were 14 percent less likely to be overweight, compared with those who ate a more American-style diet. My favorite? Brown rice and black beans.

76 | Nurse a noodle craving with shirataki

These "noodles" are mostly fiber and made out of a mixture of tofu and yam flour. They're delicious! Look for them in specialty markets or in the Asian aisle of your supermarket.

77 | Try pole walking

Walking poles, which have long been popular among hardy Scandinavian hikers, can make a boring workout more challenging. You use muscles in your shoulders, arms, and torso, and the Cooper Institute in Dallas reports that they cause you to burn 20 percent more calories.

78 | Dip smarter with endive

I love to serve endive with dips or hummus. It's crunchy and satisfying, and even looks pretty when you've got company. Who needs chips, anyway?

79 | Meet your metabolites

Ever wonder exactly how exercise makes you lose weight? In a first-of-its-kind study, scientists at the Massachusetts Institute of Technology traced the progress of fat-burning cells, called metabolites, and developed a chemical snapshot of how they break down fat during exercise. After running on a treadmill for 10 minutes, people who were relatively

number

Offer yourself a weight loss bribe

Rewards are motivating, and for some people, the more tangible they are the better. Why not buy that dress you want in a size 6 and hang it on your closet door? That way, you can look at it every day and say, "Yep, I'm almost there."

more fit had a 98 percent increase in the breakdown of stored fat, sugar, and amino acids, while less fit people had only a 48 percent increase. But the very fit had the biggest difference of all. Blood samples taken from 25 people before and after they ran the 2006 Boston Marathon showed a 1,128 percent increase in some key metabolites.

80 | Hatch a holiday strategy

The winter holidays wreak havoc on many people's healthy eating efforts. A Harris poll recently found that 40 percent of American adults say they overeat and choose unhealthy foods during the holidays—and they blame it on the stress of the season. What helps my clients most is being prepared. Once they develop an effective strategy (go to the office party late and leave early; skip the cookie swap; bring a salad and healthy vegetable dish to Grandma's for Thanksgiving), they're able to relax and enjoy all the season's good things.

81 | Jump

When athletes are boosting their conditioning level, they use moves called plyometrics, the kind of hard-core drills you might see football or soccer players do at practice. Sometimes called jump training, these moves can be done anywhere. Jump up on a step, or try a deep squat followed by a jump. (Start with a few sets of 8, and see how intensely your leg muscles feel it the next day.) If you are already reasonably fit, you'll benefit from these leaps.

   In addition to the big jump in confidence, you'll get health benefits. Even a few minutes of plyometrics a week can increase your fitness, build your bones, and protect you from injury. The American Council on Exercise says high-intensity, power-based exercises are effective for burning a high number of calories in a short period of time. They also promote the anabolic hormones such as HGH and IGF-1, which are responsible for muscular growth and can actually have an antiaging effect.

82 | *Nutritious Life-ism:*

Enjoy your meals! "Nothing would be more tiresome than eating and drinking if God had not made them a pleasure as well as a necessity." —VOLTAIRE

83 | Stage a side-by-side tasting

One way to teach yourself to concentrate more on how foods taste is to really give your tastebuds a challenge. For fun, organize your own personal tasting. What you taste doesn't matter—it could be three types of olive oil, four different varieties of plums, even those tiny chocolate pastilles you can buy at stores such as Whole Foods and Central Market. Sit down and go slow. Are the textures different? The aromas? The aftertaste? It takes a little effort, but you can become a connoisseur of anything if you learn to slow down and savor the subtle differences.

85 | Make a good plan to be bad

I think one reason people get off track sometimes is that no matter how sincerely we commit to losing weight, there's a limit to how well behaved any of us can be. Sooner or later, we want to be a little defiant, sort of naughty, or just downright bad. I say, "Go for it." If being on too short a leash makes you feel crazy, it's important that you know you can eat whatever you want every now and then. I promise, the world won't end, and one reckless meal won't erase all your hard work. Promise me this, though: Make all your splurges splendid. I'd much rather know that you kicked up your heels with a crème brûlée than an ordinary bag of chips.

86 | Get South African at Starbucks

In South Africa, the native rooibos tea is very popular. It has a natural sweetness. Starbucks uses it in lattes and also sells Tazo's African Red Bush brewed tea, which has a tangy jolt of hibiscus flowers.

87 | Time a massage to a big event

At this point, dozens of studies have demonstrated that massage—one of my favorite ways to pamper myself—really does reduce stress levels. And since we can't eliminate stress from our lives, treat yourself right and schedule a massage right after an event that you think may leave you feeling depleted, such as a big work deadline, finals, or a visit with difficult family members.

88 | Rethink your approach to "fake" food

I certainly don't like the idea of eating highly engineered "fake" foods in order to avoid extra fat or calories. Some of them are scarier than Frankenstein! Instead, I encourage you to roll up your sleeves and experiment a little with real food. Try tuna with Greek yogurt or low-fat cottage cheese. And instead of vegetable oil, try pumpkin puree, applesauce, or mashed bananas in baked goods.

number

Picture it

Visual cues are often more powerful than words. Use that to help you lose weight. Is there a picture of you that makes you shudder and think, "Aack—how did I get so heavy?" Put it up on your fridge to curb temptation. Maybe you're hoping to slim down for a trip? Tape a picture of the beach you're going to near your computer, so you can keep your eyes on the prize.

89 | Arm yourself with apples

I love apples because they're an amazingly good source of fiber and antioxidants, and there are so many varieties that it's impossible to get bored. But they're also dynamite snacks. A Pennsylvania State University study found that people who ate an apple 15 minutes before a meal took in about 187 fewer calories.

90 | Stake out a tea shop

Test panel secrets: Even though it's a 45-minute drive from her home, test panelist Teresa Klein occasionally heads to a specialty tea shop that's stocked with constantly changing varieties. "I really love tea," she says. "I challenge myself to buy at least one I've never tried before every time I go there."

91 | Sneak off with a book

When it comes to taming stress, there are lots of ways to relax, but reading a book you enjoy—like this one—is most effective. Researchers at the University of Sussex found that reading for just 6 minutes was enough to lower physical measures of stress by 68 percent. Listening to music reduced stress levels by 61 percent; having a cup of tea or coffee, 54 percent; and taking a walk, 42 percent.

92 | Try the love-your-lawn workout

Here's a full-body workout that's good for everyone: Use a push mower to cut your grass. Push-reel mowers have been redesigned so they're easier to use. Not only are they great exercise, but they're also better for the environment. A conventional lawn mower creates as much harmful emissions as driving a car for 100 miles.

93 | Nap like the Japanese

In ancient Japan, naps were a big part of the daily routine, and there's been a national effort to bring them back. Schools and offices encourage 30-minute midday snoozes with piped-in classical music. (You can even buy desk pillows or pay $5 to relax in a nap salon.) Use your phone alarm to make sure you don't fall into a really deep sleep. There are even apps that fake "productivity noises" so no one has to know you are snoozing in your cubicle!

94 | Reinvent the burger

"To be honest, I'm not a very good cook," says test panelist Kim Hartung. "So the Portobello Burger with cheese has been great. It's easy to make on the broiler." Fire one up yourself!

96 | Dial up your weight loss

There are literally hundreds of apps out there to help with weight loss. Why not try a few to see if they help? Two that get plenty of good buzz are Weightbot and THI Personal Trainer Lite.

97 | Subtract one thing from your to-do list

An old friend of mine swears by this stress-management technique, and it works for me whenever I remember to do it. When you're looking at your list of things to do and feel like your head is swimming, find one thing to take away. Either defer it or cancel it. Sometimes, deciding what you don't have to do makes it easier to focus on what's really essential.

98 | Don't just laugh a little—laugh a lot

Seriously, researchers at Loma Linda University have discovered that when we laugh, we actually manipulate our hunger hormones as much as when we go to the gym. The scientists asked one group of participants to watch 20 minutes of clips from *Saturday Night Live, Seinfeld,* and Bill Cosby's stand-up routine; another group watched *Saving Private Ryan.* Ghrelin, a hunger-regulating hormone, spiked in the group that got to watch the funny stuff, as it would have if they had exercised.

99 | Start your own Sabbath

The idea of devoting a whole day to rest and reflection is part of just about every religion, and it's something most of us have gotten far away from. We tend to use weekends to do chores and errands, not to relax. But every so often, you should pencil in a whole day of nothing—no housework, no errands, just downtime to relax and rejuvenate.

100 | Sniff away stress

Aromatherapy is a proven way to lower stress and anxiety, but a recent study in *Psychiatry Research* found that lavender and rosemary are especially effective in helping us feel better. (Researchers measured the amount of cortisol, the stress hormone, in participants' saliva.) Two other super-relaxing scents? Ylang-ylang oil and rose oil.

101 | Count your blessings

I know, the idea of taking time out from a stressful day to write something as hokey as a Gratitude List doesn't seem very productive. But researchers have found that doing so for just 7 days boosts your happiness level and makes everything else in your life feel better. Do it. You deserve that rosy glow.

number

95

Dust off your bike

Want an inspiration to get back on two wheels? In the Netherlands, bikes outnumber people, and 54 percent of Dutch people say they use them daily. Traffic lights are even synced to bike speed. You don't have to turn into a long-distance cyclist (those shorts aren't for everybody). Just think about using your bike for short errands whenever possible.

slim calm sexy ●
recipes

Not everyone likes to cook, which

is why the Slim Calm Sexy Diet is especially easy to follow. It also leaves plenty of room for your own creative flair. Every recipe here is delicious, and of course, I've included them because they're loaded with foods and flavors that will power your weight loss.

Many of them are nutrient dense. There's a lot of food per calorie because I want you to feel constantly satisfied. (Remember, check your hunger quotient, or HQ, frequently. This plan works best when you eat often and consistently.) Almost every ingredient is nutrient dense, and many recipes contain water-dense ingredients, as well. The idea is that these slimming recipes are jam-packed with good stuff, making them both satisfying and a calorie bargain.

If you're already a cook, you don't need my permission to be creative. Mix it up! I think you'll love all these recipes as they are, but swap grains, fruits, nuts, vegetables, and spices as you like. The more you "own" each recipe, the more empowered you'll be.

START
YOUR DAY
WITH THE
DELICIOUS
MELON-MANGO
CUP
ON PAGE 223

Beautiful
Breakfasts

If

there's one thing people who have successfully lost weight have in common, it's that they embrace breakfast. Even if you're not usually a fan, it's important that you eat something within an hour of waking up each morning while following the plan. Your body is hungry after a long night's sleep, and this critical meal jump-starts your metabolism. Truly not in the mood? Try to eat a little something—maybe a piece of fruit or a handful of nuts—then have the rest of your meal by midmorning.

These good-morning glories are surefire ways to start your day on the right foot.

Melon-Mango Cup

from previous page

½ cup diced cantaloupe
½ cup diced mango
2 teaspoons lime juice
Pinch of ground nutmeg
1 cup fat-free plain yogurt
2 tablespoons chopped pecans

1. Combine the cantaloupe, mango, lime juice, and nutmeg in a small bowl.

2. Place one-third of the yogurt in a tall glass. Top with one-third o f the fruit mixture and one-third of the pecans.

3. Repeat the layers twice, using the remaining ingredients. Garnish with additional nutmeg, if desired.

Ruby Red Slim Smoothie

1 cup fat-free Greek yogurt
½ red grapefruit, sectioned
½ cup frozen strawberries
¼ cup orange juice
2 teaspoons flaxseed or grapeseed oil
¼ teaspoon vanilla extract

1. Place all the ingredients in a blender and puree until smooth.

2. Pour into a tall glass and serve.

Banana "Bread" Oatmeal

½ cup old-fashioned rolled oats
¾ cup fat-free milk
Pinch of salt
½ ripe banana
¼ teaspoon vanilla extract
Pinch of ground cinnamon
1 tablespoon chopped walnuts

1. Combine the oats, milk, and salt in a small bowl. Microwave on high power for 2 to 3 minutes, stirring halfway.

2. In a separate bowl, mash the banana and vanilla with a fork until no large chunks remain.

3. Stir the banana mixture and the cinnamon into the oatmeal until well combined.

4. Top with the walnuts and additional cinnamon, if desired.

✳ ALL RECIPES SERVE ONE, UNLESS OTHERWISE SPECIFIED.

Western Egg Sandwich

1   slice (1 ounce) uncured, nitrate-free deli ham
     (such as Applegate Naturals)
1   whole wheat English muffin, toasted
1   large omega-3-enriched egg
     Salt
     Freshly ground black pepper
1   slice (1 ounce) Cheddar or American cheese
1-2 teaspoons ketchup

1. Fold the ham on the bottom half of the muffin. Set aside.

2. Coat a small nonstick skillet with canola oil cooking spray and place it over medium heat. Add the egg and cook it for 1 minute, breaking the yoke slightly with a spatula, until set.

3. Fold the egg in half and cook it for 1 minute longer. Season it with salt and pepper.

4. Flip the egg and place the cheese on top. Cover and cook for 2 minutes, or until the cheese is melted.

5. Place the egg on top of the ham. Spread the ketchup on the remaining muffin half and place it on top of the egg.

Calm in a FLASH

BE AN INSTANT EGGS-PERT

You can turn out perfect hard-cooked eggs every single time, courtesy of the pros at the American Egg Board.

+ Put the eggs in a saucepan large enough to hold them in a single layer. Add cold water to cover the eggs by 1 inch. Heat just to boiling, then remove from the burner and cover.

+ Let extra-large eggs stand in the hot water for about 18 minutes, large eggs for 15 minutes, and medium eggs for 12 minutes.

+ Drain immediately and serve warm. Or cool completely under cold running water or in a bowl of ice water, then refrigerate.

Raspberry-Ricotta French Toast

1   cup raspberries
1   teaspoon honey
¼   cup fat-free ricotta cheese
1   large omega-3–enriched egg
1   tablespoon fat-free milk
¼   teaspoon ground cinnamon
1   slice multigrain bread
1   tablespoon chopped pecans

1. Mash ¼ cup of the raspberries with ½ teaspoon of the honey in a small bowl with a fork. Add the ricotta and stir to combine. Set aside.

2. Coat a small nonstick skillet with canola oil cooking spray and place it over medium heat.

3. Beat the egg, milk, and cinnamon in a shallow bowl. Dip the bread in the egg mixture and flip to coat both sides.

4. Transfer the bread to the skillet and cook for 1 to 2 minutes per side, or until the egg is lightly browned.

5. Top it with the reserved ricotta mixture, and sprinkle on the pecans and ¼ cup of the remaining raspberries. Drizzle with the remaining ½ teaspoon of honey and garnish with additional cinnamon, if desired. Serve with the remaining ½ cup of raspberries on the side.

BAKE
ON THE
WEEKEND FOR A
GRAB-
AND-GO
MORNING

Slim Calm Sexy Squares

2	cups old-fashioned rolled oats
¼	cup ground flaxseed
¾	teaspoon ground cinnamon
¼	teaspoon ground cloves
¼	teaspoon salt
½	cup almond butter
¼	cup honey
1	teaspoon vanilla extract
½	cup finely chopped and pitted Medjool dates
½	cup dried cherries or goji berries

1. Preheat the oven to 350°F. Coat an 8″ x 8″ pan with canola oil cooking spray.

2. Combine the oats, flaxseed meal, cinnamon, cloves, and salt in a large bowl.

3. Combine the almond butter, honey, and vanilla in a small bowl. Add to the dry ingredients and stir to combine. Stir in the dates and cherries until well combined.

4. Press the mixture firmly into the prepared pan. Bake for 25 minutes, or until the edges are browned. Let it cool completely before cutting into 8 bars. Store in an airtight container. Serve with 1 cup fat-free milk.

MAKES 8 SERVINGS

There's an old Chinese proverb that I love: "Sour, sweet, bitter, pungent—all must be tasted." Try it— even if you can only pull it off for one meal each day, eat as slowly as you can, appreciating every separate flavor in each dish.

Luscious Lunches

SAVOR A QUICK AND CRUNCHY CHEF SALAD ON PAGE 232

When

it comes to timing, lunch is usually all about what works for your schedule and not so much about what works for your body. (Believe me, I know— I'm constantly squeezing in lunch between appointments, and I eat at my desk a lot more than I'd like.) So while I understand that on some days you'll just grab lunch whenever you can, I hope that sometimes you'll take it slow. Step away from your desk and try to spend at least 20 minutes eating.

There are two reasons for that time frame. First, it takes about that long for the hunger hormones to quiet down and let your brain know you're full. Second, while most Americans eat way too fast, mindfulness experts say it actually takes 20 minutes to fully appreciate a meal. Hard for you to eat that slowly? Think about chewing each bite 30 times. Try to savor each bite for about 30 seconds, really enjoying the flavor (even if it's a simple sandwich). Take the time to think about something you're really looking forward to, like an after-work date with your friends or an upcoming vacation. Letting your mind drift to happy thoughts will keep you from downing the entire meal in one bite.

Quick and Crunchy Chef Salad

1 tablespoon red wine vinegar
1 teaspoon grapeseed oil or cold-pressed olive oil
  Salt
  Freshly ground black pepper
2 cups chopped romaine or
  iceberg lettuce
½ cup cherry tomatoes, halved
2 slices (2 ounces) roasted all-natural turkey breast or nitrate-free ham,
  cut into ½" pieces
3 tablespoons shredded Cheddar or Monterey Jack cheese
2 tablespoons chopped red onion
2 teaspoons raw or toasted sunflower seeds

1. Combine the vinegar and oil in a small bowl. Season with salt and pepper.

2. Place the lettuce, tomatoes, turkey, cheese, onion, and sunflower seeds in a serving bowl. Toss with the dressing.

Pear and Nut Butter Sandwich with Spiced Pear Yogurt

1 small pear
2 teaspoons nut butter (peanut, cashew, or almond)
1 slice multigrain bread
  Pinch of ground cinnamon
  Pinch of ground nutmeg
¾ cup fat-free plain yogurt

1. Cut two ⅛"-thick slices from the pear. Chop the remaining pear into ½" pieces. Set aside.

2. Spread the nut butter on the bread, and sprinkle with cinnamon and nutmeg. Place the reserved pear slices flat on top.

3. Mix the yogurt with a pinch of cinnamon and nutmeg in a small bowl. Top with the reserved pear pieces and sprinkle with additional nutmeg and cinnamon, if desired. Serve with the sandwich.

Tuscan White Bean and Artichoke Salad

2 teaspoons cold-pressed olive oil
2 teaspoons lemon juice
  Salt
  Freshly ground black pepper
2 cups baby arugula
½ cup canned cannellini beans, rinsed and drained
½ cup canned artichoke hearts in water, drained and chopped
3 ounces water-packed chunk light tuna (about ⅓ cup)
2 tablespoons grated Parmesan cheese

1. Combine the oil and lemon juice in a small bowl. Season with salt and pepper.

2. Place the arugula, beans, artichokes, tuna, and cheese in a serving bowl. Toss with the dressing.

Tuna and Roasted Red Pepper Wrap

2 tablespoons roasted red pepper hummus (such as Tribe)
1 (10″) multigrain wrap (such as La Tortilla Factory Smart & Delicious Multigrain Soft Wrap)
½ cup baby spinach
1 jarred roasted red pepper, seeded and cut into thin strips
3 ounces water-packed chunk light tuna (about ⅓ cup)
½ teaspoon red wine vinegar (optional)
  Freshly ground black pepper

1. Spread the hummus on one side of the wrap, leaving a 2″ border around the edges.

2. Top with the spinach and red pepper strips, and then add the tuna.

3. Drizzle with the vinegar (if using) and season with black pepper.

4. Fold the sides of the wrap toward the filling, and roll the filling end toward the center, keeping the ends tucked in. Serve with 1 low-fat mozzarella string cheese.

Open-Faced Herbed Egg Salad Sandwich

2 tablespoons fat-free plain yogurt
1 teaspoon Dijon mustard
1 large hard-cooked omega-3-enriched egg, chopped
¼ cup finely chopped celery (about 1 rib)
1 teaspoon lemon juice (optional)
1 tablespoon minced fresh parsley
1 multigrain English muffin, toasted
  Salt
  Freshly ground black pepper

1. Combine the yogurt and mustard in a small bowl.

2. Add the egg, celery, lemon juice (if using), and 2 teaspoons of the parsley to the bowl and gently mix to combine. Season with salt and pepper.

3. Divide the egg salad between the English muffin halves and garnish with the remaining 1 teaspoon parsley. Serve with 1 sliced apple.

CUBED
WATERMELON
SAVES TIME
AND DOUBLES
AS A
SNACK

234

Watermelon and Spinach Salad *with* Mint Dressing

2	teaspoons balsamic or fig vinegar
1	teaspoon grapeseed oil
1	teaspoon finely chopped fresh mint
2	cups baby spinach
1	cup cubed watermelon, cut into ½" pieces
2	tablespoons (1 ounce) goat cheese, crumbled
2	tablespoons slivered pecans

1. Combine the vinegar, oil, and mint in a small bowl.

2. Place the spinach, watermelon, goat cheese, and pecans in a serving bowl.

3. Toss with the dressing. Serve with 2 Wasa Crispbreads.

TAKE IT FROM Keri

TRY "MINDFUL COOKING"

You've heard me talk a lot about mindful eating, which means slowing down and paying attention to every part of a meal—the tastes, the aromas, the textures, how it all comes together in your mouth. But you can be a mindful cook, too. Slice that scallion a little slower, put your nose closer to the oatmeal pot when you add the cinnamon, or enjoy the texture of lettuce as you shred it. Preparing food can be incredibly sexy and sensual, too, if we take the time to slow down and feel it.

Italian Bulgur Bowl

2   teaspoons balsamic vinegar
1   teaspoon cold-pressed olive oil
¼   teaspoon dried basil or oregano
     Salt
     Freshly ground black pepper
1 ½ cups baby arugula
⅓   cup cooked bulgur (such as Bob's Red Mill Quick Cooking), cooled to room temperature
1   low-fat mozzarella string cheese, cut into thin rounds
2   ounces precooked all-natural grilled chicken breast strips, diced (about ½ cup)
1   jarred roasted red pepper, seeded and chopped

1. Combine the vinegar, oil, and basil in a small bowl. Season with salt and pepper.

2. Place the arugula, bulgur, cheese, chicken, and red pepper in a serving bowl. Toss with the dressing.

Greek Lentil and Feta Salad

2   teaspoons red wine vinegar
1   teaspoon lemon juice
1   teaspoon cold-pressed olive oil
¼   teaspoon dried oregano
½   cup canned lentils, rinsed and drained
½   cup cherry tomatoes, cut into quarters
⅓   cup peeled and chopped cucumber
¼   cup (2 ounces) crumbled feta cheese
1   tablespoon finely chopped red onion
     Salt
     Freshly ground black pepper

1. Combine the vinegar, lemon juice, oil, and oregano in a small bowl.

2. Place the lentils, tomatoes, cucumber, cheese, and onion in a serving bowl. Toss with the dressing. Season with salt and pepper to taste.

Thai Tofu Wrap

2	teaspoons natural chunky peanut butter
1	teaspoon reduced-sodium soy sauce
1	teaspoon honey
1	(10") multigrain wrap (such as La Tortilla Factory Smart & Delicious Multigrain Soft Wrap)
½	cup bagged coleslaw mix (shredded cabbage and carrots)
¼	cup bean sprouts (optional)
3	ounces extra-firm tofu, drained and cut into ½" cubes (about ½ cup)
⅓	cup peeled and chopped cucumber

1. Combine the peanut butter, soy sauce, and honey in a small bowl.

2. Place the wrap flat on a plate. Top with the coleslaw mix and bean sprouts (if using), leaving a 2" border around the edges.

3. Add the tofu and cucumber. Drizzle the peanut sauce on top.

4. Fold the sides of the wrap toward the filling, and roll the filling end toward the center, keeping the ends tucked in.

TAKE IT FROM Keri

HOW TO GOOSE AN AVOCADO

Avocados don't actually ripen on trees. They get soft enough to use after they've been picked. If you've got an avocado that's rock hard, put it in a brown paper bag. That captures ethylene gas and speeds up ripening. It should be ready within 3 to 6 days. Add a banana, apple, or tomato to the bag, and it will ripen in about half the time.

TLT Pita and Edamame Salad

½	ripe tomato
½	cup shelled frozen and thawed edamame
½	teaspoon cold-pressed olive oil
½	teaspoon red wine vinegar
	Salt
	Freshly ground black pepper
2	pieces (2 ounces) uncured nitrate-free turkey bacon (such as Applegate Organics), or 2 slices (2 ounces) all-natural roasted turkey breast
¼	Hass avocado
1	whole wheat mini pita (such as Thomas' Sahara)
1	leaf romaine or iceberg lettuce

1. Cut a ¼"-thick slice from the tomato and set it aside. Chop the remaining tomato and toss it with the edamame, oil, and vinegar in a small bowl. Season with salt and pepper to taste and set aside.

2. Prepare the turkey bacon, if using, according to package directions to desired crispness.

3. Mash the avocado in a small bowl and season with pepper. Split the pita and spread the avocado inside.

4. Fold the lettuce to fit inside the pita. Layer the bacon or turkey and tomato slice on top of the lettuce. Serve with the reserved edamame salad on the side or in a pita.

A
PERFECT
BRING-TO-WORK
LUNCH

DATES
ADD A
SPECIAL
SWEETNESS
TO
LUNCH

240

Date-Nut Mesclun Mix

1	tablespoon balsamic vinegar
1	teaspoon grapeseed oil
2	cups baby mixed greens
2	ounces precooked grilled chicken strips, diced, or 2 slices all-natural roasted turkey breast, cut into $\frac{1}{2}$″ pieces
2	tablespoons (1 ounce) goat cheese, crumbled
1	Medjool date, pitted and finely chopped
1	tablespoon chopped walnuts

1. Combine the vinegar and oil in a small bowl.

2. Place the mixed greens, chicken or turkey, cheese, date, and walnuts in a serving bowl.

3. Toss with the dressing.

Black Bean Burger *with* Mango-Avocado Medley

½	cup diced mango
¼	cup chopped tomato
¼	avocado, diced
1	tablespoon minced red onion
2	teaspoons finely chopped cilantro
2	teaspoons lime juice
1	black bean veggie burger (such as Gardenburger Black Bean Chipotle)
2	tablespoons shredded Monterey Jack cheese
1	whole wheat mini pita (such as Thomas' Sahara)
1	leaf romaine lettuce

1. Combine the mango, tomato, avocado, onion, cilantro, and lime juice in a small bowl.

2. Prepare the burger according to package directions. Top with the cheese and microwave on high power for 30 seconds, or until the cheese is melted.

3. Split the pita and fold the lettuce to fit inside. Place the veggie burger on top of the lettuce. Serve with the mango-avocado mixture on the side or on top of the burger.

Delicious
Dinners

SPICY SHRIMP AND SQUASH SAUTÉ **IS READY** IN LESS THAN **10 MINUTES** ON PAGE 246

Most of us are a little extra vulnerable at dinnertime.

Often, we head into the kitchen after we've been worn out from the day—a little too tired, a little too hungry—making it easy to snack mindlessly while we're cooking. The best way to go into dinner is to make sure you have a Happy Hour food at least a half hour beforehand. (I advise super-busy clients to set a reminder on their online calendars to eat a midafternoon snack.) I also like to keep a bowl of fresh-cut veggies nearby to nibble on when I have to cook on an empty stomach.

Spicy Shrimp and Squash Sauté

2	teaspoons pine nuts
1	teaspoon extra-virgin olive oil
$\frac{1}{2}$	cup chopped plum tomato
1	cup yellow squash, cut into $\frac{1}{8}$"-thick rounds and sliced into half moons
	Salt
	Freshly ground black pepper
4	ounces wild rock shrimp, shelled and deveined
$\frac{1}{2}$	teaspoon minced garlic (about 1 clove)
	Splash of white wine (optional)
$\frac{1}{8}$	teaspoon red-pepper flakes
1	tablespoon chopped fresh basil
2	tablespoons grated Parmesan cheese

1. Place a medium nonstick skillet over medium heat. Add the pine nuts and cook, stirring, for 1 to 2 minutes, or until lightly browned. Remove from the skillet and set aside.

2. Add the oil to the same skillet, then add the tomato and squash. Season with salt and black pepper. Cook, stirring, for 5 to 7 minutes, or until the squash is softened and golden.

3. Add the shrimp, garlic, wine (if using), and red-pepper flakes. Cook for 3 to 4 minutes, flipping the shrimp halfway, until opaque and firm throughout. Stir in the reserved pine nuts and 2 teaspoons of the basil before transferring to a serving bowl.

4. Top with the cheese and the remaining 1 teaspoon of basil before serving.

THE POWER OF PINE NUTS

These tender seeds of pine trees have been part of the human diet for hundreds of years. Recently, researchers have found that pine nuts produce a polyunsaturated fat that suppresses the appetite of the women who eat them, more so than other seeds or nuts. Study participants reported a 29 percent drop in their desire to eat after a meal that included the tasty little treats. Toast them in a dry skillet to bring out their flavor (be careful and shake the pan often—they burn quickly).

Four-Veggie Frittata

2	large egg whites
1	large omega-3–enriched egg
1/3	cup fat-free milk
1/4	teaspoon garlic powder
1/4	teaspoon dried oregano
3	tablespoons Parmesan cheese
1/4	cup cherry tomatoes, cut into quarters
1/4	cup chopped canned and drained or frozen and thawed artichoke hearts
	Salt
	Freshly ground black pepper
1/2	teaspoon extra-virgin olive oil
1/2	cup chopped button mushrooms
1/4	cup chopped onion

1. Preheat the broiler.

2. Whisk the egg whites, egg, milk, garlic powder, oregano, and 1 tablespoon of the cheese in a medium bowl. Stir in the tomatoes and artichokes. Season with salt and pepper. Set aside.

3. Heat the oil in a small nonstick, ovenproof skillet over medium heat. Add the mushrooms and onion to the skillet and cook, stirring, for 3 to 5 minutes, or until the onion is slightly softened. Spread the vegetables evenly in the skillet.

4. Pour the reserved egg mixture on top of the vegetables. Cook for 3 minutes, or until the edges are set and the center is still runny.

5. Sprinkle with the remaining 2 tablespoons of cheese. Place the skillet under the broiler for 3 to 5 minutes, or until the top is golden and bubbling. Let the frittata stand for 2 minutes before using a rubber spatula to loosen it onto a serving plate.

Philly-Style Burrito

1/2	teaspoon canola oil
1/2	cup thinly sliced button mushrooms
1/3	cup thinly sliced yellow onion
1	cup baby spinach
	Salt
	Freshly ground black pepper
1	(10") multigrain wrap (such as La Tortilla Factory Smart & Delicious Multigrain Soft Wrap)
1	slice (1 ounce) Cheddar or American cheese
2–3	slices (2 ounces) thinly sliced roast beef, cut into 1/2"-wide strips lengthwise
1	tablespoon ketchup (optional)

1. Heat the oil in a small nonstick skillet over medium heat.

2. Add the mushrooms and onion to the skillet and cook, stirring, for 3 to 5 minutes, or until softened.

3. Add the spinach to the skillet and cook for 1 to 2 minutes, or just until wilted. Season with salt and pepper to taste.

4. Place the wrap flat on a serving plate. Lay the cheese flat on one side of the wrap. Microwave on high power for 30 seconds, or until the cheese starts to melt.

5. Place the cooked vegetables on top of the cheese. Set aside.

6. Add the roast beef to the skillet and cook for 1 minute, or until heated through. Place the meat on top of the vegetables. Top with ketchup (if using). Fold the sides of the wrap toward the filling, and roll the filling end toward the center, keeping the ends tucked in.

Two-Step Broccoli and Turkey Rotelle

1 ½   cups frozen broccoli florets
½   cup hot cooked quinoa-blend rotelle pasta
      (such as Ancient Harvest)
2   slices (2 ounces) roasted all-natural turkey
      breast, cut into ½" pieces
3   tablespoons grated Parmesan cheese
2   teaspoons cold-pressed olive oil
      Pinch of red pepper flakes
      Salt
      Freshly ground black pepper

1. Microwave the broccoli according to package directions.

2. Toss the pasta, turkey, cheese, and broccoli in a serving bowl. Drizzle with the oil and red-pepper flakes. Season with salt and pepper, and toss before serving.

RED
PEPPER
GIVES YOUR
METABOLISM
A
BOOST

Moroccan Chicken Platter with Roasted Cauliflower

¼   cup fat-free plain yogurt
1   tablespoon finely chopped cilantro plus additional for garnish
½   teaspoon minced garlic (about 1 clove)
¼   teaspoon ground paprika
    Pinch of ground cumin
2   teaspoons lemon juice
2   teaspoons extra-virgin olive oil
    Salt
    Freshly ground black pepper
4–5 ounces boneless, skinless chicken breast (about ½"–¾" thick)
2   cups cauliflower florets

1. Preheat the oven to 400°F. Coat an 8" x 11" baking dish with canola oil cooking spray.

2. Combine the yogurt, cilantro, garlic, paprika, cumin, 1 teaspoon of the lemon juice, and 1 teaspoon of the oil in a small bowl. Season with salt and pepper.

3. Place 2 tablespoons of the yogurt mixture in a resealable plastic bag and add the chicken breast, tossing to coat. Refrigerate until ready for use. Cover and refrigerate the remaining yogurt mixture in the bowl.

4. Toss the cauliflower with the remaining 1 teaspoon of oil and 1 teaspoon of lemon juice, a pinch of paprika, and a pinch of cumin in a small bowl. Season to taste with salt and pepper. Transfer to the prepared baking dish in a single layer and roast for 20 minutes.

5. Flip the cauliflower and move it to one side of the baking dish. Add the reserved chicken to the opposite side of the baking dish, discarding the excess marinade. Bake for 20 to 25 minutes, or until a thermometer inserted in the thickest portion registers 160°F. Remove the remaining yogurt mixture from the refrigerator and let stand at room temperature.

6. Transfer the chicken and cauliflower to a serving plate, drizzle with the remaining yogurt mixture, and garnish with cilantro.

Southwestern Quinoa Salad

½   cup canned black beans, rinsed and drained
⅓   cup cooked quinoa
⅓   cup chopped tomato
¼   cup thick and chunky salsa
¼   avocado, cut into ½" cubes
2   tablespoons shredded Monterey Jack cheese
1   tablespoon chopped cilantro
2   tablespoons fat-free Greek yogurt

1. Toss the black beans, quinoa, and tomato with 3 tablespoons of the salsa in a small bowl.

2. Stir in the avocado, cheese, and 2 teaspoons of the cilantro.

3. Top with the yogurt and the remaining 1 tablespoon of salsa. Sprinkle with the remaining 1 teaspoon of cilantro.

Mexican Tortilla Pizzas

2   (6") corn tortillas
¼   cup (1 ounce) shredded Monterey Jack or Mexican blend cheese
1   link Al Fresco All Natural Chipotle Chorizo Chicken Sausage, cut into ¼"-thick rounds
2   tablespoons chopped red onion
¼   cup thick and chunky salsa

1. Preheat the oven to 350°F. Line a baking sheet with parchment paper and place the tortillas flat on the baking sheet.

2. Divide the cheese between the tortillas.

3. Place the sausage pieces flat on top of the cheese. Sprinkle the onion around the sausage.

4. Bake for 15 minutes, or until the cheese is melted and the tortilla edges are crisp. Transfer to a serving plate using a spatula.

5. Top the tortillas with the salsa.

Fast Fried Rice

1   large omega-3–enriched egg*
    Salt
    Freshly ground black pepper
1   teaspoon grapeseed oil
¼   cup finely chopped onion
1   cup bagged coleslaw mix (shredded cabbage and carrots)
⅓   cup cooked brown rice
⅓   cup frozen and thawed peas
½   teaspoon minced garlic
2   teaspoons reduced-sodium soy sauce

1. Coat a small nonstick skillet with canola oil cooking spray and place over low heat.

2. Whisk the egg in a small bowl and add it to the skillet. Season with salt and pepper and cook for 1 to 2 minutes, using a spatula to break up the egg into small pieces. Set the egg aside and scrape the skillet clean with the spatula.

3. Return the skillet to medium-low heat and add the oil. Add the onion and coleslaw mix and cook for 3 to 5 minutes, or until softened.

4. Add the rice, peas, and garlic. Cook, stirring, for 1 to 2 minutes. Stir in the soy sauce and the reserved egg and cook for 1 minute longer, or until heated through.

*OPTIONAL: SUBSTITUTE 3 OUNCES DICED EXTRA-FIRM TOFU IN STEP 2 AND COOK UNTIL JUST GOLDEN.

Grilled Veggie and Steak Kebabs

1   small zucchini, cut into $1/4$"-thick rounds
$1/2$ cup cherry tomatoes, cut into quarters, plus 8 whole cherry tomatoes
2   teaspoons extra-virgin olive oil
$1/2$ teaspoon minced garlic
       Salt
       Freshly ground black pepper
4   ounces beef sirloin, cut into 6 (1") cubes
2   teaspoons chopped fresh basil

1. Soak two bamboo skewers in water for 10 to 15 minutes.

2. Set aside 6 zucchini rounds. Cut the remaining zucchini rounds into quarters and toss with the quartered cherry tomatoes, 1 teaspoon of the oil, and the garlic. Season with salt and pepper. Set aside.

3. Preheat a nonstick grill pan over medium heat. Thread 1 skewer with 1 whole tomato, 1 zucchini round, and 1 beef cube. Repeat two more times, ending with a tomato. Thread the remaining tomatoes, zucchini rounds, and beef cubes onto the other skewer. Drizzle the skewers with the remaining 1 teaspoon oil, turning to coat both sides. Season with salt and pepper.

4. Place the kebabs in the center of the grill pan and cook for 6 minutes.

5. Add the reserved vegetables to one side of the grill pan and flip the kebabs. Cook the kebabs for 5 to 6 minutes for medium, turning on all sides to ensure doneness, and cook the vegetables, stirring, until softened. Stir the basil in with the vegetables. Transfer the kebabs and vegetables to a serving plate.

Bison-Stuffed Red Pepper Boats

1	large bell pepper, stemmed, halved lengthwise, and seeded
1	teaspoon extra-virgin olive oil
1/4	cup chopped onion
1/2	cup chopped mushrooms
4	ounces ground bison
1/4	teaspoon dried oregano
	Salt
	Freshly ground black pepper
2	cups spinach, chopped
1/4	cup shredded reduced-fat mozzarella cheese
1	tablespoon chopped fresh parsley

1. Preheat the oven to 400°F. Coat a baking dish with canola oil cooking spray. Place the red pepper halves, cut side up, in the dish.

2. Heat the oil in a medium nonstick skillet over medium heat. Add the onion and sauté for 3 minutes, or until softened. Add the mushrooms, bison, and oregano. Season with salt and black pepper. Cook for 3 to 5 minutes longer, or until the meat is no longer pink. Add the spinach and cook for 1 minute, or just until wilted.

3. Spoon the bison mixture into the red pepper halves and cover the dish with foil. Bake for 15 to 20 minutes, or until the peppers are tender. Remove the foil and sprinkle the cheese over the peppers. Top with parsley, and serve.

BRING HOME THE BISON

No wonder cowboys always sang about buffalo—it's a great meal. Bison meat has very little intramuscular fat, so it scores favorably lower in cholesterol, fat, and saturated fat when compared with beef, pork, skinless breast of chicken, and even most fish. It's available in many supermarkets.

Mediterranean Vegetable Soup

1	can (14.5 ounces) diced or petite diced organic tomatoes
1	small carrot, peeled and cut into $\frac{1}{8}$"-thick rounds
1	rib celery, cut into $\frac{1}{4}$"-thick slices
2	teaspoons minced garlic (about 2 cloves)
	Salt
	Freshly ground black pepper
$\frac{1}{2}$	cup thinly sliced button mushrooms (about 2 large)
1	cup baby spinach
$\frac{1}{4}$	cup finely chopped fresh basil (or 1 teaspoon dried)
2	teaspoons balsamic vinegar

1. Add the tomatoes and $\frac{1}{2}$ cup of water to a small saucepan over medium heat. Stir in the carrot, celery, and garlic. Season with salt and pepper.

2. Cover and bring to a slow boil, then reduce the heat to low and simmer, covered, for 15 minutes, or until the vegetables are tender. Stir in the mushrooms halfway through the cooking time.

3. Add the spinach and basil and cook, stirring, for 1 minute, or until the spinach wilts.

4. Stir in the vinegar and serve.

MAKES 2 SERVINGS

For a complete meal, serve the soup with a 1-ounce slice of fresh mozzarella cheese stacked with a $\frac{1}{4}$"-thick slice of tomato and fresh basil leaves, drizzled with 1 teaspoon of cold-pressed olive oil and $\frac{1}{2}$ teaspoon of balsamic vinegar.

USE
LEFTOVERS
FOR AN
APPETIZER
TOMORROW!

Honey-Ginger Glazed Salmon

4–5 ounces skinless wild salmon fillet (about ¾"–1" thick)

½ cup pineapple chunks, cut into ½" pieces

1 tablespoon lime juice

2 teaspoons honey

½ teaspoon minced ginger

1½ cups bagged coleslaw mix (shredded cabbage and carrots)

1 tablespoon roasted or raw sunflower seeds

1 tablespoon chopped cilantro

1. Place the broiler rack in the top position and preheat the broiler. Line a broiler pan with foil and mist it with canola oil cooking spray. Place the salmon next to the pineapple on the foil.

2. Combine the lime juice, honey, and ginger in a small bowl. Drizzle the salmon and pineapple with 2 teaspoons of the lime juice dressing; reserve the rest.

3. Broil the salmon and pineapple for 6 to 7 minutes, or just until the salmon is opaque throughout and the pineapple is slightly browned.

4. Meanwhile, combine the coleslaw mix, sunflower seeds, and cilantro in a small bowl.

5. Transfer the broiled pineapple to the coleslaw mixture and toss with 2 teaspoons of the reserved lime juice dressing. Drizzle the remaining dressing on top of the salmon before serving. Serve the slaw on the side.

glossary

In the world of nutrition, glossaries aren't so easy to write. That's because there is so much ongoing research in the field that defining basic and emerging terms—let alone clarifying the evidence about what each may be able to do for your health—can be confusing, even for professionals.

I've collected these definitions from some of the most reliable, acceptable sources I know. I relied heavily on Medline, which is maintained by the National Institutes of Health; the International Food Information Council Foundation; the Linus Pauling Institute at Oregon State University; and the Health and Nutrition Newsletter published by the Friedman School of Nutrition Science and Policy at Tufts University. I also looked to the American Heart Association, the American Cancer Society, the National Cancer Institute, the American Institute for Cancer Research, the U.S. Agricultural Research Service, and the Alzheimer's Association.

I like to use Web sites run by the Mayo Clinic, the Cleveland Clinic, and WebMD, and encourage you to do so, too. They cover the connection between nutrition research and health in an accurate, user-friendly way. And by all means, "friend" me at A Nutritious Life on Facebook, because I post research updates now and then that will help you continue on your journey to empowered eating.

ADENOSINE TRIPHOSPHATE (ATP) A substance present in all living cells that provides energy for many metabolic processes and is involved in making RNA. ATP made in the laboratory is being studied in patients with advanced solid tumors to see if it can decrease weight loss and improve muscle strength.

ADRENALINE Also called epinephrine, this hormone is the principal blood pressure–raising hormone secreted by the adrenal medulla. Adrenaline is prepared from adrenal extracts or made synthetically, and is used medicinally especially as a heart stimulant, as a vasoconstrictor (to treat open-angle glaucoma and life-threatening allergic reactions and to prolong the effects of local anesthetics), and as a bronchodilator.

ALLIUM, ALLIINASE ORGANOSULFUR COMPOUNDS These are currently under investigation for their potential to prevent and treat disease. Garlic is a particularly rich source of these compounds. Crushing or chopping garlic releases an enzyme called alliinase that catalyzes the formation of allicin. Allicin rapidly breaks down to form a variety of organosulfur compounds.

ALPHA-LINOLENIC ACID (ALA) A type of omega-3 fatty acid found in plants. It is similar to the omega-3 fatty acids that are in fish oil (eicosapentaenoic acid, or

EPA, and docosahexaenoic acid, or DHA). Alpha-linolenic acid can be converted into EPA and DHA in the body. ALA is highly concentrated in flaxseed oil and, to a lesser extent, in canola, soy, and walnut oils.

ALPHA-LIPOIC ACID A naturally occurring compound that is synthesized in small amounts by humans and is found in some foods. Although alpha-lipoic acid is an antioxidant itself, it also regenerates other antioxidants after they've been oxidized by their scavenging activity.

AMINO ACIDS The basic building blocks of proteins. These have traditionally been classified as either essential, which means we need them in our diet, or nonessential, which means our body can manufacture them.

ANTHOCYANINS A group of antioxidants that is a subclass of flavonoids, which provide the health benefits of neutralizing free radicals and possibly reducing the risk of cancer. Anthocyanins are found in red, blue, and purple berries; red and purple grapes; and red wine. They include cyanidin, delphinidin, malvidin, pelargonidin, peonidin, and petunidin.

ANTIOXIDANTS Substances that protect your cells against the effects of free radicals. Free radicals are molecules produced when your body breaks down food or by environmental exposures such as tobacco smoke and radiation, which damage cells and contribute to aging, heart disease, cancer, and other diseases.

ASCORBIC ACID Also known as vitamin C, this water-soluble vitamin is essential for the development and maintenance of connective tissue and for speeding the production of new cells in wound healing. It is also an antioxidant that keeps free radicals from hooking up with other molecules to form damaging compounds that might attack tissue. Vitamin C protects the immune system, helps fight off infections, reduces the severity of allergic reactions, and plays a role in the synthesis of hormones and other body chemicals. Food sources include green bell peppers, broccoli, citrus fruits, tomatoes, and strawberries.

ATHEROSCLEROSIS A condition that exists when too much cholesterol builds up in the blood and accumulates in the walls of the blood vessels.

BETA-CAROTENE A derivative of the antioxidant vitamin A. This compound is found in many foods that are orange in color, including sweet potatoes, carrots, cantaloupe, squash, apricots, pumpkin, and mangos. Some green leafy vegetables (including collard greens, spinach, and kale) are also rich in beta-carotene.

BETA GLUCANS Sugars that are found in the cell walls of bacteria, fungi, yeasts, algae, lichens, and plants such as oats and barley. They are sometimes used to treat high cholesterol, diabetes, cancer, and HIV/AIDS, as well as to boost the immune system.

BODY MASS INDEX (BMI) A calculation that divides a person's weight in pounds by height in inches, squared. Search the term "BMI" on the Internet to find a calculator. Individuals with a BMI of 25 to 29.9 are considered overweight, and those with a BMI of 30 or greater are considered obese.

CAFFEIC ACID A type of phenol found in various fruits (including citrus) and vegetables. Caffeic acid has antioxidant-like activities and may reduce the risk of degenerative diseases, heart disease, and eye disease.

CAFFEINE A naturally occurring substance found in the leaves, seeds, or fruits of more than 63 plant species worldwide. Caffeine is part of a group of compounds known as methylxanthines. The most commonly known sources of caffeine are coffee and cocoa beans, kola nuts, and tea leaves. Caffeine is a pharmacologically active substance and, depending on the dose, can be a mild central nervous system stimulant. Caffeine does not accumulate in the body over the course of time and is normally excreted within several hours of consumption.

CALCIUM A mineral that builds and strengthens bones. Calcium helps in muscle contraction and heartbeat, and assists with nerve function and blood clotting. Milk and other dairy products such as yogurt and most cheeses are the best sources of calcium. In addition, dark green leafy vegetables, fish with edible bones, and calcium-fortified foods supply significant amounts.

CALORIE A unit of heat content or energy, which is defined as the amount of heat necessary to raise the temperature of 1 gram of water by 1°C.

CAROTENOIDS Derived from the antioxidant vitamin A, these yellow, orange, and red pigments are synthesized by plants. The most common carotenoids are alpha-carotene, beta-carotene, beta-cryptoxanthin, lutein, lycopene, and zeaxanthin.

CATECHINS A type of flavonoid found in tea. Catechins provide the health benefits of neutralizing free radicals and possibly reducing the risk of cancer.

CELLULITE The dimpled appearance of skin some people have on hips, thighs, and buttocks. More common in women than men, the lumpiness is caused by fat deposits that distort connective tissues beneath skin, leading to changes in appearance.

CENTRAL OBESITY Overweight that accumulates around the midsection, often packed inside the abdominal cavity. This body type, often called "apple shaped," is linked to greater health risks than "pears," who carry their weight in the thighs and buttocks.

CHOLESTEROL A waxy, fatlike substance that occurs naturally in all parts of the body. Your body needs some cholesterol to work properly. But high levels of cholesterol in the blood can block arteries and increase the risk of heart disease.

CHOLINE An essential nutrient linked to heart health and cancer prevention. Although the body manufactures some choline, we need dietary sources, too. Beef and eggs are good sources.

COENZYME Q10 A fat-soluble compound primarily synthesized by the body and also consumed in the diet. Coenzyme Q10 acts as an antioxidant in cell membranes. Food sources include nuts, herring, trout, and soybean and canola oils.

COMPLEX CARBOHYDRATES Starchy foods that are excellent sources of energy and nutrients, such as whole grain breads, rice, and pasta. They are called "complex," as opposed to "simple," sugars because they take longer for the body to digest and absorb.

CORONARY ARTERY DISEASE The most common type of heart disease and the leading cause of death in the United States for both men and women. The arteries that supply blood to the heart muscle become hardened and narrowed because of the buildup of cholesterol and other material, called plaque, on their inner walls. As the buildup grows, less blood can flow through the arteries. As a result, the heart muscle can't get the blood or oxygen it needs. This can lead to chest pain (angina) or a heart attack.

CORTISOL A stress hormone manufactured by the adrenal and pituitary glands.

CURCUMIN A polyphenolic compound that gives turmeric its yellow color. It's also an antioxidant that may be linked to cognitive function.

DOCOSAHEXAENOIC ACID (DHA) An omega-3 fatty acid that is essential for the growth and functional development of the brain in infants and for maintenance of normal brain function in adults.

EICOSAPENTAENOIC ACID (EPA) A fatty acid found in cold-water fish, including mackerel, herring, tuna, halibut, salmon, and cod. EPA is used for high blood pressure in high-risk pregnancies (eclampsia), age-related macular degeneration, heart disease, schizophrenia, personality disorder, cystic fibrosis, Alzheimer's disease, depression, and diabetes.

ELLAGIC ACID A natural cancer-fighting agent that is found in strawberries.

EPIGALLOCATECHIN-3-GALLATE (EGCG) A type of catechin found in green tea. It has been linked to heart health, lower cancer risks, and weight loss.

ESSENTIAL FATTY ACIDS Alpha-linolenic acid (ALA), an omega-3 fatty acid, and linoleic acid (LA), an omega-6 fatty acid, are considered essential fatty acids because they cannot be synthesized by humans.

FAT-SOLUBLE VITAMINS Vitamins A, D, E, and K. Your body stores the excess in your liver and body fat, using them as needed. Unlike water-soluble vitamins, where the excess is excreted in urine, fat-soluble vitamins are potentially toxic in too-large doses and can cause nausea, vomiting, and liver and heart problems.

FERULIC ACID A type of phenol found in various fruits and vegetables and citrus fruits. Ferulic acid has antioxidant-like activities that may reduce the risk of degenerative diseases, heart disease, and eye disease.

FIBER See *soluble fiber* and *insoluble fiber*.

FLAVONOLS A type of flavonoid found in citrus fruits that provides the health benefits of neutralizing free radicals and possibly reducing the risk of cancer.

FLAVONES A type of flavonoid that includes apigenin and luteolin, found in parsley, thyme, celery, and hot peppers.

FLAVONOIDS Naturally occurring compounds found in plant-based foods recognized as conferring certain health benefits. Flavonoids are a subgroup of polyphenols. So far, there are more than 4,000 known flavonoid compounds, including anthocyanidins; flavanones, such as catechins, found in teas (particularly green and white), chocolate, grapes, berries, and apples; theaflavins and thearubigins, found in teas (particularly black and oolong); and proanthocyanidins, found in chocolate, apples, berries, red grapes, and red wine. The flavonoid category also includes the widely distributed quercetin, kaempferol, myricetin, and isorhamnetin, which are found in yellow onions, scallions, kale, broccoli, apples, berries, and teas.

FOLIC ACID This B vitamin helps the body make healthy new cells. Folic acid is critical for pregnant women, to prevent major birth defects in the baby's brain or spine.

Food sources include leafy green vegetables, fruits, dried beans, peas, and nuts. Enriched breads, cereals, and other grain products also contain folic acid.

FREE RADICALS Highly reactive substances that result from exposure to oxygen, background radiation, and other environmental factors. Free radicals cause cellular damage in the body. The damage may be repaired by antioxidants.

GHRELIN A hormone produced in the gastrointestinal tract, which stimulates appetite and hunger.

HIGH-DENSITY LIPOPROTEIN (HDL) CHOLESTEROL Known as the "good" cholesterol, HDL carries about one-fourth to one-third of blood cholesterol. High levels of HDL seem to protect against heart attack; low levels of HDL (less than 40 milligrams per deciliter) increase the risk of heart disease. Medical experts think that HDL tends to carry cholesterol away from the arteries and back to the liver, where it's passed from the body. Some experts believe that HDL removes excess cholesterol from arterial plaque, slowing its buildup.

HYDROGENATED FAT During food processing, fats may undergo a chemical process called hydrogenation. This is common in margarine and shortening. Hydrogenated fats raise blood cholesterol levels.

INFLAMMATION The way the body responds to an injury or abnormal stimulation, involving cellular changes and infiltration in affected blood vessels and surrounding tissues.

INSOLUBLE FIBER Found in foods such as wheat bran, vegetables, and whole grains. It adds bulk to the stool and appears to help food pass more quickly through the stomach and intestines.

INSULIN A hormone, secreted in the pancreas, that promotes glucose use, protein synthesis, and the formation and storage of neutral lipids. Insulin is used to treat diabetes.

INSULIN RESISTANCE The diminished effectiveness of insulin in lowering plasma glucose levels, usually due to binding of insulin or insulin receptor sites by antibodies. It's associated with obesity, ketoacidosis, and infection.

ISOFLAVONES Another subclass of flavonoids. These include daidzein, genistein, and glycitein and are found in soybeans, soy foods, and legumes.

L-CARNITINE A derivative of the amino acid lysine. Healthy individuals manufacture enough of this substance, which plays an important role in cellular activity, converting long-chain fatty acids so the body can use them.

LOW-DENSITY LIPOPROTEIN (LDL) CHOLESTEROL Known as the "bad" cholesterol, LDL cholesterol can slowly build up in the inner walls of the arteries that feed the heart and brain. Together with other substances, it can form plaque, a thick, hard deposit that can narrow the arteries and make them less flexible. This condition is known as atherosclerosis. If a clot forms and blocks a narrowed artery, a heart attack or stroke can result.

LEPTIN A hormone produced in fat cells that sends a signal to the brain when you are full.

L-ERGOTHIONEINE A powerful antioxidant linked to heart health and found in mushrooms.

LIBIDO Conscious or unconscious sexual desire.

LIGNANS Polyphenol compounds found in plants. Lignan precursors are found in a wide variety of plant-based foods, including seeds, whole grains, legumes, fruits, and vegetables. When eaten, they are converted to the mammalian lignans—enterodiol and enterolactone—by bacteria that normally colonize the human intestine. Flaxseeds are the richest dietary source of lignan precursors.

LIMBIC BRAIN A system of related neural structures in the brain that are involved in emotional and more primitive behavior, including eating and sex. It includes the hippocampus, the thalamus, and amygdala.

LUTEIN An antioxidant best known for its association with healthy eyes. Lutein, a carotenoid, is abundant in green, leafy vegetables such as collard greens, spinach, and kale.

LYCOPENE A carotenoid and potent antioxidant found in tomatoes, watermelon, guavas, papayas, apricots, pink grapefruit, blood oranges, and other foods. Estimates suggest that 85 percent of the American dietary intake of lycopene comes from tomatoes and tomato products.

METABOLIC SYNDROME Formerly called Syndrome X, metabolic syndrome refers to a group of risk factors: high blood pressure, high blood sugar, high cholesterol levels, and belly fat. Taken together as a single syndrome, it increases the risk of heart disease and diabetes.

METABOLISM The process that involves a set of chemical reactions that modify a molecule into another for storage, or for immediate use in another reaction, or as a by-product. This is the way our body uses food as energy to keep all systems functioning.

MINERALS Used by the body for many different jobs, including building bones, making hormones, and regulating heartbeat. Your body needs two kinds of minerals: macrominerals in larger amounts, including calcium, chloride, magnesium, phosphorus, potassium, sodium, and sulfur; and trace minerals in small amounts, including cobalt, copper, fluoride, iodine, iron, manganese, selenium, and zinc.

MONOUNSATURATED FATS Unsaturated fats that are heart healthy. They are liquid at room temperature but start to solidify at refrigerator temperatures. They're found in olive, canola, and peanut oils and in avocados.

NEUROTRANSMITTER Any specific chemical agent (including acetylcholine, five amines, four amino acids, two purines, and more than 28 peptides) released by an excited cell that crosses the synapse to stimulate another cell. More than one may be released at any given synapse.

NOREPINEPHRINE A hormone, like adrenalin and epinephrine, that is secreted when we are under stress. In contrast to epinephrine, it has little effect on bronchial smooth muscle, metabolic processes, and cardiac output, but has strong vasoconstrictive effects and is used pharmacologically as a vasopressor.

NUTRIENT DENSITY The ratio of nutrient content in a food to its total calories.

OBESOGENS Chemicals that alter regulation of energy balance to favor weight gain and obesity. There is growing evidence that these chemicals disrupt the endocrine process. They include bisphenol A (BPA), xenoestrogens, phthalates, and organotins.

OMEGA-3 FATTY ACIDS A type of fatty acid found in fish and marine oils. Omega-3s provide the health benefits of reduced risk of cardiovascular disease and improved mental and visual function.

OPIOIDS A class of narcotic drugs that causes addiction.

ORGANIC AGRICULTURE Farming that promotes and enhances biodiversity, biological cycles, and soil biological activity. It is based on minimal use of off-farm inputs, such as synthetic fertilizers or pesticides, and on management practices that restore, maintain, and enhance ecological harmony.

OXIDATION The loss of electrons from a compound (or element) in a chemical reaction. When one compound is oxidized, another compound is reduced—that is, the other compound must "pick up" the electrons that the first has lost. Oxidation is what causes an apple to turn brown after it is sliced and causes metal to rust.

OXYTOCIN A hormone secreted by the pituitary gland. It stimulates the contraction of the uterine muscle and the secretion of milk. Oxytocin production is stimulated by orgasm and cuddling. Oxytocin is linked to lower rates of breast cancer and has some antioxidant properties.

POLYCHLORINATED BIPHENYLS (PCBS) A mixture of chlorinated chemicals that are no longer used in U.S. manufacturing but still pollute soil and waterways. Fish are thought to be a major source of PCBs, which cause serious skin conditions and immune problems, and are likely carcinogens.

PECTIN A natural gelling agent found in ripe fruit. Pectin is an important source of fiber.

PHYTOCHEMICALS Also called phytonutrients, these are technically any chemicals produced by plants, but the term is generally used to describe compounds that may affect health but are not essential nutrients.

PHYTOSTEROLS These plant-derived compounds are similar in both structure and function to cholesterol.

POLYPHENOLS The most abundant dietary antioxidants, according to researchers. The main sources are fruits and plant-derived beverages, such as juices, tea, coffee, and red wine. Polyphenols are made up of phenols, a class of chemical compounds consisting of a hydroxyl functional group.

POLYUNSATURATED FATS Another heart-healthy fat, these oils are liquid at room temperature and in the refrigerator. They easily combine with oxygen in the air to become rancid, and can be found in safflower, sesame, soy, corn, and sunflower oil, as well as nuts and seeds.

RESVERATROL A polyphenolic compound linked to heart health and found in grapes, red wine, purple grape juice, peanuts, and some berries.

RETINOIDS Derivatives of vitamin A. Retinoids are topical and oral antioxidants that are used to prevent and reverse sun damage and signs of aging, as well as to treat acne. These medications should be prescribed and coordinated by a qualified licensed health care professional. Vitamin A supplements should not be used in tandem with these drugs because of a risk of increased toxicity.

SAPONINS The functional component of soybeans, soy foods, and soy protein. Saponins may lower LDL cholesterol and may contain anticancer enzymes.

SARCOPENIA A loss of skeletal muscle mass that may accompany aging.

SATIETY The state of feeling full and satisfied.

SATURATED FAT The main dietary cause of high blood cholesterol, found mostly in foods from animals and some plants, including beef, beef fat, veal, lamb, pork, lard, poultry fat, butter, cream, milk, cheeses, and other dairy products made from whole and 2 percent milk. All these foods also contain dietary cholesterol. Foods from plants that contain saturated fat include coconut, coconut oil, palm oil, and palm kernel oil (often called tropical oils), and cocoa butter.

SELENIUM A mineral that is a component of antioxidant enzymes but not an antioxidant nutrient. Plant foods such as rice and wheat are the major dietary sources of selenium in most countries. The amount of selenium in soil, which varies by region, determines the amount of selenium in the foods grown in that soil. Animals that eat grains or plants grown in selenium-rich soil have higher levels of selenium in their muscle. Meats, bread, and Brazil nuts are good food sources.

SEROTONIN A hormone manufactured by the brain. Serotonin is a feel-good chemical that, along with dopamine, has been shown to have antioxidant properties.

SOLUBLE FIBER Attracts water and turns to gel during digestion, which slows digestion. Soluble fiber is found in oat bran, barley, nuts, seeds, beans, lentils, peas, and some fruits and vegetables. Soluble fiber may help lower cholesterol, which can help prevent heart disease.

SUBCUTANEOUS FAT CELLS The adipose tissue under the skin. It differs from abdominal fat, which is located inside the abdominal cavity.

TRANS FATTY ACIDS Found in small amounts in various animal products such as beef, pork, and lamb and in the butterfat in butter and milk. Trans fatty acids are also formed during the process of hydrogenation, making margarine, shortening, cooking oils, and the foods made from them a major source of trans fats in the American diet. Partially hydrogenated vegetable oils provide about three-fourths of the trans fats in the U.S. diet. Trans fatty acids are also formed during the process of hydrogenation.

TRIGLYCERIDES A form of fat made in the body. Elevated triglycerides can be due to overweight/obesity, physical inactivity, cigarette smoking, excess alcohol consumption, or a diet very high in carbohydrates (60 percent of total calories or more). People with high triglycerides often have a high total cholesterol level, including a high LDL (bad) level and a low HDL (good) level. Many people with heart disease and/or diabetes also have high triglyceride levels.

UNSATURATED (POLYUNSATURATED AND MONOUNSATURATED) FATS

They're found mainly in many fish, nuts, seeds, and oils from plants. Some foods that contain these fats are salmon, trout, herring, avocados, olives, walnuts, and liquid vegetable oils such as soybean, corn, safflower, canola, olive, and sunflower. Both polyunsaturated and monounsaturated fats may help lower your blood cholesterol level when you use them in place of saturated and trans fats.

VITAMINS One of many organic compounds that are nutritionally essential in small amounts to control metabolic processes and cannot be synthesized by the body. Vitamins are usually classified by their solubility, which to some degree determines their stability; occurrence in foodstuffs; distribution in body fluids; and tissue storage capacity. While there are many vitamins, vitamins A, C, and E have the strongest antioxidant properties.

VITAMIN A A fat-soluble antioxidant vitamin that comes in two categories. One is retinol (because it produces the pigments in the retina of the eye) and is found in such foods as eggs, liver, and whole milk. The other is carotenoids, found in colorful fruits and vegetables, including dark leafy greens and carrots. It helps form and maintain healthy teeth, skeletal and soft tissue, mucous membranes, and skin.

VITAMIN C See *ascorbic acid.*

VITAMIN E Also known as alpha-tocopherol, this antioxidant is found in almonds; in many oils, including wheat germ, safflower, corn, and soybean oils; and in mangos, nuts, broccoli, and other foods. It's important in the formation of red blood cells and helps the body use vitamin K.

WATER-SOLUBLE VITAMINS

Vitamins such as B-6, C, and folic acid that are easily absorbed by the body. Your body uses the vitamins it needs, then excretes excess water-soluble vitamins in urine. Because these vitamins are not stored in the body, there is less risk of toxicity than with fat-soluble vitamins but a greater risk of deficiency.

the slim calm sexy diet

shopping list

Grocery List

PRODUCE
FRESH FRUIT:
- 1 small pear
- 1 lemon or 1 small package lemon juice
- 1 lime
- 1 avocado
- 1 small banana

FRESH VEGETABLES:
- red and yellow peppers
- carrots
- water chestnuts
- 5 cups baby spinach
- 2 cups spinach
- 1 red onion
- ¼ cup cherry tomatoes
- 1 cup sliced red cabbage
- 1 cup sliced green cabbage
- 1 cup brussels sprouts
- 6 cups romaine lettuce
- 1 cup sliced cucumbers
- 1 cup asparagus
- 1 large red tomato
- 1 small sweet potato
- ¼ cup bean sprouts
- 1 artichoke
- 4 ribs celery
- 1 portobello mushroom
- 1 small package mushrooms
- 1 cup snow peas
- 1 cup string beans

FRESH HERBS:
- 1 teaspoon basil
- 2 teaspoons mint

DAIRY
MILK:
- 1 cup/8 ounces almond milk
- 1 quart fat-free milk
- 1 cup/8 ounces fat-free chocolate milk

CHEESE:
- 3 tablespoons/1½ ounces Parmesan cheese
- 3 ounces reduced-fat Cheddar cheese
- ½ cup fat-free cottage cheese
- 2 ounces reduced-fat feta cheese
- 1 ounce low-fat Swiss cheese

YOGURT:
- 5.3 oz Acai Oikos Greek yogurt
- 3 cups organic fat-free Greek yogurt
- 2 tablespoons plain fat-free yogurt

EGGS
- 3 DHA-fortified eggs

NUTS, NUT BUTTERS, AND SEEDS
- 1 tablespoon pumpkin seeds
- 40 raw almonds
- ½ cup sliced almonds
- 10 walnut halves
- 1 tablespoon chopped walnuts
- 36 pistachios
- 2 tablespoons sunflower seeds
- 6 teaspoons natural peanut butter
- 2 tablespoons ground flaxseed

OILS
Cold-pressed olive oil
Canola oil spray

GROCERY
GRAINS:
- ½ cup steel-cut oats
- 1 ounce wild rice (⅓ cup cooked)
- 1 ounce bulgur (¼ cup cooked)
- 1 ounce brown rice (⅓ cup cooked)
- 1 ounce quinoa (⅓ cup cooked)

BREADS:
- 1 slice whole grain bread

CEREALS:
- 1½ cups SmartBran cereal

CRACKERS:
- 2 high-fiber crackers

OTHER PACKAGED FOODS:
- 4 tablespoons hummus
- 1 can pumpkin puree
- ⅛ cup/1 ounce dried mango
- ½ cup canned (or frozen) artichoke hearts
- ⅓ cup marinara sauce
- 1 small jar green olives
- 2 tablespoons guacamole
- ½ cup chickpeas
- ½ cup lentils

POULTRY
- 8 ounces skinless chicken breast
- 4 ounces fresh sliced turkey

SEAFOOD
- 4 ounces salmon
- 4 ounces cod filet
- 4 ounces shrimp
- 4 ounces canned salmon

MEATS
- 4 ounces 85% lean organic ground beef
- 4 ounces lean organic beef

VEGETARIAN
- 4 ounces firm tofu, cubed

HERBS AND SPICES
Red-pepper flakes
Sea salt
Black pepper
Cinnamon
Oregano
Matcha powder
Ground coffee beans
Seaweed gomashio (sesame salt)

CONDIMENTS
Vanilla extract
Balsamic vinegar
Lemon vinaigrette
Dijon mustard
Rice vinegar

PRODUCE

FRESH FRUIT:
- 1 cup cherries
- 2 avocados
- 1 lime
- 1 grapefruit
- ½ cup cantaloupe
- 1 small banana

FRESH VEGETABLES:
- 1 large red tomato
- ½ cup cherry tomatoes
- 4 red bell peppers
- 3 yellow bell peppers
- 5 ribs celery
- 1 small package mushrooms
- 1 cup cauliflower
- ¼ cup fresh spinach
- 1 cup red onion
- 1 cup broccoli
- 3 cups baby spinach
- 2 cups chopped kale
- 1 artichoke
- 2½ cups romaine lettuce
- ½ cup carrots
- ½ cup zucchini
- 1 small butternut squash
- 1 cucumber
- 1 cup bok choy
- 1 cup sugar snap peas
- ½ cup shredded red cabbage
- ½ cup shredded green cabbage

FRESH HERBS:
- 2 teaspoons mint

DAIRY

MILK:
- 1 cup soy milk
- 1 quart fat-free milk
- 1 cup almond milk

CHEESE:
- 2 ounces fresh mozzarella cheese
- 1 ounce reduced-fat feta cheese
- 2 ounces goat cheese
- ½ cup fat-free cottage cheese

YOGURT:
- 4½ cups organic fat-free Greek yogurt
- 5.3 oz Oikos Organic Greek Yogurt

EGGS

8 DHA-fortified eggs

NUTS, NUT BUTTERS, AND SEEDS

- 40 raw almonds
- 3 tablespoons walnuts
- 2 Brazil nuts
- 4 teaspoons natural peanut butter
- 2 teaspoons almond butter
- 2 tablespoons sunflower seeds
- 1 tablespoon pine nuts
- 2 tablespoons flaxseed
- 2 tablespoons chia seeds

OILS

Olive oil
Canola oil spray

GROCERY

GRAINS:
- 2 ounces quinoa (⅔ cup cooked)
- 1 ounce wild rice (⅓ cup cooked)

BREADS:
- 3 slices whole grain bread

CRACKERS:
- 8 high-fiber crackers

OTHER PACKAGED FOODS:
- 1 cup artichoke hearts, canned or jarred in water
- 1 cup Amy's Organic Black Bean Chili
- 4 tablespoons hummus
- 1 jar green olives
- 2 corn tortillas
- ½ cup chickpeas
- ½ cup lentils

POULTRY

- 4 ounces grilled chicken breast
- 4 ounces all-natural chicken sausage
- 4 ounces turkey

SEAFOOD

- 4 ounces scallops
- 4 ounces water-packed chunk light tuna
- 4 ounces cod

MEATS

- 4 ounces pork tenderloin
- 4 ounces beef filet

HERBS AND SPICES

Sea salt
Black pepper
Cinnamon
Dry mustard
Oregano
Matcha powder
Ground coffee beans
Thyme

CONDIMENTS

Vanilla extract
Balsamic vinegar
Lemon vinaigrette
Rice vinegar
Dijon mustard
Salsa
Guacamole

Grocery List

PRODUCE

FRESH FRUIT:
- 1 small pear
- 1 lemon or 1 small package lemon juice
- 1 lime
- 1 avocado
- 1 small banana

FRESH VEGETABLES:
- red and yellow peppers
- carrots
- water chestnuts
- 5 cups baby spinach
- 2 cups spinach
- 1 red onion
- 1/4 cup cherry tomatoes
- 1 cup sliced red cabbage
- 1 cup sliced green cabbage
- 1 cup brussels sprouts
- 6 cups romaine lettuce
- 1 cup sliced cucumbers
- 1 cup asparagus
- 1 large red tomato
- 1 small sweet potato
- 1/4 cup bean sprouts
- 1 artichoke
- 4 ribs celery
- 1 portobello mushroom
- 1 small package mushrooms
- 1 cup snow peas
- 1 cup string beans

FRESH HERBS:
- 1 teaspoon basil
- 2 teaspoons mint

DAIRY

MILK:
- 1 cup/8 ounces almond milk
- 1 quart fat-free milk
- 1 cup/8 ounces fat-free chocolate milk

CHEESE:
- 3 tablespoons/1½ ounces Parmesan cheese
- 3 ounces reduced-fat Cheddar cheese
- ½ cup fat-free cottage cheese
- 2 ounces reduced-fat feta cheese
- 1 ounce low-fat Swiss cheese

YOGURT:
- 5.3 oz Acai Oikos Greek yogurt
- 3 cups organic fat-free Greek yogurt
- 2 tablespoons plain fat-free yogurt

EGGS

- 3 DHA-fortified eggs

NUTS, NUT BUTTERS, AND SEEDS

- 1 tablespoon pumpkin seeds
- 40 raw almonds
- ½ cup sliced almonds
- 10 walnut halves
- 1 tablespoon chopped walnuts
- 36 pistachios
- 2 tablespoons sunflower seeds
- 6 teaspoons natural peanut butter
- 2 tablespoons ground flaxseed

OILS

- Cold-pressed olive oil
- Canola oil spray

GROCERY

GRAINS:
- ½ cup steel-cut oats
- 1 ounce wild rice (⅓ cup cooked)
- 1 ounce bulgur (⅓ cup cooked)
- 1 ounce brown rice (⅓ cup cooked)
- 1 ounce quinoa (⅓ cup cooked)

BREADS:
- 1 slice whole grain bread

CEREALS:
- 1½ cups SmartBran cereal

CRACKERS:
- 2 high-fiber crackers

OTHER PACKAGED FOODS:
- 4 tablespoons hummus
- 1 can pumpkin puree
- ⅛ cup/1 ounce dried mango
- ½ cup canned (or frozen) artichoke hearts
- ⅓ cup marinara sauce
- 1 small jar green olives
- 2 tablespoons guacamole
- ½ cup chickpeas
- ½ cup lentils

POULTRY

- 8 ounces skinless chicken breast
- 4 ounces fresh sliced turkey

SEAFOOD

- 4 ounces salmon
- 4 ounces cod filet
- 4 ounces shrimp
- 4 ounces canned salmon

MEATS

- 4 ounces 85% lean organic ground beef
- 4 ounces lean organic beef

VEGETARIAN

- 4 ounces firm tofu, cubed

HERBS AND SPICES

- Red-pepper flakes
- Sea salt
- Black pepper
- Cinnamon
- Oregano
- Matcha powder
- Ground coffee beans
- Seaweed gomashio (sesame salt)

CONDIMENTS

- Vanilla extract
- Balsamic vinegar
- Lemon vinaigrette
- Dijon mustard
- Rice vinegar

WEEK 4

PRODUCE

FRESH FRUIT:
1   cup cherries
2   avocados
1   lime
1   grapefruit
½   cup cantaloupe
1   small banana

FRESH VEGETABLES:
1   large red tomato
½   cup cherry tomatoes
4   red bell peppers
3   yellow bell peppers
5   ribs celery
1   small package mushrooms
1   cup cauliflower
¼   cup fresh spinach
1   cup red onion
1   cup broccoli
3   cups baby spinach
2   cups chopped kale
1   artichoke
2½ cups romaine lettuce
½   cup carrots
½   cup zucchini
1   small butternut squash
1   cucumber
1   cup bok choy
1   cup sugar snap peas
½   cup shredded red cabbage
½   cup shredded green cabbage

FRESH HERBS:
2   teaspoons mint

DAIRY

MILK:
1   cup soy milk
1   quart fat-free milk
1   cup almond milk

CHEESE:
2   ounces fresh mozzarella cheese
1   ounce reduced-fat feta cheese
2   ounces goat cheese
½   cup fat-free cottage cheese

YOGURT:
4½ cups organic fat-free Greek yogurt
5.3 oz Oikos Organic Greek Yogurt

EGGS
8 DHA-fortified eggs

NUTS, NUT BUTTERS, AND SEEDS
40 raw almonds
3   tablespoons walnuts
2   Brazil nuts
4   teaspoons natural peanut butter
2   teaspoons almond butter
2   tablespoons sunflower seeds
1   tablespoon pine nuts
2   tablespoons flaxseed
2   tablespoons chia seeds

OILS
Olive oil
Canola oil spray

GROCERY
GRAINS:
2   ounces quinoa (⅔ cup cooked)
1   ounce wild rice (⅓ cup cooked)

BREADS:
3   slices whole grain bread

CRACKERS:
8   high-fiber crackers

OTHER PACKAGED FOODS:
1   cup artichoke hearts, canned or jarred in water
1   cup Amy's Organic Black Bean Chili
4   tablespoons hummus
1   jar green olives
2   corn tortillas
½   cup chickpeas
½   cup lentils

POULTRY
4   ounces grilled chicken breast
4   ounces all-natural chicken sausage
4   ounces turkey

SEAFOOD
4   ounces scallops
4   ounces water-packed chunk light tuna
4   ounces cod

MEATS
4   ounces pork tenderloin
4   ounces beef filet

HERBS AND SPICES
Sea salt
Black pepper
Cinnamon
Dry mustard
Oregano
Matcha powder
Ground coffee beans
Thyme

CONDIMENTS
Vanilla extract
Balsamic vinegar
Lemon vinaigrette
Rice vinegar
Dijon mustard
Salsa
Guacamole

Grocery List

PRODUCE

FRESH FRUIT:
- 1 small pear
- 1 lemon or 1 small package lemon juice
- 1 lime
- 1 avocado
- 1 small banana

FRESH VEGETABLES:
- red and yellow peppers
- carrots
- water chestnuts
- 5 cups baby spinach
- 2 cups spinach
- 1 red onion
- 1/4 cup cherry tomatoes
- 1 cup sliced red cabbage
- 1 cup sliced green cabbage
- 1 cup brussels sprouts
- 6 cups romaine lettuce
- 1 cup sliced cucumbers
- 1 cup asparagus
- 1 large red tomato
- 1 small sweet potato
- 1/4 cup bean sprouts
- 1 artichoke
- 4 ribs celery
- 1 portobello mushroom
- 1 small package mushrooms
- 1 cup snow peas
- 1 cup string beans

FRESH HERBS:
- 1 teaspoon basil
- 2 teaspoons mint

DAIRY

MILK:
- 1 cup/8 ounces almond milk
- 1 quart fat-free milk
- 1 cup/8 ounces fat-free chocolate milk

CHEESE:
- 3 tablespoons/1 1/2 ounces Parmesan cheese
- 3 ounces reduced-fat Cheddar cheese
- 1/2 cup fat-free cottage cheese
- 2 ounces reduced-fat feta cheese
- 1 ounce low-fat Swiss cheese

YOGURT:
- 5.3 oz Acai Oikos Greek yogurt
- 3 cups organic fat-free Greek yogurt
- 2 tablespoons plain fat-free yogurt

EGGS
- 3 DHA-fortified eggs

NUTS, NUT BUTTERS, AND SEEDS
- 1 tablespoon pumpkin seeds
- 40 raw almonds
- 1/2 cup sliced almonds
- 10 walnut halves
- 1 tablespoon chopped walnuts
- 36 pistachios
- 2 tablespoons sunflower seeds
- 6 teaspoons natural peanut butter
- 2 tablespoons ground flaxseed

OILS
- Cold-pressed olive oil
- Canola oil spray

GROCERY

GRAINS:
- 1/2 cup steel-cut oats
- 1 ounce wild rice (1/3 cup cooked)
- 1 ounce bulgur (1/3 cup cooked)
- 1 ounce brown rice (1/3 cup cooked)
- 1 ounce quinoa (1/3 cup cooked)

BREADS:
- 1 slice whole grain bread

CEREALS:
- 1 1/2 cups SmartBran cereal

CRACKERS:
- 2 high-fiber crackers

OTHER PACKAGED FOODS:
- 4 tablespoons hummus
- 1 can pumpkin puree
- 1/8 cup/1 ounce dried mango
- 1/2 cup canned (or frozen) artichoke hearts
- 1/3 cup marinara sauce
- 1 small jar green olives
- 2 tablespoons guacamole
- 1/2 cup chickpeas
- 1/2 cup lentils

POULTRY
- 8 ounces skinless chicken breast
- 4 ounces fresh sliced turkey

SEAFOOD
- 4 ounces salmon
- 4 ounces cod filet
- 4 ounces shrimp
- 4 ounces canned salmon

MEATS
- 4 ounces 85% lean organic ground beef
- 4 ounces lean organic beef

VEGETARIAN
- 4 ounces firm tofu, cubed

HERBS AND SPICES
- Red-pepper flakes
- Sea salt
- Black pepper
- Cinnamon
- Oregano
- Matcha powder
- Ground coffee beans
- Seaweed gomashio (sesame salt)

CONDIMENTS
- Vanilla extract
- Balsamic vinegar
- Lemon vinaigrette
- Dijon mustard
- Rice vinegar

WEEK **6**

PRODUCE

FRESH FRUIT:
1 cup cherries
2 avocados
1 lime
1 grapefruit
½ cup cantaloupe
1 small banana

FRESH VEGETABLES:
1 large red tomato
½ cup cherry tomatoes
4 red bell peppers
3 yellow bell peppers
5 ribs celery
1 small package mushrooms
1 cup cauliflower
¼ cup fresh spinach
1 cup red onion
1 cup broccoli
3 cups baby spinach
2 cups chopped kale
1 artichoke
2½ cups romaine lettuce
½ cup carrots
½ cup zucchini
1 small butternut squash
1 cucumber
1 cup bok choy
1 cup sugar snap peas
½ cup shredded red cabbage
½ cup shredded green cabbage

FRESH HERBS:
2 teaspoons mint

DAIRY

MILK:
1 cup soy milk
1 quart fat-free milk
1 cup almond milk

CHEESE:
2 ounces fresh mozzarella cheese
1 ounce reduced-fat feta cheese
2 ounces goat cheese
½ cup fat-free cottage cheese

YOGURT:
4½ cups organic fat-free Greek yogurt
5.3 oz Oikos Organic Greek Yogurt

EGGS

8 DHA-fortified eggs

NUTS, NUT BUTTERS, AND SEEDS

40 raw almonds
3 tablespoons walnuts
2 Brazil nuts
4 teaspoons natural peanut butter
2 teaspoons almond butter
2 tablespoons sunflower seeds
1 tablespoon pine nuts
2 tablespoons flaxseed
2 tablespoons chia seeds

OILS

Olive oil
Canola oil spray

GROCERY

GRAINS:
2 ounces quinoa (⅔ cup cooked)
1 ounce wild rice (⅓ cup cooked)

BREADS:
3 slices whole grain bread

CRACKERS:
8 high-fiber crackers

OTHER PACKAGED FOODS:
1 cup artichoke hearts, canned or jarred in water
1 cup Amy's Organic Black Bean Chili
4 tablespoons hummus
1 jar green olives
2 corn tortillas
½ cup chickpeas
½ cup lentils

POULTRY

4 ounces grilled chicken breast
4 ounces all-natural chicken sausage
4 ounces turkey

SEAFOOD

4 ounces scallops
4 ounces water-packed chunk light tuna
4 ounces cod

MEATS

4 ounces pork tenderloin
4 ounces beef filet

HERBS AND SPICES

Sea salt
Black pepper
Cinnamon
Dry mustard
Oregano
Matcha powder
Ground coffee beans
Thyme

CONDIMENTS

Vanilla extract
Balsamic vinegar
Lemon vinaigrette
Rice vinegar
Dijon mustard
Salsa
Guacamole

More Options to Personalize Your Plan

To make this plan your own, start with the basic building blocks in the chart below: starches, proteins, milk (or milk substitute), fats, fruits, and of course, lots of vegetables. Then swap in all of your favorite foods! The following are a list of some of my favorite foods to make it super-easy to shop and stock your pantry with healthy, delicious options!

Build a breakfast that includes:

Starch or fruit
Milk or milk substitute
Fat or protein

Build a morning snack that includes:

Fat or protein
Veggie

Build a lunch that includes:

Veggie
Protein
Fat
Starch
(if you aren't having starch at dinner)

Build an afternoon snack that includes:

Milk or milk substitute
Fat

Choose a Happy Hour snack that includes:

Any vegetables. My favorite is veggie soup, but even a cup of crudités works. These add water, volume, and crunch satisfaction at the time of day you need it most.

Build a dinner that includes:

Veggie
Protein
Fat
Starch
(if you didn't have starch at lunch)

STARCHES

Cereals

Generic....................................½ cup

Arrowhead Mills Organic
  Old Fashioned Oatmeal
  Hot Cereal.................... ⅓ cup

Barbara's Bakery Puffins
  Original.........................¾ cup

Barbara's Bakery Ultima
  Organic High Fiber
  Cereal...........................½ cup

Bob's Red Mill Steel-cut
  oats ....¼ cup cooked

Ezekiel 4:9 Sprouted
  Whole Grain Cereal
  Original.........................¼ cup

General Mills
  Wheat Chex..............¾ cup

Kashi GOLEAN..............½ cup

Kashi Good Friends....¾ cup

Kashi Heart to Heart..¾ cup

Kashi 7 Whole Grain..¾ cup

Kellogg's All-Bran........½ cup

McCann's Irish Oatbran
  Hot Cereal....................¼ cup

Nature's Path Organic
  Flax Plus......................¾ cup

Nature's Path Organic
  Optimum Slim............½ cup

Nature's Path Organic
  SmartBran with Psyllium
  & Oatbran...................¾ cup

Nutritious Living
  Hi-Lo 100% Natural
  Cereal..........................½ cup

Post Shredded Wheat
  Wheat 'n Bran...........¾ cup

Quaker Instant
  Oatmeal...................1 packet

Quinoa..............⅓ cup cooked

Uncle Sam ....½ cup

Uncle Sam Instant
  Oatmeal...................1 packet

Waffles

Generic....................1 waffle

Kashi GOLEAN waffles......1

Kashi Heart to Heart
  Waffles...........................1

Nature's Path Organic
  Waffles...........................1

Van's All Natural Multigrain
  Belgian Waffles.................1

Van's Natural Foods Lite
  Totally Natural Waffle....1

Van's Natural Foods Or-
  ganics with
  Vitamin Boost.................1

Bread and Tortillas

Generic..................1 slice bread,
  ½ pita, ½ English muffin, ½ roll
  or bun, 1 small tortilla

Arnold 100% Whole
  Wheat Sandwich
  Thins.............1 sandwich thin

Damascus Bakeries
  Flax Roll-Up............1 roll-up

French Meadow Bakery
  Hemp Bread ....1 slice

French Meadow Bakery
  Men's Bread ....1 slice

La Tortilla Factory
  Smart & Delicious
  Low-Carb High-Fiber
  Tortillas......................1 tortilla

Oroweat Sandwich Thins..1

Matthew's All Natural
  Whole Wheat English
  Muffin...................... 1 muffin

Shiloh Farms Sprouted
  7 Grain Bread,
  Organic.......................1 slice

Thomas' Light Multi-Grain
  English Muffins... ½ muffin

Thomas' 100% Whole
  Wheat Bagel
  Thins .... 1 bagel

Thomas' Sahara 100%
  Whole Wheat Pita
  Bread .... ½ pita

Oroweat Sandwich
  Thins..............................1

Vermont Bread
  Company Whole
  Wheat Bread.............1 slice

Vermont Bread Company
  Soft Whole Wheat
  Bread ....1 slice

Crackers

Generic... Check the packaging
  for portions

Finn Crisp Original 4

Doctor Kracker Klassic
  3 Seed Flatbread............1

GG Scandinavian Bran
  Crispbread.......................5

Kashi TLC Original
  7 Grain Crackers............7

Kavli Hearty Thick
  Crispbread.......................2

Mary's Gone Crackers
  Organic Original......... 4

Ryvita Dark Rye
  Crispbread.......................2

Wasa Fiber Crispbread......2

Chips and Stuff

Generic..............................1 oz.

Bearitos Organic No Salt
  No Oil Microwave Pop-
  corn............. 5 cups, popped

Mary's Gone Crackers
  Sticks & Twigs.....10 pieces

Newman's Own Organics
  Pop's-Corn No-Salt 94%
  Fat Free . 3 ½ cups, popped

Flax Roll-Up.................1 roll-up

French Meadow Bakery
  Hemp Bread ....1 slice

French Meadow Bakery
Men's Bread ....1 slice

La Tortilla Factory
Smart & Delicious
Low-Carb High-Fiber
Tortillas....................1 tortilla

Matthew's All Natural
Whole Wheat English
Muffin........................ 1 muffin

Shiloh Farms Sprouted
7 Grain Bread,
Organic ....1 slice

Thomas' Light Multi-Grain
English Muffins... $\frac{1}{2}$ muffin

Thomas' 100% Whole
Wheat Bagel
Thins .... 1 bagel

Thomas' Sahara 100%
Whole Wheat Pita
Bread .... $\frac{1}{2}$ pita

Vermont Bread
Company Whole
Wheat Bread..............1 slice

Vermont Bread Company
Soft Whole Wheat
Bread ....1 slice

Crackers

Generic...Check the packaging
for portions

Finn Crisp Original 4

Doctor Kracker Klassic
3 Seed Flatbread 1

GG Scandinavian Bran
Crispbread..........................5

Kashi TLC Original
7 Grain Crackers 7

Kavli Hearty Thick
Crispbread 2

Mary's Gone Crackers ....

Organic Original 4

Ryvita Dark Rye
Crispbread.........................2

Wasa Fiber Crispbread......2

Chips and Stuff

Generic................................1 oz.

Bearitos Organic No Salt
No Oil Microwave Pop-
corn .... 5 cups, popped

Mary's Gone Crackers
Sticks & Twigs.....10 pieces

Newman's Own Organics
Pop's-Corn No-Salt 94%
Fat Free ..3 $\frac{1}{2}$ cups, popped

Grains

Generic.............................. $\frac{1}{3}$ cup

Brown rice.........$\frac{1}{3}$ cup cooked

Kamut ....$\frac{1}{3}$ cup cooked

Millet (whole)...$\frac{1}{3}$ cup cooked

Quinoa ....$\frac{1}{3}$ cup cooked

Arrowhead Mills Pearled
Barley..............$\frac{1}{3}$ cup cooked

Barilla Plus Pasta ....$\frac{1}{2}$ cup
cooked

Bob's Red Mill 100% Whole
Grain Quick Cooking
Bulgur Wheat .... $\frac{1}{3}$ cup
cooked

DeBoles Organic
Whole Wheat
Penne ....$\frac{1}{3}$ cup cooked

Eden Organic
Soba Pasta...$\frac{1}{2}$ cup cooked

Hodgson Mill Certified
Organic Whole Wheat
Fettuccine with Milled
Flaxseed........$\frac{1}{2}$ cup cooked

Ian's Panko Breadcrumbs,
Whole Wheat............$\frac{1}{4}$ cup

Kretschmer Original
Toasted Wheat
Germ .... 3 Tbsp

Near East Long Grain &
Wild Rice.......$\frac{1}{3}$ cup cooked

Near East Whole
Grain Blends Brown
Rice Pilaf ....$\frac{1}{3}$ cup cooked

Near East Whole
Grain Blends Wheat
Couscous, Original
Plain................$\frac{1}{3}$ cup cooked

Starchy Vegetables

Generic......................... $\frac{1}{2}$–1 cup

Acorn Squash..$\frac{1}{2}$ cup cooked

Butternut Squash..........1 cup
cooked

Corn (ear) ....1 small

Corn (frozen)................$\frac{1}{2}$ cup

Peas.................................$\frac{1}{2}$ cup

Potato (baked with
skin) ....1 small

Spaghetti Squash..........1 cup
cooked

Sweet Potato (baked
with skin) ....1 small

Amy's Organic Light
in Sodium Split Pea
Soup ....1 cup

Dr. Praeger's Pancakes
(Spinach, Broccoli,
Sweet Potato)....1 pancake

Pacific Organic Light
Sodium Creamy
Butternut Squash
Soup ....1 cup

Imagine Organic Creamy
Butternut Squash or
Creamy Sweet Pea
Soup ....1 cup

Legumes

Generic................................$\frac{1}{2}$ cup

Black Beans.....................$\frac{1}{2}$ cup

Black-Eyed Peas..........$\frac{1}{2}$ cup

Chickpeas........................$\frac{1}{2}$ cup

Kidney Beans..................$\frac{1}{2}$ cup

Lentils...............................$\frac{1}{2}$ cup

Pinto Beans.....................$\frac{1}{2}$ cup

Split Peas ....$\frac{1}{2}$ cup

White (Cannellini)
Beans...........................$\frac{1}{2}$ cup

Amy's Organic Chili
Medium Black Bean1 cup

Tribe All Natural
Hummus Classic.... 2 Tbsp

MILK OR MILK SUBSTITUTE

Generic................................ 6-8 oz

Almond Dream Almond
   Milk (original)............... 8 oz

Chobani Non-Fat Greek
   Yogurt (plain)............. 6 oz

Emmi Swiss Premium Lowfat
   Plain Yogurt................. 5.3 oz

Fage Total 0% Greek
   Yogurt (plain)............. 6 oz

Friendship Lowfat 1%
   Cottage Cheese ...... ½ cup

Horizon Organic
   Skim Milk........................ 1 oz

Lactaid Fat Free Milk ... 1 cup

Light n' Lively Lowfat
   Cottage Cheese ..... ½ cup

Oikos Organic Greek
   Yogurt (plain).......................

Rice Dream Rice Drink. 4 oz

Silk Live! Soy Yogurt ..... 8 oz

Silk Original Soymilk ..... 8 oz

Silk Soy DHA Omega-3
   Milk...................................... 8 oz

Skim Plus Milk .... 1 cup

Stonyfield Organic

0% Plain Yogurt.......... 8 oz

Stonyfield Organic
   Fat Free Milk................. 4 oz

Tempt Original
   Hemp Milk...................... 8 oz

WestSoy Lite Plain
   Soymilk Drink............... 8 oz

VEGETABLES

Generic No portion when there
             is no added fat

Alfalfa Sprouts

Artichokes

Artichoke Hearts

Arugula

Asparagus

Bamboo Shoots

Bean Sprouts

Beets

Broccoli

Brussels Sprouts

Cabbage

Carrots

Cauliflower

Celery

Cherry Tomatoes

Cucumber

Dandelion Greens

Eggplant

Escarole

Green Beans

Green Onions/Scallions

Hearts of Palm

Iceberg Lettuce

Jicama

Kabul Seaweed Noodles

Kale

Leeks

Mushrooms

Onion

Peppers, Bell
   (green and red)

Radish

Romaine Lettuce

Sauerkraut

Snow Peas

Spaghetti Squash

Spinach (cooked and raw)

Swiss Chard

Tomato

Turnips

Water Chestnut

Watercress

Yellow Squash

Zucchini

Amy's Organic Chunky
   Vegetable Soup.......... 1 cup

Bird's Eye Artichoke
   Hearts (frozen)........... 1 cup

Colavita Marinara
   Sauce .... ½ cup

Healthy Delites Souffle
   (Roasted Vegetable,
   Zucchini, Spinach, or
   Broccoli)................. 1 souffle

Imagine Organic Light in
   Sodium Creamy Garden
   Broccoli Soup or Tomato
   Soup .... 1 cup

Imagine Natural Creamy
   Portobello Mushroom
   Soup .... 1 cup

Pacific Organic Light So-
   dium Creamy Tomato or
   Roasted Red Pepper and
   Tomato Soup.............. 1 cup

Seapoint Farms
   Veggie Blends with
   Edamame.................... 1 cup

V8 Juice............................. 8 oz

PROTEIN

Poultry

Chicken Breast

Cornish Hen

Turkey Breast

Aidells Chicken & Turkey Meatballs

Applegate Organics Roasted Chicken Breast (deli slices)

Applegate Organics Roasted Turkey Breast (deli slices)

Applegate Organics Turkey Bacon

Applegate Organics Turkey Burgers (frozen)

Bell & Evans Grilled Chicken Breasts (fully cooked, plain)

FreeBird Seasoned Grilled Chicken Breast Strips

Shady Brook Farms 93/7 Lean Ground Turkey

SnackMasters Range Grown Turkey Jerky, Original

Fish

Clams

Cod

Flounder

Halibut

Imitation Crab (Surimi)

King Crab

Lobster

Mahi Mahi

Mussels

Red Snapper

Salmon (wild)

Scallops (large sea)

Shrimp (fresh or frozen)

Sole

Swordfish

Trout

Tuna (bluefin, raw)

Tuna (canned chunk light in water), Tongol, Crown Prince

Tuna (fresh, cooked)

Henry & Lisa's Uncooked Natural Shrimp, Farm Raised

Sardines in Pure Spring Water

SnackMasters Natural Ahi Tuna Jerky

SnackMasters Natural Salmon Jerky

Whole Foods Whole Catch Wild Alaskan Sockeye Salmon Fillets (frozen)

St. Dalfour Ready to Eat Gourmet to Go Wild Salmon with Vegetables

Meat

Beef, 95% Lean Ground

Beef, Sirloin

Beef, T-Bone

Beef, Tenderloin

Canadian Bacon

Ham, Extra Lean

Lamb Loin

Pork, Center Loin Chops

Pork, Cutlet

Pork, Tenderloin

Veal, Loin

All Natural Great Range Brand Bison Patties

Applegate Organics Roast Beef (deli slices)

Laura's 92% Lean Frozen Ground Beef Patties

Eggs

Eggology 100% Egg Whites

Eggology On-the-Go 100% Egg Whites

Papetti's Better'n Eggs

Hot Dogs and Sausages

Aidells Chicken & Apple Sausage

Applegate The Great Organic Uncured Chicken Hot Dog

Applegate The Great Organic Uncured Turkey Hot Dog Applegate Organics Chicken and Apple Sausage

Bilinski's Organic or All Natural Chicken Sausage

Casual Gourmet Chicken Sausage

The Original Brat Hans Organic Breakfast Links Chicken Sausage

Wellshire Farms Chicken Sausage or Turkey Kielbasa

Soy Products

Tempeh

Dr. Praeger's California Veggie Burger

House Foods Tofu Shirataki noodles

House Foods Tofu Steak
Grilled

Lightlife Organic Tempeh

Woodstock Farms Organic
Firm Tofu

Whole Foods Market
Whole Kitchen Vegan
Meatballs

Legumes

Black Beans....................½ cup

Black-Eyed Peas............½ cup

Chickpeas........................½ cup

Kidney Beans..................½ cup

Lentils................................½ cup

Pinto Beans.....................½ cup

Split Peas........................½ cup

White (Cannellini)
Beans..........................½ cup

Health Valley Organic
40% Less Sodium
Black Bean
Vegetable Soup.........1 cup

Tribe All Natural
Hummus..........................4 T

Cheese

Cottage Cheese (low-fat
or fat-free)..................½ cup

Feta Cheese.....................3 oz

Mozzarella Cheese.........3 oz

Other Reduced-Fat
Cheeses

Whole-milk cheeses,
especially goat or feta
cheeses..........................3 oz

FATS

Oils and Dressings

Canola oil spray................ 2 tsp

Coconut Oil, Spectrum
    or Nutiva .... 2 tsp

Corn Oil.............................. 2 tsp

Flaxseed Oil...................... 2 tsp

Grapeseed Oil .... 2 tsp

Olive Oil .... 2 tsp

Safflower Oil .... 2 tsp

Salad Dressing
    (oil-based) .... 1 Tbsp

Sunflower Oil.................... 2 tsp

Walnut Oil......................... 2 tsp

Olives and Cheese

American Cheese .... 1 slice
        (Note: higher in fat)

Goat cheese...................... 1 oz

Olives (large) 6

Olives (small)...................... 10

Parmesan Cheese
    (grated) .... 3 Tbsp

Alpine Lace Reduced
    Sodium Muenster
    Cheese .... 1 slice

Alpine Lace Reduced
    Fat Swiss Cheese ... 1 slice

Athenos Crumbled
    Feta................................ 1/4 cup

Athenos Reduced-Fat
    Crumbled Feta .... 1/4 cup

Cabot 50% Reduced Fat
    Sharp Cheddar
    Cheese .... 1 oz cube

Cabot Reduced Fat with
    Omega 3 DHA .... 1 oz

Friendship All Natural
    Farmer Cheese....... 2 Tbsp

Horizon Organic Shredded
    Part-Skim Mozzarella
    Cheese .... 1/4 cup

Horizon Organic
    Mozzarella String
    Cheese .... 1 stick

The Laughing Cow
    Light Cheese
    Wedges .... 2 wedges

The Laughing Cow
    Mini Babybel Light
    Cheese .... 1 piece

Organic Valley Stringles
    Part Skim Mozzarella
    Cheese 1

Nuts, Nut Butters, and Seeds

Almonds................................. 8

Barney Butter............... 2 tsp

Brazil Nuts............................. 2

Ground Flaxseed........ 2 Tbsp

Hazelnuts.............................. 8

Nuttzo Nut Butter........ 2 tsp

Peanuts............................... 15

Pecan Halves....................... 8

Pine Nuts .... 1 Tbsp

Pistachio Nuts................... 18

Pumpkin Seeds .... 1 Tbsp

Sunflower Seeds .... 1 Tbsp

Soy Nuts......................... 1 Tbsp

Walnut Halves....... 7 or 1 Tbsp
                chopped

Arrowhead Mills
    Organic Valencia
    Peanut Butter .... 2 tsp

Blue Diamond Whole
    Natural Almonds 100
    Calories Per Bag...... 1 pack

Carrington Farms
    Flax Paks................. 1 packet

Health Warrior Chia
    Seeds .... 2 Tbsp

Justin's All-Natural Classic
    Almond Butter .... 2 tsp

Justin's Organic Classic
    Peanut Butter .... 2 tsp

MaraNatha Organic
    Almond Butter .... 2 tsp

Naturally More Natural
    Peanut Butter .... 2 tsp

Smucker's Natural
    Peanut Butter .... 2 tsp

Eggs

Country Hen Organic
    Omega-3 Eggs ...... 1 extra
                    large

Horizon Organic Eggs........ 1

Land O Lakes Omega 3
    All-Natural Eggs .... 1 large

Fruit

Avocado.................. 1/4 medium

FRUITS

Generic...... 1 small fruit or 1 cup cubes or berries

Apple.................................... 1 small

Apricot (dried) .... 9 halves

Apricot (fresh)............. 3 small

Banana .... 1 small

Blackberries ....1 cup

Blueberries......................1 cup

Cantaloupe ....1 cup

Cherries.............................½ cup

Figs .... 2 medium

Grapefruit .... ½ fruit

Grapes (seedless)............... 15

Honeydew ....1 cup

Kiwi..1

Mango .... ½ medium

Mixed Fruit Cup ....1 cup

Orange .... 1 medium

Papaya...............................1 cup

Passion Fruit .... 3 medium

Peach .... 1 medium

Pear ....1 small

Pineapple...........................1 cup

Plum................................. 1 large

Pomegranate......... ½ medium

Prunes.......................................3

Raspberries ....1 cup

Strawberries (sliced)....1 cup

Watermelon ....1 cup

Santa Cruz Organic Apple Sauce .... 4 oz

index

Boldface page references indicate photographs. Underscored references indicate boxed text.

examination, yet its verbal nature makes it seem analogous to objects of literary criticism. And while it is true that a critic viewing a painting takes in first one part, then another, and the critic of music hears sounds in sequence in time, the critic of a live speech faces a more exacting assignment. He must see and hear sequences. Often he will not even have the drama critic's advantage of being able to consult a script before or after seeing and hearing the object he is to criticize.

The speech critic deals with a critical object which usually exists once and only once. There may be no public preview of it, and there may be no subsequent record. Speeches may be on identical subjects and in identical words, but exact duplication is impossible. The components in the speech situation are constantly shifting; the critic can perceive a whole speech only once. He may record judgments and reactions, but he cannot depend upon repeated exposures to the critical object.

To complicate matters further, the speech critic cannot always be present when the speech he wishes to criticize takes place. For example, he may choose to criticize a speech delivered in the past. Or he may decide to criticize oral utterance only after finding that it was of some importance to society or exerted some particular influence. In these situations he is unable to experience the *real* speech. Nonetheless, several alternative critical objects are available to him.

The most advantageous of these alternatives rarely exists. It is conceivable, though not very likely, that our would-be critic could obtain a sound motion picture that made all possible observations of visual and audible elements. A film of this sort would come closest to reproducing the real speech, but it cannot reproduce the speech situation because it will lack three-dimensional factors. The film is obviously not as reliable as on-the-spot observation for assessing such factors as environment and audience reaction. And this alternative will seldom be open to the critic, for even where films are available they usually contain only portions of major speeches.

A second alternative critical object is some form of electrical transcription of the sounds of the speech. This form of the speech

knowledge as possible to bear when we respond to discourse. To equip us for such informed responses is a general object of all liberal education and a special object of speech courses.

The broad aims of a liberal education are to stimulate you to think in a variety of ways, to increase your ability to judge, to enable you to choose among alternatives, and to prepare you to take a responsible place in the world. We have explored theories with you to enlarge your understanding and described procedures and methods to enable you to fill your roles as public speaker and listener to speeches. As a final matter we invite you to consider how to form useful critical judgments.

We know there are those who believe that students are too young and inexperienced to be critics. But we believe criticism of live speeches is an important and necessary aspect of your study of public speaking. You were not prepared to function as a critic during the first rounds of speaking, but with some theories at your command you are ready and able to evaluate speeches with regard to those principles at least. Most important, critical activity will benefit you both as a speaker and as a private person.

The audience reactions revealed to you in early speeches are valuable. By knowing what your audience thought of your first speeches, you can improve your adaptation to the group in your later efforts. We are not saying audiences ever remain the same. By living a day longer your classroom audience changes each time you meet. Nonetheless, there are some criteria by which they measure effective speaking which do not change from session to session. Their consistent standards and recurring judgments can teach you much about speech and yourself.

Criticism in the classroom is a reciprocal activity. By openly registering your responses to your peers, you will aid immensely in their improvement, just as their frank responses to your speech-making will provide you with directions for improvement and always with insights into how others judge speaking.

To exercise full responsibility as a critic, you need to develop powers of discrimination and to know the methods and standards for criticism. We believe that preparing oral and written criticisms of live speeches and written criticisms of the texts of outstanding speeches are constructive experiences. We say with Dean Everett L. Hunt that

> . . . we might be better satisfied with the returns from the money and energy spent on rhetorical training if we cared more about producing educated and critical audiences. . . . Critical and analytical study of rhetoric and oratory should not be limited to those who expect to become professional speakers or writers, or to those who expect to teach it; it should be offered to all students who desire to understand the significance of rhetoric in modern life.[1]

Whether or not you are invited to criticize spoken or written public speeches at any juncture in your public speaking course, you owe it to yourself as a part of liberal education to develop standards of judgment and critical acuity toward the speeches you will hear, read, or deliver in future days or years. For this you must understand criticism, the standards and methods commonly employed in evaluating speeches, and the tasks you can effectively undertake as a critic of the speeches you will find in the laboratory of the classroom and elsewhere.

The Nature of Speech
Criticism

Criticism of any kind is judgment and/or appreciation. To evaluate or criticize implies analysis and comparison, approval or disapproval, commendation or censure. All reactions to objects, ideas, actions, and persons are critical or noncritical. Assessments or evaluations are criticism. Descriptions, reviews, commentaries, and surveys, unless interpretative, are not.

Criticism is essentially a comparative activity involving discrimination. Whenever we make a judgment or register appreciation, we do so with some standards of perfection in mind.

---

[1] "Editorial: 'From Rhetoric Deliver Us,'" *The Quarterly Journal of Speech*, XIV (April 1928), 266–267.

Where we are subjective in our judgments, our standards likely to be very personal. We may not even be conscious of t' Where we become objective, we tend to become consciously a of our norms and to identify them in our minds or on p Whichever cast of mind characterizes our criticism, we have standards and our judgments place what we judge some along a continuum of excellence. The object of our appra contrasted to norms, or measured by them, and found to spond in some degree. Either the item corresponds closely standards or it does not.

The Critical Object

A focus upon some object is essential in any type of critici object may be tangible or intangible. It may be a material bination of materials, an action or an idea. In aesthetic this object may be a specific painting such as Picass Lovers''; a pattern of sounds such as Beethoven's Fifth S interpreted by a great orchestra; or physical action perf dancers, such as the *pas de deux* from *The Firebird*. C literary criticism are novels, short stories, poems, or essa in the tangible form of printed words on a page. Wh kind of criticism, some object exists to be appreciat evaluated and perhaps to be praised or condemned.

The critic who assesses a live speech, the speech as ered, deals with a distinctive critical object. What h appreciates, and judges consists of a combination of actions symbolizing ideas, existing in time, and cutt air. This object is in constant flight, not static, not a unlike some other critical objects. It is not a statue placed on a pedestal and viewed from all sides. It is score nor a play script which can be consulted. It is r which can be gazed at for hours. It is not print which over. The critical object in speech-making cannot be either eye or ear alone. It must be seen and hea moments of its creation. Like the dance, it does no eliminates all possibilities for considering its visual aspects, but it does allow some evaluation of vocal performance. The current practice of many speech critics is to tape speeches at the time of observation and then to use the tapes as checks on the accuracy of their impressions. If a critic cannot make his own electrical recording, he may try to obtain one through a radio or television station or buy one which has been commercially marketed. The availability of such recordings is limited, and, of course, obtaining a recording of an orator who spoke in the early days of sound recording provides a critical object of dubious quality.

More often, the critic who was not present when a speech was delivered will have to content himself with some written record: a handwritten manuscript, a typed or mimeographed script, or a printed page. Fortunately, he may pore over, analyze, outline, and study this kind of record. He may be able to supplement a script with other written accounts that help him reconstruct the milieu, the occasion, and audience reaction. He may be able to read the criticisms others wrote after the speech was delivered. He may, and often does, use the various methods of historical, literary, and experimental studies. But even with all these aids his critical object remains the least satisfactory of those we have discussed.

The critical objects for critics of speeches, then, are four. The object may be the live, pulsating, reacted-to utterance of the moment; a film; an electrical transcription; or a manuscript or printed text. These critical objects chiefly distinguish rhetorical criticism from other kinds of criticism.

The purpose of public speaking also influences speech criticism. Public speaking seeks to gain immediate or long-range response or both, and it must be judged in the light of its purpose. It is possible to judge the literary value, the historical significance, and the moral qualities of speeches, but these judgments alone cannot yield full appreciation or analysis of a speech. They do not produce evaluations recognizing that the primary purpose of speech-making is practical.

Wichelns, in his essay entitled "The Literary Criticism of Oratory," says of rhetorical criticism:

> . . . we find that its point of view is patently single. It is not concerned with permanence, nor yet with beauty [as may be the case in the judgment of literature]. It is concerned with effect. It regards a speech as a communication to a specific audience and holds its business to be the analysis and appreciation of the orator's method of imparting his ideas to his hearers.[2]

Wichelns was thinking mainly of criticism as a scholarly activity involving the analysis of speech texts, but what he says applies to critics who hear and see speeches as well as to those who read them. His elaboration of rhetorical criticism bears quotation.

> Rhetorical criticism is necessarily analytical. The scheme of a rhetorical study includes the elements of the speaker's personality as a conditioning factor; it includes also the public character of the man—not what he was, but what he was thought to be. It requires a description of the speaker's audience, and of the leading ideas with which he plied his hearers—his topics, the motives to which he appealed, the nature of the proofs he offered. These will reveal his own judgment of human nature in his audiences, and also his judgment on the questions which he discussed. Attention must be paid, too, to the relation of the surviving texts to what was actually uttered: in case the nature of the changes is known, there may be occasion to consider adaptation to two audiences—that which heard and that which read. Nor can rhetorical criticism omit the speaker's mode of arrangement and his mode of expression, nor his habit of preparation and his manner of delivery from the platform; though the last two are perhaps less significant. "Style"—in the sense which corresponds to diction and sentence movement—must receive attention, but only as one among various means that secure for the speaker ready access to the minds of his auditors. Finally, the effect of the discourse on its immediate hearers is not to be ignored, either in the testimony of witnesses, nor in the record of events. And throughout such a study one must conceive of the public man as influencing the men of his own times by the power of his discourse.[3]

---

[2] Herbert A. Wichelns, "The Literary Criticism of Oratory," in *Studies in Rhetoric and Public Speaking in Honor of James Albert Winans* (New York: Century, 1925), p. 209. Reprinted in Donald C. Bryant, ed., *The Rhetorical Idiom* (Ithaca: Cornell University Press, 1958), pp. 1–42.

[3] *Ibid.*, pp. 212–213 or pp. 38–39.

As a critic analyzes and evaluates he ought to keep the demands of the audience, the material, the occasion, and the speaker uppermost in his mind. The assignment that faced the speaker should be a primary consideration as the critic describes and then sets forth what ought to have been said and how it ought to have been said under the peculiar circumstances which constituted the demands of the speaker's situation.

It is also of value to turn to what rhetorical criticism is not. Loren D. Reid, in reflecting upon the myopia of young critics, warns:

> Rhetorical criticism is not simply a discussion of the speaker's ideas, . . . not simply a narrative of the circumstances under which a speech is delivered, . . . not simply a classification or tabulation of rhetorical devices, . . . [and] not primarily an excursion into other fields of learning.[4]

The perils Reid enumerates all lead to mere description or too-simple comment on a speech. A preoccupation with any of them will produce something less than significant critical judgments. Constructive criticism, as we have said, involves evaluation as well as description. Accordingly, the critic's values—his point of view —inevitably color his criticism.

Critical Points of View

THE PRAGMATIC VIEWPOINT

Value systems underlie all our judgments of speech-making. Whether we wish to call them critical standards or philosophies, we all hold basic tenets which determine qualities we emphasize in our assessments. Perhaps the most important of these viewpoints is the pragmatic, that which in speech criticism stresses the speech's effects. This emphasis underlies Wichelns' distinction between

---

[4] "The Perils of Rhetorical Criticism," *The Quarterly Journal of Speech,* XXX (December 1944), 416–422.

rhetorical criticism and other kinds of comment about speeches. Weaver, Borchers, and Smith call it the "empirical standard."[5] McBurney and Wrage label it "the results theory" of criticism.[6]

Under this philosophy the consideration of the speech becomes an especially practical matter. We ask, "Was the speech effective? Did it elicit the response sought? Did it achieve the intended result? Did it fulfill its purpose?" In the classroom we are also likely to ask, "Did the speech fulfill the assignment for which it was designed?"

We tend to measure the success of a speech on the basis of immediate rather than long-range effectiveness, forgetting that failure to attain an immediate, visible response may not mean the speech was a failure. A speech may not elicit immediate response; its effects may operate over a period of time. Who can declare that the speeches proposing the St. Lawrence Seaway in the 1920's had absolutely no favorable effect? Some of the persuasive speeches given a generation ago may have contributed toward producing the eventual decision to build the seaway. To base judgment of over-all quality on immediate response alone is not entirely fair. The speeches of a political campaigner may be excellent in many respects, but due to extrinsic forces it may be impossible for any speaking to win an electoral victory.

Of course, we cannot dismiss effect completely. Practically, the speech must get an effect to do its work. Yet, to consider only immediate or even long-range effects will produce but a partial evaluation.

THE ETHICAL VIEWPOINT[7]

A second value system underlying speech judgments arises from a special interest in judging intention. If the motives of a

---

[5] See Andrew T. Weaver, Gladys L. Borchers and Donald K. Smith, *The Teaching of Speech* (Englewood Cliffs, N.J.: Prentice-Hall, 1952), pp. 497–498.

[6] See James H. McBurney and Ernest J. Wrage, *The Art of Good Speech* (New York: Prentice-Hall, 1953), pp. 22–24.

[7] This viewpoint, as we discuss it, involves both ethical and truth considerations. McBurney and Wrage see these as separate theories. See *ibid.*, pp. 24–28.

speaker are in line with ours and if his intentions are admirable, we may praise him for upholding what we think is the right position. In viewing a speech from such a vantage point we ask, "Is the speaker honest, sincere, courageous in the beliefs he enunciates? Is he truthful? Is he consistent? Is he on the side of good?"

These are all good questions which should not be overlooked by any thoughtful critic. Certainly, as critics, we would not wish to hold up as exemplary that which is untrue, biased, or designed to hurt the audience. We cannot underscore strongly enough that lying, cheating, plagiarizing, and speaking with bad intent are reprehensible. We must pause, however, to consider that an oral discourse may be filled with truths and be based on the soundest motives and still not represent an intelligent or artistic use of the resources of human speech. Who would deny that some clergymen and professors honorably present what they believe to be truth and still prove poor preachers and lecturers?

So, we say first, that ethical merit, even though highly prized, cannot guarantee quality or even competence in speech making. Secondly, it is very hard in some instances to discover a speaker's motives. It is not always possible to declare he is sincere, honest, acting with good will, or appealing ethically to the feelings of his auditors. Lastly, it is well to bear in mind that ethical standards vary from society to society, group to group, era to era, and age level to age level. Ethical standards are relative. And the question, "How can we know truth?" is still in dispute among philosophers. This is not to say that we, as critics, can dodge responsibility for making those ethical judgments that are plainly and defensibly open to us. A function of humane education is to aid discovery of truth and formulation of a system of values. Still, even where we can make fair and supportable judgments on the ethical merits of a speech, these cannot be made the sole standards of judgment applied to rhetorical efforts.

THE ARTISTIC VIEWPOINT

A third value system esteems artistic excellence. It calls upon the critic to judge on the basis of the skill with which the theories and principles of an art have been applied. The artistic viewpoint

> . . . holds that speech is an art reducible to principles. Good speech is constructed on these principles, exhibits these principles to the discerning critic, and may be judged by these principles. Any speech in any situation for any purpose is good in the degree to which it measures up to or incorporates these principles, and is poor speech in the degree to which it does not.[8]

An artistic value system sometimes places great weight upon the skill with which the resources of an act have been used. Such a system is really eclectic, for it formulates criteria to be applied with an eye to both effectiveness and ethical worth. It calls upon the critic (1) to know the particular methods and norms to be applied to speeches, (2) to perceive whether or not these standards have been applied skillfully and unobtrusively, and (3) to offer what judgments he can fairly defend concerning the public worth of the speech as a whole. To the authors of this book the artistic viewpoint seems most likely to produce comprehensive and practically useful speech criticism.

Critical Criteria

It is not enough to base criticism of speeches upon a value system. You must also be specific in passing judgment on the choices a speaker makes, and this entails accurate, fair description of what the speaker did. Your description need not always involve detailed or intricate observations, but there must be awareness of the speaker's matter and method. Particularly in classroom criticism, where one goal of criticism is to teach, it is essential to know each speaker's purpose. Purpose will determine which aspects of speaking were crucial to success and which were not. As you move from awareness of the total speech to specific judgments on how well principles and techniques were applied, the facts of the speech, its purpose, and relevant circumstances need to be held in your mind. But the relative importance of these descriptive data will alter as you move from speech to speech.

[8] *Ibid.*, pp. 28–29.

364

CRITICAL HIERARCHIES

The aspects of speaking which you choose to evaluate will form a hierarchy in your mind as you approach the task of judging. On one occasion the organization of the speech may be the item at the top of your hierarchy, the most important aspect of the speech to be judged. On another, structure will be far down the list. This is particularly true when you are judging classroom speeches. When you have been concentrating on organization and outlining in class, structure may loom as the most important thing to be considered in oral criticism or in the notes you provide for the speaker. In listening to a lecture by a learned professor or to a court plea, structure may be important but not as important as the speaker's selection of topics or arguments or the evidence he uses as support. Structure then moves down from the head of the list of rhetorical resources under critical consideration to second or third place. In criticizing another speech, you may find yourself discounting both disposition and invention while heavily weighing the speaker's stylistic achievements. You may conclude that the ideas are worn, that structure was dictated so the speaker had little choice of patterns, given his situation. The topical or chronological patterns may seem to you about the only appropriate ones for this speaker to use. Given such circumstances, you may decide that originality in wordings and use of images were the chief resources open to the speaker in his effort to produce response through artistic utterance. So you may move style, delivery, invention, and all their attendant aspects ahead of structure in your evaluation of this speaker's accomplishments.

Thus, a critic's hierarchy of criteria shifts constantly depending upon the aims of the speaker, his subject matter, and the occasion. You must decide upon your critical hierarchy each time you criticize a speech. As you listen or read to describe and evaluate, you must separate the important from the unimportant qualities of discourse. If you do not, you may end by concentrating on trivial matters to the neglect of items that deserved most attention.

You will need to guard against developing fixations. For some, voice or bodily action always occupies first place. They seem easiest to comment on. In your critiques of classmates the danger sign is present if you always say: "Jim doesn't make any gestures," or "John has too many breaks in fluency," or "Sandra mispronounces cement, column, and coupon," or "George rattled the keys and change in his pocket—most distracting!" All you have said may be true, but you also must focus on the total speech or its most important aspects, unless delivery is your only concern.

DETAILING THE CRITERIA

Once you decide which matters are most important in criticizing a specific speech, you will become concerned with other specific judgments. Usually you will start with the broader aspects of the speech and work to the details. In assessing a speech of information, for example, you will want first to ask yourself questions about the speech as a speech: Did it have an identifiable central purpose? Did it have a recognizable introduction, body, and conclusion? What was the quality of its total impact? Descriptive data thus become bases for specific evaluations.

Next, you will want to ask questions about the speech as a speech of information. You might ask, "Does the audience understand the subject better now that they have heard this speech?" Then you may pose questions relating directly to expository techniques: "Was there justification in the subject matter and in the audience's interest for the way this speaker used exposition, description, and narration at various points? Did this speech meet the special demands for good expository speaking by being accurate, clear, and interesting? Were visual aids used to clarify points or for their own sake?"

From these kinds of questions you may turn to specific details which may or may not be exclusively applicable to informative speeches. Here you will ask such questions as: "Did the story of the male student who knitted his own socks and ate light bulbs illustrate originality or peculiarity?" "Were reliable statistics used to show the relation between monetary support and the quality of higher education? Were they truly representative?" "Were appropriate gestures used to support the idea that schools are bursting with students? Well coordinated? Definite enough?" "Isn't the word pronounced gri-*mace*, not *grim*-ace?" These and like questions complete your movement: evaluating the speech as a speech, then as a particular kind of speech, and finally as a work consisting of detailed strengths and weaknesses.

Criticism sheets used to assess classroom speaking will sometimes assist you in deciding which questions to ask and which questions are most important. The criticism sheet we have designed for classroom use is reproduced on p. 368. It provides for both structured and unstructured comment. Aspects of speech-making that need constant attention when considering any kind of speech are arranged along the left side of the paper with spaces in which quick reactions can be entered while the speech is being delivered. The right half of the sheet provides space for personal notations and revised, final reactions to the speech. The box in the lower right-hand corner encourages the user to recommend areas for improvement and so points up the constructive aspect of the critic's task.

The Critical Act

IN THE CLASSROOM

A good classroom critic, like a good speaker, considers the import his observations will have for his audience. He aims for and expresses judgments which cast the most light for the largest number. In public evaluations he side-steps purely personal preferences and those problems of concern only to a particular speaker. Instead of commenting orally on one speaker's peculiar vocal habit, he dwells on problems common to all speakers. He concentrates only on strengths or faults often found in the speeches heard in class. All faults are fair game for the critic to treat constructively, but in the classroom as elsewhere matters having general applica-

NAME: SPEECH NO.:   Symbols:
SUBJECT: DATE: X—No
                                                 √—Yes
SUBJECT AND PURPOSE   Grades:
   Subject worthwhile? _____   Papers:
   Purpose delimited? _____   Speech:
                                                 For the round:
CONTENT AND ORGANIZATION   Consult Instruc-
  Introduction   tor? _____
   Get attention? _____
   Needed information given? _____   _____
   Purpose made clear? _____
  Development
   Organization—soundly planned? _____
    —easily followed? _____
    —transitions effective? _____
    —internal summaries appropriate? _____
   Supporting Material—clear? _____
    —interesting? _____
    —convincing? _____
    —visual aids effective? _____
  Conclusion
   Provide a note of finality? _____
   Whole speech in focus? _____

DELIVERY
  Mental Alertness
   Realize each idea as uttered? _____
   Keen sense of communication? _____
  Body
   Eye contact adequate? _____
   Posture acceptable? _____
   Movement meaningful? _____
   Gestures effective? _____
  Voice
   Distinct? _____
   Vocal variety adequate? _____
    Rate? _____ Pitch? _____ Volume? _____
   Fluency adequate? _____

LANGUAGE
  Have good oral qualities? _____
  Convey ideas clearly? _____
  Grammar correct? _____   NEXT TIME work especially for:
  Pronunciation correct? _____
  Increase interest and impact? _____

OVERALL EVALUATION
  Adapted to situation and audience? _____
  Purpose fulfilled? _____
  Make good personal impression? _____
  Interesting? _____

tion deserve public comment; basically personal matters are best criticized in private conferences or in tactful notes.

Your education as a speech critic begins in the classroom. To make the most of it and to give others greatest benefit from it we suggest you approach classroom criticism in the following ways.

1. *Ready yourself for your critical task by preparing to concentrate on what you will see and hear.* Focus, visually and aurally, upon the speech being made. You must listen intently (See Chapter 3, pp. 67–70). Try to rid yourself of distractions from without and within. Exclude all bids for attention except those of the speaker.

2. *Locate your critical criteria consciously.* Decide what you are listening for, what aspects of the speech deserve your special consideration because of their importance in this speaking situation. In other words, decide which aspects will rank highest in your critical hierarchy. By attending to the facets of speech-making which you are currently studying in class, you will give your criticism purpose. The more specific you can be in determining your critical purposes, the more specific will be your description, hence your evaluation.

Do not try to observe every aspect of the speech at once. Try to feel its full impact, of course, but select several important items for observation, analysis, and critical description. You cannot describe and evaluate all the phenomena of a speech, so let your critical criteria define the scope of your analysis and register your reactions accordingly. Scattering your attention over too many items will be of little service to the speaker and will impede the development of your own critical faculties. A speaker will not be helped by superficial comments about a dozen things. You will not be helped by trying to judge a host of items in haphazard fashion. Aim to substantiate and develop a few major critical judgments.

3. *Adopt a constructive attitude.* As you try to detect the choices the speaker has made, consider the alternatives. As you note merits and flaws, ask: "What might have been done in this situation given the speaker's purpose?" "What constructive sug-

gestions can I offer for future improvement?" Negative comment registering only personal impressions without substantiating evidence or affirmative suggestions will be of little help. To say, "Your speech was poorly organized" or even, "Your economic argument was unsound" does not get to the heart of the matter, because it does not get to the "why" of the trouble. It does not offer *full* analysis of the critical object. "You didn't look at your audience," "Your sentences were clumsy," or "You committed several grammatical errors" may be useful lead-off generalizations in evaluating a speech, but unless they are accompanied by suggestions for correction they offer no help. Such comments illustrate criticism but not rhetorical criticism.

Starting speech criticisms with the positive things, the strong points of the speech, and leading to the less praiseworthy works well. The speaker will listen to what you say, will know that you are not picking him apart for selfish reasons, and will be likely to remember both the things he did well and those he did poorly. It has been said, "Only those who have the heart to help have a right to criticize."

4. *Measure the speech against the criteria you are applying.* Set clearly in mind the three basic aspects to be examined in a speech: effectiveness, ethical worth, and artistry. Measure what the speaker does against specific criteria relating to ideas, proofs, arrangement, style, and delivery. Keep the situation uppermost in your mind as you make your educated guesses on the effectiveness, truth, and skill of what the speaker is doing.

As you listen, jot down reminders of your descriptive observations and the criteria you are applying, then note your judgments along with the most pertinent examples and illustrations. A few notes to serve as reminders will do. Do not become a stenographer. You are a member of an audience as well as a critic and should remember that no speaker can be at his best when trying to address a roomful of bowed heads. Neither can a critic function effectively without giving himself opportunity to take in the visual as well as the aural elements of communication.

Remember that your job is to judge the speech-making, not the personality of the speaker. Of course, there is never a speech without a speaker, but your business is to assess his platform personality as a part of the speech. Consider how his ethos contributes to the speech, not what contributes to your like or dislike for him as a person.

5. *Make a judgment.* This admonition may sound superfluous, but we make it because we have found it is often needed. In too many cases you will be tempted merely to describe what you see and hear. Description is, to be sure, a first step in fruitful criticism, but not your main business as a critic. Your ultimate function is to deliver a decision—a judgment—based upon the relationship between what you perceive and what you know. To be an effective critic you must avoid straddling the fence. Decide whether the aspect of speech which you are considering is effective or ineffective, true or untrue, adequate or inadequate, skillfully or unskillfully handled, successful or unsuccessful, and why.

6. *Be as specific as possible in formulating your judgment.* Document your criticism with descriptive evidence. Refer directly to the speech whenever you can, to specific arguments, illustrations, and wordings. Provide examples to back up both favorable and unfavorable evaluations. If you are criticizing style, strive to identify portions of the speech where style was effective and portions where it was not. Refer to specific sentence structures, phrasings, and images. This will reveal that you have been both perceptive and thorough in arriving at your judgments. It will also be constructively useful to all who hear your criticism. Find segments of the speech illustrating strengths and weaknesses in clarity, liveliness, force, and the like. The more precisely you can put your finger upon exactly what was done and exactly why it was effective or ineffective, the more worthy of attention your observations will be.

7. *Register your judgment.* When you present your critical assessments orally or in writing, articulate your convictions. Silence during an oral criticism period following a speech or submitting doodlings on a scrap of paper will contribute nothing to the speaker or to your own development as an intelligent, informed critic. Do not feel that you must couch your judgments in rhetorical jargon. Do feel that you must be tactful in wording and

frank in your remarks. Clear, direct, precise expression of your position and the data and criteria on which it rests are required.

EVALUATING TEXTS OF SPEECHES

Your task as a critic of a tape-recorded, printed, or manuscript speech will be more complicated than your task as critic of the live utterance in the classroom. What appears before you on paper or what you hear over the amplifier is all that remains of a speech. It is as if an archaeologist gave you only some of the pieces of a Greek vase and then asked your opinion of the whole.

Most differences in your critical procedure will result from your lack of knowledge about the speaker and about the historical and immediate settings for his speech. You will find it necessary to substitute reading for listening. You will be taking words in with only the eye *or* ear, not seeing and hearing a speaker as he delivers his speech. Delivery cannot be described fully, if at all. Voice may be judged from a recording, but not bodily action, unless you have access to a sound film. Most judgments on delivery will be far from satisfactory since they must usually be based on accounts written by others who saw and heard the speaker in action.

In all ways your criticism of texts will be post-mortem evaluation. This means that you will substitute "read" for "listen" in the steps of criticism we have already given, and your perceptions will be restricted to word symbols since you are denied the stimuli of the real situation.

Your tasks in evaluating texts must precede those necessary for evaluating classroom speeches. These duties are:

1. *Determine the authenticity of your speech text.* Determining the genuineness of the text may not be easy. Unless you are convinced of the trustworthiness of the editor or of the accuracy of the source, you will have to match the text you use with others in order to produce a reliable one of your own. You will wish to work with the best text available. You must also be as sure as possible that this speech was actually composed and delivered by the orator in question.

2. *Inform yourself of the milieu.* For a full understanding of the speech you must have knowledge of the time in which it was given. You must learn what ideas were in the air, what philosophies prevailed, what historic events occurred, and what were the day-to-day concerns of the people. In other words, you must reconstruct the temper of the times if your educated guesses about the importance of the speech and the possible effects it had are to be of any worth. To accomplish this you will have to read historical and interpretative accounts of the cultural, economic, religious, and moral activities of the particular society in which the speaker moved. You will also have to acquire a sense of the chronology of events. This is a large order, but only by filling it to the best of your ability can you hope to describe and judge fairly a rhetorical effort designed for a particular audience, particular place, and particular time in the past.

3. *Inform yourself of the immediate speech setting.* Once again, to make judgments you must know the particularities of the situation. You must know where the speech was delivered, when it was delivered, and to whom it was delivered. Gaining this knowledge, like gaining knowledge about the milieu, calls for historical research. This research will lead you to sources bearing more directly upon the speech than the research you will do on the temper of the times. You will peruse those writings that specifically concern the subject of the speech, the circumstances determining its composition and delivery, the physical setting, and the particular audience which assembled to listen to it.

4. *Inform yourself about the speaker.* A study of the speaker will further your understanding of the recorded or printed speech. You will need to acquire information as to his identity, his place in society, his habits of mind and life, his sense of values, and his impact on other people. To gain insights into the speaker as a person you will need to study autobiographical and biographical materials, diaries, memoirs, photographs, and books of letters. Your task will be to produce a portrait of the speaker as a speaker. To do this you will have to sift through your resource materials to find whatever information is available on the orator's speech training, his methods of speech composition, his way of thinking, and what people influenced him in ways that might have affected his

speaking. You will also need to look for descriptions and evaluations of his speaking and of his speeches.

5. *Read the criticism written by others.* Turning to see what others have done or how they have treated the speech will reward you. The amount of published speech criticism is not great and you will sometimes find it difficult to locate. But there are essays, headnotes, and journal articles containing critical evaluations of many speeches and speakers of the past and present. Often you have only to turn to the newspapers published the day after the speech to find an appraisal of what was said and of the orator's performance. You are not reading the criticism of others so that you can parrot or imitate. Your purpose is to synthesize what you have read and then to arrive at your own point of view.

You can see that criticizing a speech when only the recorded or written text is available is much more difficult than criticizing speeches you can personally witness and hear. In the latter case, you hear and see the speaker and are normally acquainted with the historical and immediate settings because you are a part of them. You may even know a good deal about the personality who addresses you. The job of criticizing a speech from a text adds many preliminary tasks to all the things you do to criticize a live speech. The object of most of this research is simply description— re-creation of the attendant circumstances. These attempts at re-creation will lead you into many fields of knowledge—history, philosophy, literature, sociology, psychology, religion. You can readily see why some argue that no one is ready to criticize speeches until he has passed considerably beyond a beginning public speaking course. Yet, we think such research and criticism benefit all who undertake them.

Criticism is judgment and/or appreciation based on informed description. It is essentially comparative. In every art the critical act calls into play one's full knowledge of the art's resources and potentialities and one's capacity to take in or understand the critical object to be examined. When this critical object is a speech, whoever would judge must understand what is possible in speaking and how to analyze the constituents of a speech.